THE
ENGLAND
COAST
PATH

For the People of the Path: Ann McLaren, Kate Conto, Richard Benyon, Neil Constable, Nick Clegg and every landowner, surveyor, walker, volunteer, and politician that shared some goodwill or ground or both. This is the best story – fact or fiction – I've ever told.

CONWAY
Bloomsbury Publishing Plc
50 Bedford Square, London, WC1B 3DP, UK
29 Earlsfort Terrace, Dublin 2, Ireland

BLOOMSBURY, CONWAY and the Conway logo are trademarks of Bloomsbury Publishing Plc

First published in Great Britain 2022

Copyright © Stephen Neale, 2022
Map illustration © David Broadbent, 2022

All images not belonging to the author have been sourced from Shutterstock, with the exception of pp19, 131 © Rod Teasdale; p326 © Getty

Stephen Neale has asserted his right under the Copyright, Designs and Patents Act, 1988, to be identified as Author of this work

A catalogue record for this book is available from the British Library Library of Congress Cataloguing-in-Publication data has been applied fo

ISBN: PB: 978-1-8448-6619-9;
      ePub: 978-1-8448-6620-5;
      ePDF: 978-1-8448-6618-2

10 9 8 7 6 5 4 3 2 1

Typeset in IBM Plex Sans by Rod Teasdale
Based on design by Austin Taylor
Printed and bound in India by Replika Press Pvt. Ltd.

MIX
Paper from responsible sources
FSC® C016779

To find out more about our authors and books visit www.bloomsbury.com and sign up for our newsletters

Mullion Cove, Cornwall

THE
ENGLAND
COAST PATH

1,100 mini adventures around the
world's longest coastal path

2nd Edition

STEPHEN NEALE

CONWAY

NORTHUMBERLAND

TYNE & WEAR

DURHAM

CUMBRIA

NORTH YORKSHIRE

EAST RIDING OF YORKSHIRE

LANCASHIRE

CHESHIRE & LIVERPOOL

SOUTH YORKSHIRE

LINCOLNSHIRE

NORFOLK

SUFFOLK

GLOUCESTER & NORTH SOMERSET

ESSEX

GREATER LONDON

KENT

SOUTH SOMERSET

HAMPSHIRE

NORTH DEVON

DORSET

NORTH CORNWALL

SOUTH DEVON

ISLE OF WIGHT

WEST SUSSEX

EAST SUSSEX

SOUTH CORNWALL

CONTENTS

Hartland Quay

PART 1

THE
MAGIC
PATH

THE MAGIC PATH

Something amazing is happening near Liverpool. Human footprints are appearing at low tide along Formby Beach. What's incredible is that they are 8,000 years old.

The beach was a little siltier, and the sun was a bit hotter in Formby back in 6000BC. The footprints baked hard before they were covered in many layers of mud by the returning tides over thousands of years. 'Scouring tides' now erode, rake and scrape the hard-silt seabed to expose the prehistoric footprints to the air again. Like magic.

The prints really make you think. Who were these people? How did they live? What was their story? What did they eat?

Part of the magic of Formby is linked to what happens next. The exposed prints vanish on the very next tide. As fast as they appear, they're gone. Loved and then lost. It's almost heartbreaking. No more than a memory, or maybe a photo, for those who were there to see them.

This an English tale – about a coast path of memories. Everything from the histories of prehistoric animals that hunted and fed here to ephemeral footprints in the sand. The memories of the great castles and hills forts, Arthurian legends, caves, coves, shipwrecks, tin mines, gold and adventures.

Most importantly, this book is about you. Your place on one of the greatest coastlines in the world. A path of wild flowers in spring, storms in winter; autumn leaves, navigating the tides aboard a canoe or raft, the gulls of the Grain, basking sharks around North Cornwall; or the rainbows over Formby. Any of the stuff our ancestors might have seen and gasped at 8,000 years ago.

If memories and stories are the magic – then your access to the coast is the key that unlocks them.

This guide sets the scene for a million new stories. There are 1,000 locations over the next 330-odd pages. Everything from coffee shops to

EXPLORE RESPONSIBLY

This book is an adventure guide to help with only basic planning. In many cases, you will be alone. Any terrain or water can become either unsafe or subject to changeable conditions. While every care has been taken with the compilation of locations within this book, it may contain inaccuracies. This book is not a substitute for your own assessment of conditions, or any expert advice available, when visiting a location. Any decision to visit must be taken by you, assessing and checking the risks and directions each time before setting off. If you are unsure about or uncomfortable with the risks involved in visiting a location then you should seek more advice and/or delay a visit. The author, publishers, editors and their agents accept no responsibility for any error or omissions, or for any accident, loss or damage (including without limitation any indirect, consequential, special of exemplary damages) arising from the use or misuse of, or reliance upon, the information contained in this publication.

The decision to use and rely on any of the information and guidance in this publication is entirely your responsibility and at your discretion.

View over Chesil Beach

caves, B&Bs to beaches and hill forts to hotels. Any of these places are the scene for your own memories. Sometimes you'll leave a footprint in the sand yourself. It'll probably be washed away on the next tide. But a memory can live forever.

What follows is a real story. It's linked to the theme of an England path: the English coast and its memories. It's a tale about a strange and varied group of people who came together just after 2000 to pull down the 'Keep Out' signs around almost 3,000 miles of England's shoreline.

This act of vandalism was aided and abetted not by anarchists or dispossessed protestors, but by a collective of England's largest landowners, the politicians of the richest, most powerful and largest political parties, conservationists, campaigners, ramblers, canoeists, youth groups, mountaineers. I'm not sure there wasn't any group or community around the coast that wasn't involved in some way.

They say they did it for the future generations. Our kids, and our kids' kids, they say. And that it couldn't have happened anywhere else in the world but England. You can be the judge of that. The result, though, was something more amazing than those Formby footprints. The 'People of the Path' created the longest coast path in world: the England Coast Path.

This book is a guide to getting to the best bits on the path. It's like a treasure map on how to find the gold. I'm not saying it's the definitive map. Just one of many more I hope others will create after this one.

What follows, then, is the story of how the path was brought to life on a scouring tide of collective purpose by people who cared. People who have literally and metaphorically scraped back time.

This is their story – their footprint in the sand.

PEOPLE OF THE PATH

1 THE JAM JAR KID

Ann McLaren

Ann McLaren was only a kid when she decided she was a walker. As she got a bit older, she explored Epping Forest at night with other teenagers from the local youth club.

'We called them Jam Jar Rallies back in the '50s,' she said, 'because we carried candles inside jam jars. We just kept going until it was light.'

Walking is still in Ann's blood. She can't walk much any more but she's got memories.

The first thing she noticed on those night rallies when the sun came up was the wild flowers: bluebells and primroses. As she got older, she started to pay attention to the trees.

'I noticed the shapes of oak trees in winter, without their leaves. And then how the leaves moved in summer,' she recalls. 'Walking is full of memories. It's something you don't fully appreciate until you've lost it.'

Ann became interested in the state of paths and access when she realised as a kid that there were 'funny gaps' in the paths.

England's coastal access is hampered in some way for nearly half of its length.
DEFRA/Natural England

Wringapeak

'As I got older I started to wonder whether those gaps could be traced back to lost footpaths that had been missed off the definitive Ordnance Survey map of 1945.'

She joined an Essex Ramblers group in 1974 and a year later she was on committee. Together with fellow ramblers, she helped create a vast network of 100-mile walks around Essex by joining together the apparently broken links between footpaths, permissive paths and lanes. By the 1980s, the '100-mile walks' were being used by groups of more than 100 people at a time, who would walk the entire route in nine or ten days. These organised excursions did not always have the blessing of landowners – but some would join in.

Ann follows in a long line of access and rights-of-way campaigners. In 1932, hundreds of ramblers took part in a mass trespass of Kinder Scout in the Peak District to highlight the fact that large swathes of open countryside across England and Wales were not accessible.

'We did our bit of trespassing!' she says. 'It seemed important to be able to get into certain areas that had been closed for too long.'

Her campaigning success and work with both landowners and local authorities saw her rise to become president of Essex Area Ramblers.

During the late 1990s, Ann began to talk to other campaigners in Essex about improving access to the Essex coast.

She remembers, 'Achieving a coastal path was the most exciting project we got involved with back then. Actually, it was the most important thing I've undertaken in my walking lifetime.

'It's in keeping with the spirit of the Kinder mass trespass all those years ago. It didn't seem right that there were so many parts of coast people couldn't walk.'

Knoll Beach

Ann started looking more closely at creating an Essex Coast Path in 2000. A fellow Essex Rambler was doing the same thing. His name was Dave Hitchman.

2 THE ARCHITECT
Dave Hitchman

Dave Hitchman was a schoolboy at Bournemouth Park School, in Southend-on-Sea. He later became office boy at the Southend-on-Sea Borough Council's architect department, and rose to become the council's chief quantity surveyor.

Dave's passion for joining things up extended into the outdoors, especially to footpaths. Together with Ann, he helped create more than 20 of the 100-mile walks around Essex in the 1980s and 1990s. He also linked a series of footpaths between Southend's famous pier and Saffron Walden, 70 miles away – a path known today as the Saffron Way.

The growth of walking and linking up paths in Essex coincided with what was happening all over England in the '80s and '90s – so much so that the Labour Party made expanding public access to the outdoors a manifesto pledge.

Blackpool Sands

From 2009–2015 an average of £18 was spent on coastal visits, compared to £6 on a visit to the countryside.
DEFRA/Natural England

That pledge was realised by the Blair government, with unanimous cross-party support, by the Countryside and Rights of Way (CRoW) Act. This gave people in England and Wales the right of access to mountain, moor, heath, down and registered common land for the first time ever.

This was good news for England. But not for Essex, where there is virtually no heath, and zero mountain or moor.

'I wasn't happy and my argument was simple,' said David Hitchman. 'We haven't got any mountains or moor in Essex. And they've left most of the coast out of the CRoW Act. Our coast is like our mountains.'

Around 2000, Dave spent 12 months walking the Essex coast, mapping it in detail and looking at how he could join it up. In 2001, he presented a motion to fellow Essex committee members, including Ann, to support an Essex Coast Path campaign.

The case was submitted by Essex Ramblers to Ramblers HQ in 2003. But rather than asking for just another Essex path, they did something unexpected: Essex asked for a coast path around all of England.

The motion was picked up by ramblers in other counties who supported Essex's idea. In 2004, Ramblers head office agreed to run a national campaign.

Ramblers HQ, in London, handed the job of petitioning the government for coast access to their top campaigner – an American called Kate Conto.

3 THE AMERICAN
Kate Conto

Kate Conto grew up in New England, just outside New York City. If the moral case for a coast path had been made by Ann McLaren, Dave Hitchman and Essex Ramblers, it was Kate who set about convincing government to make it law. She did that in her nine-to-five day job as Ramblers' campaigns officer.

She was well placed to lead on the coast path campaign. She was a graduate in politics; she was a keen walker; she had worked on the right to roam campaign and the implementation of the CRoW Act in 2004; and she was an environmentalist. Most importantly, she was an outsider.

'I always loved playing in the woods. Did that a lot when I was little. I love the outdoors. The job combined politics and the outdoors. It was perfect for me really.

'When the CRoW Act came along the Essex Ramblers were kind of saying, "What about us?" There was this big beautiful coastline and I think, quite rightly, they thought, "We want something too."

'So they gave us this thick report and we started thinking, "OK … well. If we're going to do this, how could it be done?"'

This ability to look in from outside put her in a position where she could talk to all sides when in 2004 the Essex Ramblers put their motion to the Ramblers General Counsel for the coast path. But even for an outsider, it wasn't easy.

'It was difficult trying to balance everything,' she said. 'Officials from Natural England would be meeting people on the coast of North Yorkshire whose houses were falling into the sea. They were having to say to them, "Well, errr … we're planning on putting a walking route through here." And … you know. It's really kind of sensitive stuff. I probably didn't appreciate how big a role politics plays in walking and access.

Within less than three years, Kate had secured cross-party support for a coast path and DEFRA produced a consultation paper in 2007 setting out the options.

'It was quite incredible that so many people worked to make it happen,' she said. 'It's a story about people sharing a finite resource and about balancing all their different interests.'

Kate believes the longest coast path in the world could have only happened in England.

'I think it's unique to England,' she says. 'Being part of an island nation is a key. Then there's the Rights of Way network. I mean … as far as I know there's nothing like it anywhere else in the world.

'I think there's a tradition of kind of allowing access that I know in the US, for instance, is a completely alien concept.

'I've discussed the England Coast Path with my family and they said, "Well, surely all these landowners will have to be paid?" And I say, "Well no, they're mostly willing to allow it." And I hear the sound of silverware dropping on plates! People outside of the UK just can't get the concept in their head: that somebody would just be able to use someone's land and not give them any money for it.'

Not everyone has welcomed the path. There have been problems, mostly in the south-west: the Isle of Wight, Hampshire.

First, Isle of Wight was in the government's draft coast path plan. Then it was out. Then, thanks to its Isle of Wight access campaigners, ramblers and Kate, it was back in again.

But whenever there has been doubt, there has been a breakthrough. One of the biggest happened in 2007 when an announcement was made by politician David Miliband on the White Cliffs of Dover.

It was the culmination of almost eight years' work.

Woody Bay

4 THE SOCIALIST
David Miliband

David Miliband is one of two brothers. His younger brother went on to become leader of the Labour Party after Gordon Brown failed to win the 2010 election and was replaced by David Cameron.

David has the distinction of being the Secretary of State for the Environment who formally announced the ECP in June 2007, just before being promoted to Foreign Secretary.

Standing on the White Cliffs footpath over Dover he said, 'We are an island nation. The coast is our birthright and everyone should be able to enjoy it.'

The England Coast Path became a legal entity as part of the Marine and Coastal Access Act in 2009. The job of making the path a reality and defining its exact route was handed to Natural England, the government quango responsible for protecting and improving England's natural environment.

Natural England worked with 421 landowners and 150 businesses between Camber and Ramsgate, including beachside properties, commercial ports and farmers before the path section was opened in 2016.

DEFRA/Natural England

5 THE MECHANIC
Natural England

The man in charge of Natural England in 2009 was Sir Martin Doughty, whose father had taken part in the Kinder mass trespass at the age of 15. Tragically, Sir Martin died of cancer on 9 March, eight months before the coast path's status passed into law in November 2009.

Christchurch

He was replaced as Chair by Oxford dairy farmer Poul Christensen, and then by Andrew Sells in 2013.

Christensen, and later Sells, sent out an army of officials who went into the English hinterlands with a fervent enthusiasm to explain why people should be allowed to cross along the bottom of their back gardens and estates. It was a monumental task.

When Sells left in January 2019, he listed the England Coast Path as one of his organisation's greatest achievements.

In his final blog post on 18 January 2019, he wrote: 'I have opened three stretches of the England Coast Path which, when it is complete, will be a wonderful symbol of the connection between people and the natural environment.'

6 THE FIXER

Neil Constable

Neil Constable was a project manager for Natural England in 2010. He was The Fixer. It was his job to map the path's 2,800 miles – and, more importantly, get thousands of landowners to agree to Natural England's chosen coastal route, or propose a better one. The team was destined to encounter incalculable problems and obstacles.

Neil was given a team of 20 made up of five groups working around England, while liaising with a small army of Rambler volunteers.

Every journey starts with the first footstep. For The Fixer and his teams it was more a giant leap. They were instructed to open the first section of path for the Olympics 2012 sailing events at Weymouth Bay in Dorset.

'We asked for a delay in the Games start date, but the Olympic Committee said, "No". I was joking.'

The land around Weymouth Bay has been owned by the Weld family, part of the Lulworth Estate, for generations. The path and its foreshore, beaches and cliffs would be opened in their entirety to provide a viewing gallery where people could watch the Olympic sailing event for free. The new access would then remain open forever as part of the ECP.

It was one of only a handful of Games events where there was no entry fee. It was arguably the most important – and the path's opening would chime perfectly with the Games' opening ceremony celebration of the people's games, innovation, unity – a united country delivering a spectacle.

There were issues – erosion, lack of public access – to negotiate, but together, Neil, his team, landowners and other statutory authorities, Dorset County Council, did it.

'We delivered the whole thing from scratch in two years,' said Neil. 'Now you might think, "Well, that was pretty easy". But it wasn't.

'We had to go through the whole new process of creating the first piece of England Coast Path. We were the ones who piloted it and effectively forged it. We drew out all the issues to template the rest of the path. And we did that collectively, with the supreme help of Dorset County Council, the landowners and all other stakeholders.

'To see all those people on the foreshore waving in the sunshine at the sailing events. It was so bloomin' perfect. It meant something even more than we might have anticipated because it directly tied it in with the Games. We couldn't have had a more fitting opening to the path than Weymouth.

'Weymouth and the Olympic opening ceremony pulled all that together. That and that whole summer of 2012. The Games were just phenomenal in terms of the people, and their input and the whole volunteering thing. It was a good, good moment.'

So then is was time to get real. Post Games 2012, the rest of England's virgin coast had to be surveyed, mapped and made accessible without an Olympic imperative. 'Just' several thousand miles, fast-eroding land and thousands more landowners to navigate.

7 THE CONSERVATIONIST

Kate Ashbrook

If universal support from every landowner was never a reality, it was fake 'conservationists' – in a limited sense – who made the moral claim for retaining the 'Keep Out' signs.

Conservation has been used as a justification to control land and access all around the world for thousands of years.

Tom Fewins, Head of Government Affairs at the Wildfowl & Wetlands Trust (WWT), says: 'There's a clear tension between conservation and public access. But at the end of the day there needs to be that recognition that it's vital to include people into conservation projects, rather than keeping them out.'

Conservation – fake or not – is routinely the Trojan horse used to justify barring public access. Yet many of the largest conservation agencies and landowners have also been at the forefront of the ECP campaign.

Kate Conto secured the support of both the National Trust and the Wildlife Trusts, whose early optimism was crucial to the path's progress. She then recruited other outdoor organisations, including British Waterways (later renamed the Canal and River Trust by Richard Benyon MP), British Canoe Union (now called British Canoeing), and the British Mountaineering Council.

Kate Ashbrook is General Secretary of the Open Spaces Society, Britain's oldest national conservation body, founded in 1865, whose founders went on to create the National Trust in 1895.

She has joined Conto at many of the path openings and is one of its leading advocates.

She said, 'The coast path will give people the confidence of being able to plan a journey. It's important to know they can do the whole thing, and not just dip in and out. You don't want to be walking and then find you're being pushed inland miles along a road.'

There have been problems along the way: environmental pinch points of unique habitat have compromised the vision of a single joined-up path clinging to the shore, without trailing many miles inland.

However, concessions along the way on both sides have kept the project moving forwards. The actions of the Tory Environment Secretary in 2013 are an example of that cooperative, progressive spirit.

8 THE BLUE BLOOD

Richard Benyon

Richard Benyon is officially one of the richest MPs in Parliament. He is also one of the largest landowners, with an estate in Berkshire and Hampshire. More importantly, he was Environment Secretary in charge of overseeing the ECP after his appointment to the Department for Environment, Food and Rural Affairs (DEFRA) when the Tories entered government after the 2010 general election.

In 2013, Benyon made a statement that sent a shudder through the walking world. Coast campaigners call it the 'Benyon Wobble' because of the seismic shock it caused.

Speaking to farmers at the Royal Cornwall Show, Benyon stated, 'The England Coast Path is a sledgehammer to miss a nut.'

There was worse to follow in July 2013, when Benyon announced that he was not extending coastal access to the Isle of Wight.

Dear God, what could possibly go wrong from there? Well actually, nothing.

Despite pressure from a select few of Benyon's constituents and supporters, he in fact oversaw important advances in ECP development, and refused to abandon it. Perhaps most importantly, Isle of Wight remained inside the project.

'I was a sceptic, but I went along with it and I'm very glad I did,' he said.

Benyon claims his light bulb moment came when he realised that the coast path had the potential to generate revenue for thousands of businesses along its length.

'I realised that this had huge potential for tourism, for added value, for inward investment and for a general benefit to coastal communities,' he stated.

Benyon also says that landowners are not only social-minded, but that they are also socially smart when it comes to monetising public access. Increased footfall is most often good news for business.

'In an uncertain economic climate, what s there not to like about that?' he said.

'Maybe we could see farmers providing green gyms. Disused barns where people with certain health conditions can go and improve their health. People having more access to the countryside. I think there's huge potential here.

'The sort of "gerr orff my land" image that is portrayed by a character called Farmer Palmer in *Viz* magazine is now the joke that it should be. Because I didn't think it applies anymore.'

It's not all good news for Benyon and fellow landowners, though. He still worries about dogs chasing sheep and damage to rural business when people don't respect the land.

'There will be certain farmers who will be hearing me say this stuff about access and they will be rolling their eyes and thinking, "This person is not living in the real world." And I entirely accept that there are certain boneheaded walkers and some ridiculously politically motivated activists who feel they can justify the stupid things they do.

'But in the main, and in the majority – particularly younger farmers now coming and taking over businesses – we're seeing different attitudes. I think it's all to the good.'

In spite of Benyon being won over by the end of 2013, there was inevitably more trouble ahead. Money. Post the 2008-banking collapse, government departments like DEFRA were by 2013 under masses of pressure to cut back spending.

'We were in the teeth of austerity,' said Tom Fewins, who joined Ramblers as a campaign officer in 2013. 'We thought we were going to lose the path.'

Appledore

Meinek, Land's End

9 THE CAMPAIGNER

Tom Fewins

Tom Fewins arrived at Ramblers as policy and advocacy manager. He had worked in Westminster. He knew the political landscape. Most importantly, he still had contacts within the Liberal Democrat Party, now in coalition with the Tories.

But all was not well. The coast path had been left to wither on the vine, and progress had almost ground to a halt.

'Maybe only two or three stages had been completed,' recalls Tom. 'It looked like the government would rather let it die quietly in the corner.'

Ramblers began talking to ministers and raising pressure in Westminster with a variety of campaigns and stunts. One included parking an ice-cream van outside the doors of Portcullis House in Westminster, to serve ices to MPs to raise awareness of the commercial benefits the path would bring to costal resorts.

Many MPs signed up, but by 2014, the need for a cash injection had reached crisis point.

Tom's insider knowledge meant he knew that both the Tory and Lib Dem parties were moving into election mode and drawing up their manifestos for the 2015 election. He also knew that the Lib Dems were specifically looking at environmental policies.

Nick Clegg was the Deputy Prime Minister in 2014, second-in-charge of the Tory/ Lib Dem coalition government that had replaced Gordon Brown's Labour Party at the 2010 general election.

Realising urgent action was needed to save the path, Tom drove Ramblers' chief executive, Benedict Southworth, to Nick Clegg's Peak District home in September 2014. His intention was to present the economic case for the coast path, and to ramp up pressure on the government to set aside funding.

They arrived late, after getting stuck in traffic. But their timing was spot on.

'Clegg's patch extended up on to the moors,' said Tom. 'So we decided to drive up there from London. The traffic was appalling. We met him up by a reservoir. We had a walk over the moors, and we raised the coast path with him.

'Clegg couldn't have been more enthusiastic about walking. He could see the benefits of the path to rural and coastal communities. And the timing was perfect with the election coming up, and the environmental policies the Lib Dems were drafting.'

They returned to London and crossed their fingers.

From 2009–2015 an average of £18 was spent on coastal visits, compared to £6 on a visit to the countryside.

DEFRA/ Natural England

10 THE POLITICIAN

Nick Clegg

Nick Clegg's parliamentary constituency of Sheffield Hallam reached into the Peak District, and is just 7 miles from Kinder Scout, where the 1932 mass trespass had occurred. Clegg was not of the coast – but he was an avid walker, passionate about access and a regular hiker over the Peak District.

He will likely go down in history as a political disaster – mostly on account of his 'betrayal' of students and the 'hike' in fees that allowed university vice-chancellors to push their salaries to obscene highs. He sold the kids out in return for a referendum on electoral reform. Less than 14 per cent of the population voted for it in 2011 – a monumental error that saw his party crash from 57 to eight MPs in 2015. Clegg was voted out of his Sheffield Hallam seat in the 2017 general election.

'You live by the sword, you die by the sword,' he said.

Five years earlier, however, in 2014, as the cash had drained away from the coast path project, he had shone like a lighthouse beacon over the rocks of austerity.

After the meeting with Ramblers in September 2014, he ordered his advisors to draft a strategy.

In November 2014, those same advisors made a press announcement on the cliffs of North Cornwall. Tom Fewins at Ramblers received a phone call to get down there.

Tom recounts, 'We got the call from the Lib Dems' central office. They said, "This Coast Path thing! We'd quite like to do something with it. Would you like to come down and join us in Cornwall? We're going to say something about it." So we said, "OK!"'

Fewins drove a van to Cornwall with Ramblers' director of advocacy and engagement, Nicky Philpott and others, where they met Clegg and the local Lib Dem MP, Daniel Rogerson, literally at the cliff edge. (Rogerson had by this point replaced Benyon as Minister at DEFRA.)

Tom recalls, 'We were all waiting around in a van handing out tea to Clegg's security detail. And then their spin doctor gets his email. And he's says, "It's just come in! It's £5.5m pounds for the coast path!"

'And I say: "Oh my god!! Wow."

'And that was it. Clegg gets the message, stands up and makes the announcement with his back to the Atlantic Ocean. That's what saved

Ilfracombe

Kimmeridge Bay

it. That was the turning the point. That's the moment the coast path was saved.'

This, however, wasn't the full story. While the background to Clegg's intervention had been fast and calculated, it had not been entirely partisan.

According to Lib Dem party staff, Clegg had wanted to make a key speech on the environment to help boost his party's 2015 manifesto campaign. He had therefore asked his personal advisors for a list of important environmental projects that needed urgent remedy.

He was presented with six projects. He chose three for an immediate announcement. One was to restrict the use of pesticides. The second was funding to keep Kew Gardens open (featured on page 56). The third was cash for the England Coast Path.

Adam Pritchard was Nick Clegg's special advisor at the time.

'The bad news from a "dramatic" storytelling point of view, as there was no battle at all over the Coast Path funding.

'I wish I could tell you a Tory minister dug his heels in or refused to move. Or the Treasury demanded costings. But I can't. It received universal support from all parties. Even the most curmudgeonly members in the House of Lords were happy with extra funding for the Coast Path.'

'I mean ... we had to fight tooth and nail to get plastic bags adopted as a policy and the 5p charge. You wouldn't believe the amount of crawling over broken glass and the concessions we had to make to get that policy over the line.

'But it wasn't anything like that with the Coast Path.'

So, while Clegg is the man who many believe dismantled the fortunes of the Lib Dems, he will always be remembered by access campaigners as the man who saved the ECP.

Today, they call him 'Saint Clegg of the Coast Path'. Time will judge whether history was harsh or kind on him. But this it not Clegg's story. There was a path to build.

England Coast Path walkers supported more than 6,000 full-time jobs in 2017.
DEFRA/Natural England

11 THE SURVEYOR

Ian Wild

Ian Wild is a sailor, fisherman, windsurfer, kayaker and rambler. He was one of more than 100 surveyors who volunteered to walk and map the coast path. These surveys were used as a comparison to judge the quality of the formal works and surveys carried out by the army of DEFRA surveyors.

Based in Kent, Ian walked all 350 miles of the Kent coast ... in both directions. He then produced a survey of where the ECP should go and published it online.

'I volunteered because I feel strongly the coast should be made available for everyone to enjoy. It took me 16 days of walking, and a darn sight longer to write it up,' he said.

> More than 20 per cent of England's population cannot use public rights of way, either because they cannot use stiles or kissing gates themselves, or they are accompanying someone who can't.
> DEFRA/Natural England

The job of the surveyors was to complement the work done by the mechanics from Natural England. The mechanics were now carrying out their own surveys with increasing speed. Once complete, the mechanics would sit down with the local Rambler surveyors to decide which final version to send off to the Secretary of State for final approval.

Where there was a difference of opinion between the Rambler and Natural England surveys, an application could be made to the Secretary of State for a change. This rarely, if ever, happened.

The crucial role played here was the diplomacy between Ramblers and Natural England surveyors and the landowners. Most of the credit for that must go to Natural England, Neil Constable and his team, and the landowners themselves.

Of almost 10,000 landowners who were consulted about the proposed England Coast Path over their land by 2018, around 4 per cent objected. This equated to about 300 formal objections. Of those 300 objections, less than 1 per cent – around three – were upheld, requiring minor diversions.

12 THE CHAIR

Alan Goffee

Having got things going back in 2000, Essex was some way behind Kent and other counties when it came to implementation, mainly because Natural England prioritised other areas first.

Alan Goffee took over as chair of Essex Ramblers in 2014. He was a bit cross as a result of the delays in Essex, so he decided to shake things up.

To do so, he took on the role of coordinator between his area's Ramblers surveyors and Natural England surveyors in 2015. More importantly, he became a fixer for occasional conflicts now emerging between landowners and his own members, as the path's progress picked up pace.

The Essex surveyors were completely committed. Maybe too much so: they complained about the refusal of some landowners to compromise more. Natural England surveyors, meanwhile, were able to talk to Alan about things they were not happy with and disparities in the two groups' wants and needs.

'A range of disagreements were solved at local level,' said Alan. 'People came to understand that it was not about: "I want, I get." It was a more pragmatic approach.

'I sat in meetings where people were not happy, but by the end they were willing to budge. They said: "OK. I'm not going to argue about 200 yards of path when the whole thing is almost 3,000 miles long."

'It all went remarkably well. A lot easier than I thought it might from the beginning.'

Dave Hitchman, now in his 80s, was unable to survey the Southend-on-Sea section so another

Bournemouth Park School boy was asked. Me. I was recruited by Ann McClaren and Alan Goffee to survey the section of the Southend-on-Sea path between Great Wakering and Canvey Island.

More than 10 years after Ann McClaren and Dave Hitchman had pushed a motion to General Council about an England Coast Path, the Essex path was finally taking shape on the ground.

In June 2017, the first section of path opened at Maldon, 18 months after Kent's first section.

By September 2017, Natural England announced that work had started on every stretch of coast in every county.

Alan added: 'Very few things in my life will still be here hundreds of years after I'm dead. This is one of them.

'It makes me feel quite small in terms of how big it all is. And it's a nice feeling being a small part of something this big. If I go on a protest I'm protesting, and that's a negative. This is all positive. I've done a small part in a big thing. I've persuaded a few people.

'A lot of people will be feeling they've done something.

'And we will be leaving something to our children and our children's children.'

South West Coast Path generates £400 million a year – £630,000 per mile.
DEFRA/Natural England

13 THE FUTURIST

Alison Hallass

Alison Hallass comes from the private sector: she was an environmental consultant working with DEFRA and the Environment Agency until she moved to Ramblers in September 2016 to take over from Kate Conto.

She remains excited about the path's progress, despite the fact that, as I write in August 2022, not all 67 sections are fully open. A combination of both Brexit and Covid-19 pushed works back. Alison said, 'It's really important as people are desperate to return to the coast and walk.' Alison is confident we can all play a part in

Bosahan Cove, Helford River Estuary

walking and talking this path into existence, now and long into the future. We all have a role to play in this remarkable story. 'People of the Path' who can walk, visit and applaud its creation. Alison predicts the path will never stop growing; that it will continue to evolve to link up inland towns and villages with the coast.

'I believe the coast path will eventually be joined to the entire footpath network,' she says.

'People who haven't ever given it a thought before will be saying, "Do you know what, I can walk from my town, which is miles from the beach, and can explore the coast. I can do that from my own doorstep."'

'It has a huge amount of potential. And the connecting up of all the communities along the coast is going to be absolutely lovely, too.'

Much like Richard Benyon, Alison says some of the biggest beneficiaries of the path will be coastal towns and communities that have suffered from lack of investment and seen a slow decay over the last century.

'There are so many bits of the coast that don't get any investment today, and this is going to make a big difference to them,' she claims.

'They're really excited about it in Northumberland because they know their coast is spectacular but is nowhere near as well known as the likes of the Devons and Cornwalls of this world.

'The path will bring people in to see how spectacular these other places are.'

This is not a fiction or a fancy. Or a perfect storm of coincidences, from the Kinder mass trespass to Jam Jar Ann through to Socialist Miliband, Blue Blood Benyon, landowning lords to the Deputy Prime Minster of England. This is a fact. England is a nation of walkers. It is not a political thing. It's a thread that joins us together. A communion of dog walkers, hikers, landowners, birdwatchers, wild campers, ramblers and strollers. A lost legacy, part-trampled by the Norman yoke, restored by the Anglo-Saxon spirit, and revived through the action of a spoken truth: the coast path is officially open; sometime soon it will all be linked.

Just like those footprints at Formby. Ephemeral, real and part of who we are, who we have been and what we will become.

What follows is a list of 1,100 places that you can visit today. Most are on the England Coast Path, many are not. One day soon, they could all be.

18 WONDERS OF THE ENGLAND COAST PATH

BEST FOR...

1 HIDDEN BEACHES
2 SECRET SWIMS
3 WILD WOODS
4 CANOES AND WILD CAMPING
5 SACRED ISLES
6 CAVES, SEA ARCHES AND TUNNELS
7 MOTHER NATURE
8 FORAGING
9 HISTORIC AND RUINED
10 SACRED AND HOLY
11 STAR WATCHING
12 FOSSIL HUNTING
13 SUNSETS AND CLIFF TOP VIEWS
14 WATERFALLS, SPRINGS AND WELLS
15 SUMMER SOLSTICE
16 MABON – AUTUMN EQUINOX
17 WINTER SOLSTICE
18 OSTARA – SPRING EQUINOX

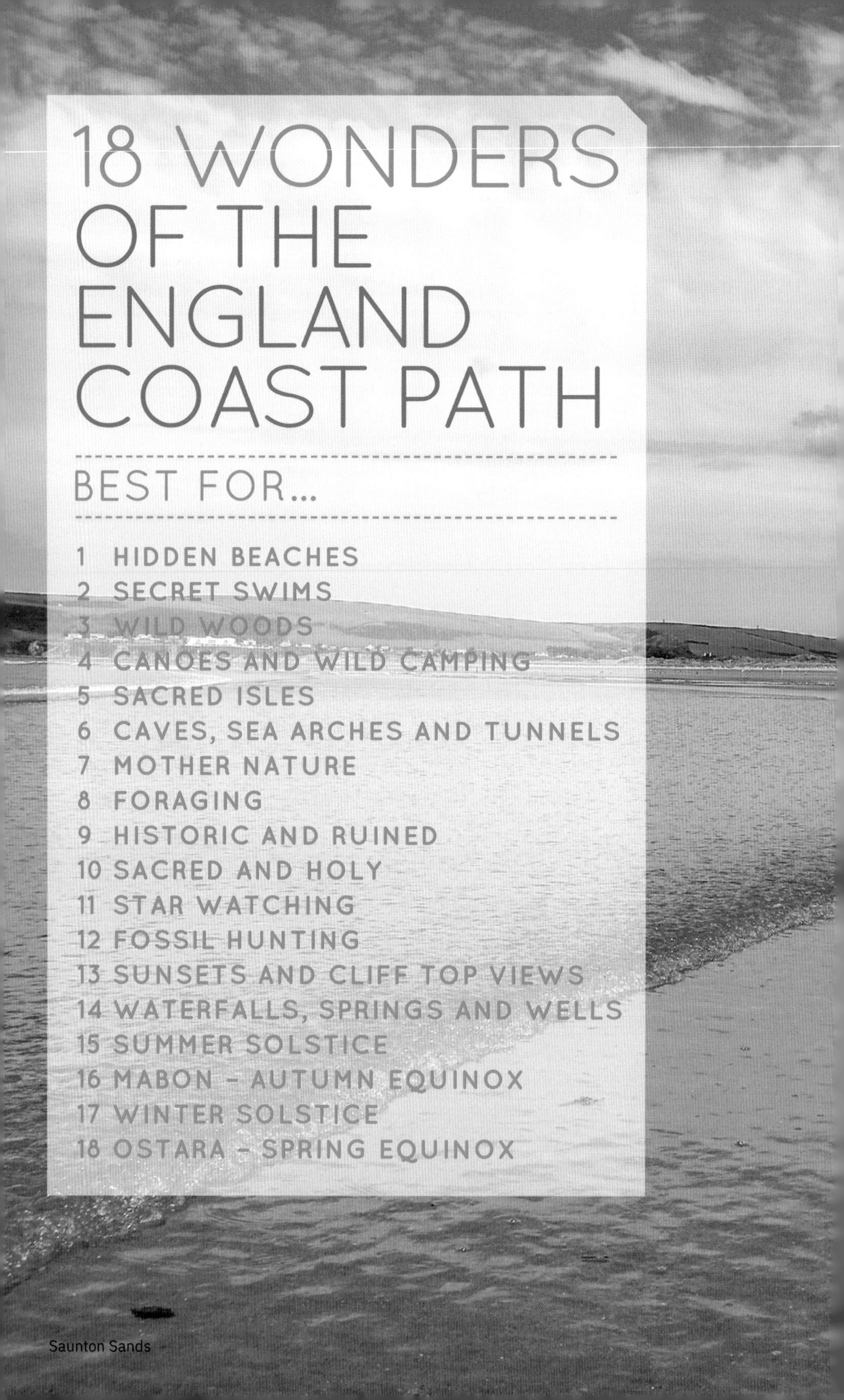

Saunton Sands

1 Best for...
HIDDEN BEACHES

The coast of England has the most spectacular variety of beaches in the world. From the sunken sands of Weston-super-Mare and Yorkshire to the secret coves, caves and bays of Cornwall and Devon.

Finding quiet places means different things in different areas. Sometimes it will entail a 45-minute hike around a cliff edge to where a tiny path zigzags down to the clear waters on a white sand bay. At other times it can mean skipping down from one of the busiest beach car parks at Padstow in Cornwall, St Bees in Cumbria, or Margate in Kent, and then walking from cove to cove at low tide to places others don't know or care about. If you're not overloaded with deckchairs and heavy hampers for six, it's all good fun.

Learn about the tides and the moon. This is the key to finding 'hidden places'. What can appear dull, rocky and littered at high tide can look like a deserted paradise on the low. Research spring tides and the lowest equinox tides. It doesn't take much nowadays. At the very least, search the web for tide times and extreme lows. Try to arrange your coastal trips to coincide with the moons and the tides. That way you get to see it all at both high and low tide.

Reaching a remote beach doesn't always require a canoe or kayak, and there's a huge sense of empowerment and freedom to be had from being able to get to somewhere that's isolated by feet alone – especially if it involves an old rope ladder or a scramble down a worn cliff path. A secret swim followed by a hot coffee warmed on a campfire or out of a flask is a moment beyond magical.

STAY SAFE
Make a note of when low tide occurs, and make sure you're back before the water starts to come in. It will always return more quickly than it goes out – psychologically speaking at least.

South East
Covehithe Broad – *Suffolk*
Covehurst Wood – *East Sussex*
Egypt Bay Beach – *Kent*

South West
Allwoods Copse – *Hampshire*
Ryde East Sands – *Isle of Wight*
Lee Bay – *North Devon*

North East
Long Nanny Bridge – *Northumberland*
Huttoft Beach – *Lincolnshire*
Black Buoy Sand – *Lincolnshire*

North West
Jenny Brown's Point – *Lancashire*
Gutterby – *Cumbria*
Longton Sands – *Lancashire*

2 Best for...
SECRET SWIMS

The coastal waters around England are mostly clean, navigable and amazingly varied.

There is very little connection between the overwhelming enjoyment of relaxing on a secret beach and taking the plunge into cool waves on a warm day. They are as different as gaping in awe at gannets and albatross gliding on thermals from cliffs over an azure sea to launching yourself from the top of the cliffs aboard a hang glider.

If the active enjoyment of allowing the five senses to be overwhelmed by the passive relaxation of nature is nirvana-like, taking the plunge into water, floating on the surface or simply dipping bare feet into surf maximises the sensations by multiples impossible to quantify. It is a magic beyond eating, music and good company. Because it overwhelms the senses of touch, hearing, taste and smell in an alien environment – much like flying – that is potentially fraught with danger and the unknown.

South East
The Ray, River Thames – *Essex*
Ken Cliff – *Suffolk*
Waveney Forest, River Waveney – *Norfolk*

South West
Black Point and Sandy Point – *Hampshire*
Nodes Point – *Isle of Wight*
Wild Pear Beach, Combe Martin – *N Devon*

North East
Cresswell Foreshore and Pond – *Northumberland*
High Scar Rocks – *Yorkshire*
Huttoft Beach – *Lincolnshire*

North West
Brighton-le-Sands, Crosby Channel – *Cheshire*
Sambo's Grave, Sunderland Point – *Lancashire*
Banks Marsh – *Lancashire*

Swimming overwhelms the senses

STAY SAFE
If in any doubt about safety, enjoy the view and stay back from the water's edge.

- Never swim alone.
- Take local advice wherever possible.
- Even when wearing a wetsuit, be wary of cold water, which can cause limbs to seize up and panic inhalation of water.
- Beware waves and currents that can sweep you out from the shore.
- Look out for motor craft – wear a bright swim hat or tag a float behind you.
- Look out for dangerous obstacles below the surface of the water that can cause injury.

3 Best for...
WILD WOODS

Coastal woodland is England's rarest habitat, and a powerful reminder of England's ancient past – a primeval intuition that you can touch when in the presence of crashing waves and the leafy canopy of even a single elder bush.

The last ice age entirely wiped out all England's trees. When the changing climate thawed things out about 10,000 years ago, pine and birch seeds blew in on the southerly winds.

Those same trees composted the cold barren ground and paved the way in leaf compost for almost 40 native trees that returned to these shores, including: alder, elder, ash, aspen, bay willow, crab apple, hawthorn, hazel, holly, hornbeam, large-leaved lime, rowan, sessile oak, small-leaved lime, wild cherry, wild service tree, elm and yew.

South East
Alresford Grange, River Colne – *Essex*
Dunwich Forest – *Suffolk*
The Warren, Folkestone – *Kent*

South West
Fal-Ruan – *South Cornwall*
Clovelley woods – *North Devon*
Rousdon woods – *South Devon*

North East
High Pool, River Tweed – *Northumberland*
Saltburn – *Yorkshire*
Brunswick Bay – *Yorkshire*

North West
Formby – *Cheshire*
Nut Wood – *Lancashire*
Roudsea Tarn – *Cumbria*

Black Heath Wood

4 Best for...
CANOES AND WILD CAMPING

Kayaks and canoes open up many more possibilities when it comes to camping and exploring areas that are inaccessible to swimmers and walkers. Tidal navigation in England, apart from one or two exceptions around the Norfolk Broads and Hampshire, is a right enshrined in law. Although this book is largely about the access provided by the ECP, those coastal areas that have been kept out for now are almost always accessible from a kayak launching from somewhere on the ECP. That's the magic of combining two rights: public rights of way and rights of navigation.

The best areas for kayaks tend to be the creek and river estuaries of Norfolk, Suffolk and Essex, and the southern coasts of Cornwall and Devon, where walking on tidal rias and rivers provides limited access.

The coast is the best place in England for wild camping. There are several reasons: many parts of the coast are isolated, no one will notice, and there are many places in which to hide. What's more, sleeping on a beach, hammocking in trees or resting beside a campfire provides limitless opportunities for night swims, star watching, and getting closer to nature.

The two most important justifications for wild camping around England's coast are enshrined in English law: tidal fishing and tidal navigation.

Fishing and kayaking are not rights limited by daylight or, more

> ### STAY SAFE
> • Check tide times.
> • Do not kayak alone.
> • Always carry warm clothing and spare sets.
> • Always let other people know where you are going.
> • Carry a radio or, at the very least, a well-charged phone with spare batteries.

Eype Mouth

Hope's Nose

importantly, time. That's a crucial distinction, because most of our domesticated world outside of the four walls of our home is controlled by time. Things close: libraries, shops, the gym, pubs, parking spaces, school, the work place.

Around the tidal coast, however, time is of no consequence. So, if we choose to fish for cod or mackerel on a beach for three weeks that's perfectly reasonable thing to do... And it's legal, 24 hours a day. As is the activity of sleep. There is no right to sleep, but it is a legitimate pursuit to sleep in a bivvie on the foreshore (below the high-tide mark) while waiting for the tide, and the fish, to return.

The same goes for kayaking or canoes. There is a right in law to be allowed to wait in the foreshore with your boat for the tide to return in six or seven hours' time before navigating off to your next destination. The function of sleeping forms a legitimate part of that travel on the foreshore, below the high-tide mark.

RULES ON WILD CAMPING

- Keep it to small groups.
- Leave no trace.
- Take all rubbish home.
- Stay below the high-tide mark (foreshore).
- Pitch after dusk and pack down before dawn.
- Keep fires well below the high-tide mark.

> 94 per cent of the public agrees there should be a legal right of access to the coast.
> Ramblers survey

South East
Bradwell Shell Bank, Ray Sand, Dengie
    – *Essex*
River Cuckmere – *East Sussex*
Seapoint Canoe Centre – *Kent*

South West
Beaulieu River West – *Hampshire*
Bembridge Foreland – *Isle of Wight*
Chapman's Pool – *Dorset*

North East
Waterfront Harbour & Church
    – *Lincolnshire*
The Parish Church of St Mary Magdalene,
    Whitgift, River Ouse – *Yorkshire*
Mablethorpe – *Lincolnshire*

North West
River Ribble – *Lancashire*
King Edward I Monument, Solway Estuary
    – *Cumbria*
River Duddon – *Cumbria*

5 Best for...
SACRED ISLES

England is a nation of islands. And much like the nation itself, these places hold a special status.

There are permanent large islands, like the Isle of Wight in Hampshire, and Canvey in Essex, and the Isles of Scilly, 30 miles off the Cornish coast.

And then there are temporal islands – those that appear at low tide when the receding waters reveal them. Many of these are flooded land that once joined us up to mainland Europe before the ice thawed during the end of the last ice age in 10,000BC.

There are thought to be more than 1,000 pieces of land in England that at some point of the tide will be surrounded by water. Essex has the most islands of any county, with 22. No one really knows how many of these are islands, however, because one person's island is another person's sunken sandbank.

There are probably four categories of island:

1 islands that are always visible without a bridge (Farne Islands, Brownsea Island)
2 islands that are always visible with a bridge (Canvey Island, Walney Island)
3 islands that are always visible with a low tide causeway (Holy Island, St Michael's Island, Mersea Island)
4 islands that only appear after high tide but can be walked and swum to at low tide (mostly sandbanks)

South East
Skipper's Island, Walton Backwaters – *Essex*
Pilsey Island – *West Sussex*
Chiswick Eyot – *London*

South West
Brownsea Island – *Dorset*
Burgh Island – *South Devon*
St Michael's Mount – *South Cornwall*

North East
The Coves, Holy Island – *Northumberland*
Farne Islands – *Northumberland*
St Mary's Island, Whitley Bay – *Tyne and Wear*

North West
Hilbre Island – *Cheshire*
Sheep Island (joined at low tide to Piel Island and to Walney Island) – *Cumbria*
Foulney Island – *Cumbria*

Most of our islands are uninhabited. However, like any property, some islands are private. That means walking on the land above the high-tide mark without permission isn't usually a good idea, or polite. That said, the foreshore around the island is almost always public, and when the tide is out that means a hike around the foreshore is an exciting and fun opportunity to explore sunken beaches, wrecks, rocks pools or to forage.

Similarly, when the tide is in, islands are great places to explore by kayak or canoe. Wild camping on an island's foreshore at low tide is a great way to seek wildlife or star watch after dark. The highest part of the foreshore, a few metres below the mean high-tide mark is usually a good place to pitch your tent. This is particularly wonderful if the island in question is surrounded by islands of salt marsh.

In June, for instance, once an 8pm high tide has fallen back enough to justify setting up camp to watch a 10pm sunset, the next high tide isn't going to return until 9am the next morning. That gives plenty of time for sleep and to pack up by 7am, before paddling away on the next tide.

Holy Island

6 Best for...
CAVES, SEA ARCHES AND TUNNELS

England's most dramatic coasts are around the rocky headlands at high tide. The power, energy and force of crashing waves against rocky crop that has been battered for millions of years is inspiring. But once the tide has receded, the opportunity to explore the calm of low-tide pools, arches and caves after the torrent of surf has subsided is irresistible.

England's caves, stacks and arches are almost all tied up in myth, magic, tragedy and triumph. You don't even need to know the stories associated with them, because you can feel the power and energy and stories all around them.

The most magical rocks and caves – like Merlin's in North Cornwall – are almost always linked to fresh water. They will contain freshwater wells, waterfalls or springs that have sustained life – some since the last ice age, many others since long before humans arrived on the scene. After then,

these sites, perhaps inevitably, became sacred, precious and protected. Don't be surprised to find waterfalls, springs and dry caves above the waterline close to or under castles and hill forts peppered around the England coast. Fortification isn't always about fighting; mostly it's about defence, and protecting what was historically most precious: shelter, warmth and fresh water next to a food source.

Fort Henry

STAY SAFE

Caves and tunnels pose a risk – seek local advice before entering or exploring them.

- Visit caves and tunnels on calm days.
- Do not enter caves that contain moving tides.
- Always wear a helmet to protect you against banging your head on overhangs, falling rocks or other hazards.
- Do not explore deep caves or tunnels without back-up torches.
- Beware caves that contain pipework, streams or flowing water that might be used by water companies as emergency flush for large amounts of water.
- Beware of becoming trapped in a cave on either a high or low tide if it suddenly floods quickly.
- Do not enter mine tunnels without professional assistance or advice.
- Use only bona fide companies and groups and wear life jackets, wetsuits and helmets if carrying out sea cave explorations.

South East
Grain Fort, Isle of Grain – *Kent*
Botany Bay, Broadstairs – *Kent*
Kingsgate Bay – *Kent*

South West
Mullion Cove – *South Cornwall*
Blackchurch Rock Arch Woods – *North Devon*
Baggy Point sea caves – *North Devon*

North East
Nose's Point, Seaham – *Northumberland*
Blackhall Rocks & Cross Gill – *Northumberland*
Thornwick Bay caves – *Yorkshire*

North West
Humphrey Head Point – *Cumbria*
Badger Hole, Warton Crag – *Lancashire*
Dog Holes caves – *Lancashire*

7 Best for…
MOTHER NATURE

For a country with a relatively small land mass, England is one of the most important places in the world for wildlife. For instance, it is home to the largest dune systems, vast bogs and unique tidal marsh and estuarine salt systems that attract the largest collection of migratory birds in the world.

South East
The Broadway – *Essex*
RSPB Minsmere – *Suffolk*
Blakeney Eye – *Norfolk*

South West
Farlington Marshes – *Hampshire*
Hook Lane – *Hampshire*
Exe Estuary – *South Devon*

North East
Humber Estuary – *Yorkshire*
Donna Nook – *Lincolnshire*
Anderby Creek – *Lincolnshire*

North West
Burton Mere Wetlands – *Cheshire*
South Walney Nature Reserve – *Cumbria*
Freeman's Wood – *Lancashire*

Cornwall is a hot spot for basking sharks. These huge but harmless plankton eaters turn up in springtime, often staying until the end of summer.

Here, and elsewhere, porpoises, dolphins and seals feed and play among kelp forests in the sea. Underwater, there are crustaceans, starfish and anemones.

Deer are an important part of the countryside, especially around the autumn rutting season when stags can be heard roaring. Otters have returned to almost all English rivers after the pesticide DDT was banned in 1984, and now beavers are being reintroduced into some rivers on a trial basis. Everywhere you look, there is something to spot.

England's coastline already attracts 313 million visits a year.
DEFRA/Natural England

Red Admiral, Freeman's Wood, Lancashire

8 Best for...
FORAGING

The English coast is awash with free food – fish, crabs, shrimps, clams, oysters, samphire and purslane.

And of course seaweed, many types of which are edible. This isn't a guide to foraging, however, so do a little research and take a book. You should also check in advance that foraging is permitted; generally, it's fine if the food is harvested in a responsible manner and, crucially, is for personal use only.

Shingle Street, Suffolk

When you know what you are looking for, you'll soon become adept at spotting tasty, salted green stuff that is better than most of the tame leaf inland. Samphire and purslane are the most common, and their raw flavours are incredible. There's also sea kale, sea cabbage and so much more. Many of the edible plants have been overpicked in recent decades, though, so take care not to pull plants up and always use scissors or a knife to trim them, leaving at least one-third of the length and the foot or claw intact where it is.

Shellfish is something to get excited about. Mussels, cockles, winkles, whelks and even oysters are easily found all around the coast. There are some areas where farmed oysters are protected by bylaws, so look out for signs. But in many cases, large Atlantic or native oysters are easy to find.

Crabs make a tasty meal or snack, whatever their size. Shrimps netted out of a rock pool are more a tasty buzz than a meal. Then there are the fish. Either use a telescopic rod or a small crayfish pot, which can be bought cheaply online and pack down really small.

Foraging for most people is less about survival and more about interacting with the outdoors while either camping or exploring. But whether it's cooking a crab on a fire or eating raw samphire on the move, wild food is one of the magic ingredients that connects us to the natural world.

BASIC RULES

- Check with the beach owner before removing shellfish, plants or seaweed.
- Don't eat anything you haven't positively identified as being safe.
- Check the status of waters to ensure they're not polluted by outfalls or recent sewage.
- Ensure all foods – especially oysters and some seaweeds – are thoroughly soaked, washed and cleaned before cooking them in line with expert advice.

South East
Copperas Bay, River Stour – *Essex*
Thorpeness – *Suffolk*
Humberstone Marshes – *Norfolk*

South West
South Efford Marsh – *South Devon*
Langstone Harbour – *Hampshire*
Taddiford Gap – *Hampshire*

North East
Staithes Harbour – *Yorkshire*
RSPB Frampton Marsh – *Lincolnshire*
The Coomb, Scarborough – *Yorkshire*

North West
White Creek – *Cumbria*
Penwortham, River Ribble – *Lancashire*
Thurstaton Beach – *Cheshire*

Grove Cliff

9 Best for...
HISTORIC AND RUINED

England's ruins come in different forms: from Roman burial sites, Norman castles, Saxon abbeys and Iron Age hill forts to the discarded, industrial fringes of tin mines, lost quays, pits and quarries.

Humans first inhabited the land along (what is now) the east coast more than half-a-million years ago, but the largest mammals thrived here millions of years before that. It's something close to incredible to search for and find – around Essex, Shropshire, Norfolk, Yorkshire, Somerset and Dorset – flints and footprints of our earliest ancestors, along with megalodon teeth, mammoth tusks and ammonites.

Enjoy staring at a shell that has been around for millions of years, or sit alone on a deserted, derelict stone quayside or tin mine, miles from the nearest road or house, and remember how less than 100 years ago that place would have been a thriving hub of labour, trade, dreams, crimes and activity. As William Blake so brilliantly put it, seek to 'see a World in a Grain of Sand' and 'Hold infinity in the palm of your hand'.

South East
Colchester Castle Museum – *Essex*
Hastings Castle, View Point – *East Sussex*
Dover Castle – *Kent*

South West
Fort Cumberland – *Hampshire*
Portchester Castle – *Hampshire*
Hurst Castle – *Hampshire*

North East
Berwick-upon-Tweed Castle, River Tweed
  – *Northumberland*
Founding Fathers Stone, the Wash
  – *Lincolnshire*
Dunstanburgh Castle – *Northumberland*

North West
Muncaster Castle, River Esk – *Cumbria*
Lytham Windmill Museum – *Lancashire*
Lancaster Castle – *Lancashire*

10 Best for...
SACRED AND HOLY

From the boat burials at Sutton Hoo pointing eastwards to the Saxon homelands and Seahenges on the Norfolk coast, to the tiny village churches around the Devonshire tidal rivers and holy islands of the north and south, the large number of henges, standing stones, churches, chapels and burial cairns located around England's edge tells us how important the coast has always been considered to be.

Much like the caves listed previously, 'non-earthly', 'spiritual', 'sacred' and 'holy' are all terms that have been historically linked to sites where there was both a source of pure fresh water and proximity to the tides: something that we know today as the merging of the yin and yang. This is because these geographically and geologically rich places have by a combination of fate and good fortune provided the greatest number of people with the greatest and best opportunity to live and breathe and breed before passing back to the ground.

Yet despite this, as a class, these coastal sacred places are often less popular and less visited in 21st-century England than the historic ruins and fossil beaches listed on pages 34 and 37. Which is really quite nice. Because in an understated and thoroughly peaceful way for anyone who stumbles upon them by chance, you'll often find yourself alone.

South East
Sutton Hoo – *Suffolk*
Chapel of St Peter-on-the-Wall, Bradwell-on-Sea – *Essex*
Seahenge – *Norfolk*

South West
Wain's Hill – *Gloucestershire*
Merlin's Cave – *North Cornwall*
Chapel Porth, St Agnes – *North Cornwall*

North East
St Ebba's Chapel – *Northumberland*
St John's Chapel, Temple Hirst – *Yorkshire*
St Oswald's Church, Althorpe – *Lincolnshire*

North West
The Godstone, St Luke's churchyard – *Cheshire*
Rock-cut tombs, St Peter's Church, Heysham – *Lancashire*
St Cuthbert's Church – *Cumbria*

The Cross on Coastguard Hill, Budleigh Salterton

STAR WATCHING

The English coast is the best place in the country for watching stars because outside of resort towns and cities it's totally unaffected by light pollution.

Wait for a clear night to visit an out-of-town location. It doesn't matter whether you're down on the beach waterside or high on a cliff top.

Take a torch, but keep it off. If you've got the time, arrive before sunset and allow your eyes to adjust to the changing phases. The skies, light and water can combine to create unique reflections of unimaginable beauty. Auras, green flashes, rainbows and unique cloud formations are common. Nature begins to do something strange and you'll start to see and hear things that are not entirely in keeping with the daylight norm. It can be unnerving, but it's good to walk into the darkness. Once your eyes have adjusted enough and the full moon lights up the way, look skywards for the North Star – the anchor around which it's possible to start exploring the celestial map on a regular basis.

On a clear coastal night, anywhere will do, but some of the best places in England are Dengie Marshes in Essex, the Wash in Lincolnshire and Norfolk, Spurn Head in Yorkshire, Solway Firth and Morecambe Bay in Cumbria, the Severn Estuary, Hartland in North Devon, the Lizard Peninsula in South Cornwall, and Birling Gap in Sussex.

Otherwise, consider combining stargazing with night-time nature walks for bat watching, listening to natterjack toads and nightjars, or looking for glow-worms.

South East
Easton Broad – *Suffolk*
Salthouse Marshes – *Norfolk*
Broad Rife Sands – *West Sussex*

South West
Golden Cap – *Dorset*
Beer Head – *South Devon*
Kemyel Cliff – *South Cornwall*

North East
Bamburgh Castle – *Northumberland*
Scremerston – *Northumberland*
Filey Brigg – *Yorkshire*

North West
Birkrigg Common – *Cumbria*
Roanhead Beach – *Cumbria*
Giant's Grave – *Cumbria*

Ventnor, Isle of Wight

Kimmeridge

12 Best for...
FOSSIL HUNTING

Time is an elastic concept that humanity has yet to come to terms with. All we know is that there remain a vast number of things about the past that we don't know. Fossils are a reminder of that lack of knowledge. Of our limits. All we can do, then, as we stand at Walton Cliffs holding a 5-million-year-old shell picked from the chalk red sand or stroke an ammonite on Lyme Regis beach, is imagine what it was like on earth back then, transporting ourselves back through time and space to a bygone era when the world was very different from how it is now.

Hunting for fossils is, therefore, a way we can best encounter time without understanding it. It also provides us with a first-hand, tangible experience of the geological changes that have happened, and are happening, beneath our feet.

The geology and history of England is evident everywhere, from London clay and the rainbow sands of the Isle of Wight to the rocky crags of Cornwall, Devon and Somerset, the sandy cliffs of Lancaster and the Dover chalk streams, if we just scratch beneath the surface.

What's more, the combination of seeing into a window of the past in a tidal setting and witnessing the impact of timeless movement and change is incredibly humbling, in a good way.

South East
Walton-on-the-Naze cliffs – *Essex*
Corton cliffs – *Suffolk*
Bognor Regis – *West Sussex*

South West
Yaverland – *Isle of Wight*
Lyme Regis – *Dorset*
Taddiford Gap – *Hampshire*

North East
Sugar Sands – *Northumberland*
South Ferriby cliff – *Lincolnshire*
Chapel Point – *Lincolnshire*

North West
Parton Bay, Whitehaven – *Cumbria*

13 Best for…
SUNSETS AND CLIFF TOP VIEWS

High tops and coastal hill forts are the places to be to find England's best coastal views – from the Chalk Cliffs or Beachy Head in Sussex and the Valley of Rocks in Devon, to Lancashire's Warton Crag and Hunt Cliff in Yorkshire.

The point where the peaks fall into the sea provides some of the most dramatic landscapes in England, and in turn are highly visible from land and sea. For this reason, these lofty summits also serve as beacons – landmarks that have been used for thousands of years as way markers and lookouts.

Three of the top four views in Yorkshire are along the England Coast Path. And now there's a new England Coast Path view from Staithes.

DEFRA/ Natural England

South East
Birling Gap – *East Sussex*
St Margaret's Bay – *Kent*
London Bridge – *London*

South West
Watershoot Bay – *Isle of Wight*
Hengistbury Head – *Dorset*
Valley of Rocks – *North Devon*

North East
St Mary's Lighthouse – *Northumberland*
Hunt Cliff – *Yorkshire*
St Bees – *Cumbria*

North West
The Barrows, Heysham – *Lancashire*
Warton Crag – *Lancashire*
West Pier Lighthouse, Whitehaven – *Cumbria*

Daddyhole

14 Best for…
WATERFALLS, SPRINGS AND WELLS

Fresh water is one of the most exciting things to discover around the coast. The fresh is yang to the tidal yin: where nature gives birth to life in a marriage of two worlds coming together. Little wonder, then, that wells, streams and waterfalls are commonly associated with ancient settlements and holy places.

Waterfalls perhaps best epitomise the conjunction of the two worlds. Certainly, showering in a waterfall is unlike anything else – an opportunity to experience a natural wonder. The English coast isn't peppered with Niagara-style features, but look around at the OS map and you'll be surprised at how many small waterfalls there are.

Most are found around the craggy south-west coast of Somerset, Devon and Cornwall. These are at their best after a long, wet winter.

Springs and wells are similarly surprisingly numerous, if you take the time to look, and searching out these sources of fresh water is an obvious follow-up to foraging for food. However, it's better not to drink at the waterfalls and fresh water streams today unless there is a very clear message that it's safe to do so. The chances of drinking contaminated or toxic water is extremely slim – our dogs are testament to that; they are the canaries in the cage that drink puddle water from dawn to dusk and never seem to get ill. But it's a personal thing. At the very least, boil or sterilise and filter the water before you drink it.

Hollow Brook Waterfall

South East
Beeleigh Falls, River Chelmer – *Essex*
Wolferton Creek – *Norfolk*
Holywell Ledge – *East Sussex*

South West
Kimmeridge Bay – *Dorset*
Osmington Mills – *Dorset*
Speke's Mill Mouth – *North Devon*

North East
Beast Cliff – *Yorkshire*
Nose's Point – *Northumberland*
Danes Dyke – *Yorkshire*

North West
Gutterby Spa – *Cumbria*
Warburton's Wood, River Weaver – *Cheshire*
Woodwell Holy Well – *Lancashire*

SUMMER SOLSTICE

English summers at the coast – much like the winters – are uniquely wonderful. Somewhere to explore nature without worrying too much about sunstroke, wild animals, getting lost or flash floods, all of which can be a problem in many of the countries we visit for traditional beach holidays. That's not to say there are no risks in England, but if you can arrive prepared and keep your wits about you, our wild coast comes with more of the fruits of Eden than the thistles of Gomorrah.

Indeed, few countries in the world enjoy such a perfectly temperate climate for walking, climbing, exploring and camping, being neither too hot, nor too cold. English summers are infamously wet, yet outside of Cumbria this reputation is based on cliché and unimaginative tales of washed-out holidays rather than the reality of a yearly average of four hours of sunshine per day and an average maximum temperature of 13°C (55°F).

Nevertheless, if guaranteed sunbathing and hours of unbroken sunshine is your idea of a perfect holiday then the English coast in summer is a coin toss and may not be right for you.

There are around 519 million visits to paths, cycleways and bridleways in England each year.
DEFRA/Natural England

Clevedon

But if swimming, cycling, rock pooling, coasteering, horse riding, climbing or kayaking, with lots of sunshine breaks in between, is more your thing then there's nowhere better than England. Pack the wetsuit and go wild in a summer storm over Northumberland dunes, or go commando in a secluded bay during a heatwave. Ride bikes over miles of hard sand in Somerset, Essex and Lancashire or climb around the wooded hills of North Devon and Cornwall. Pack your binoculars and your patience and see if you can spot dragonflies, orchids, glow-worms, blue butterflies, whales, basking sharks and dolphins.

Summer is a time for late-night picnics and campfires under tarp or tree; walks through meadows and cliff top rambles awash with butterflies and wild flowers; the screeching sound of playful swallows and swifts at dusk, and mewing buzzards over ripe cornfields in the weeks before the combine harvesters are sent out over another golden harvest.

If you measure value for money in daylight hours, then the summer solstice is the most valuable day of the year. It usually occurs around 21 June with sunrise before 5am and sunset around 9.30pm. Which means you have all day to get out there out there and soak it all in.

South East
East Head Spit (sunbathing lizards and
  wild flowers) – *West Sussex*
Sovereign Harbour and Beach (swallows
  and house martins) – *East Sussex*
Cley Marshes (spoonbills) – *Norfolk*

South West
Godrevy (butterflies) – *North Cornwall*
Chapel Port (flowering purple heath) –
  North Cornwall
Looe Island (grey seals) – *South Cornwall*

North East
Tynemouth Castle and Priory (swifts) –
  Tyne
Noah's Wood (tree fossils) – *Yorkshire*
Annstead Dunes (sunbathing adders and
  lizards) – *Northumberland*

North West
Arnside (butterflies) – *Cumbria*
Freshfield Dune Heath (summer heather)
  – *Cheshire*
Sandscale Haws National Nature Reserve
  (croaking natterjack toads) – *Cumbria*

MABON – AUTUMN EQUINOX

Marking the end of the English summer, the September equinox occurs between 21 and 24 September when the sun crosses the celestial equator, and rises directly in the east and sets directly in the west. Before this date, the sun rises and sets more to the north, and after the equinox it rises and sets more to the south.

Around the equinox, the sun dips lower and lower in the sky, making this the best time to explore wooded shores where beams of sunlight creep beneath the green leaf canopy on to the floor. Hedgerows still hang heavy with late berries, fruits and slow-moving dragonflies. As the autumn season moves on, look out for the dewy dawns and mist-filled mornings.

Late October and November are the best times to visit the wooded river valleys around South Devon, Somerset and Suffolk; bathed in sunshine and leaves dappled reds, yellows, browns and oranges that seem to have the ability to hang forever ... until winter gales finally blow in on the first winter storms. October and November see the return of thousands of geese and migrant waders flying in on their famous V-formations from Iceland and the Arctic colds.

This is also probably the best season for foraging. Apart from shellfish, there are mushrooms, the last of the fattest and sweetest blackberries and elderberries, chestnuts, hazelnuts and the early sloes after an early frost.

Paignton

South East

Pagham Harbour (brent geese arrive in October) – *West Sussex*

Normans Bay (quiet swims with seals) – *East Sussex*

Bawdsey Manor (autumn woodland) – *Suffolk*

South West

Bossington (roaring red deer) – *Somerset*

Arne Nature Reserve (rutting sika deer) – *Dorset*

Bouldnor Forest (red squirrels) – *Isle of Wight*

North East

Gibraltar Point (flocks of waders, fieldfares and redwings) – *Lincolnshire*

Saltwick Bay (fossil hunt after storm tides) – *Yorkshire*

Farne Islands (seal pups born) – *Northumberland*

North West

Leasowe Lighthouse (redstarts and ring ouzels) – *Cheshire*

Jack Scout (autumn woodland) – *Lancashire*

Piel Castle, Barrow-in-Furness (migratory curlew and pink-footed geese arrive) – *Cumbria*

17 Best for…
WINTER SOLSTICE

England's best-kept secret is winter. Yet all too often, we miss its magic while tied up in thoughts of de-icing the car, grumbling about the cold and the dark, and shopping for Christmas. For many, in fact, the chaos of Christmas has probably become more associated with 'wishing away' the shorter days, pining instead for spring and summer holidays, with their more easy-going pace.

Our ancient ancestors saw things a bit differently. Instead of mourning the changing seasons, they celebrated them. The 'deathly hallows' of modern winters were a celebration of nature, represented by the iconic motifs of holly, mistletoe and sloes.

Waxwing feeding on rowan berry

South East
Blakeney Point (thousands of seal pups born) – *Norfolk*
Hickling Broad (common cranes) – *Norfolk*
Fobbing Marsh (starling murmurations) – *Essex*

South West
Compton Bay (flocks of dunlin) – *Isle of Wight*
Mullion Island (storm watching) – *South Cornwall*
Berrow Beach (migratory snipe and oystercatchers) – *Somerset*

North East
Gibraltar Point (80,000 dark-bellied brent geese) – *Lincolnshire*
Craster Harbour wall (pink-footed geese flying in V-formation) – *Northumberland*
Druridge Bay (otters) – *Northumberland*

North West
Dee Estuary – (short-eared owls hunting) – *Cheshire*
Campfield Marsh (thousands of teals, wigeons, pintails and shovelers feeding) – *Cumbria*
Sunbrick Stone Circle, Birkrigg Common (solstice) – *Cumbria*

We can learn from their example: dark footpaths and hedgerows in our coastal parts often lead out to the bright light of midday winter sun sparkling on an estuary or a seascape alive with the millions of wintering birds that flock to our shores from all around the world. This is especially the case along the east coast.

Solstice – from the Latin *sol* (sun) and *sistere* (to stand still) – occurs a few days before Christmas, usually on 21 December, on the shortest day. It's literally a reference to the sun dying or appearing to stand still, its daily movement resting at its most northerly point before reversing its direction and moving south. Much like a giant tanker on a sea that can't turn so quickly in the heavenly void, the sun appears motionless for a few days before it picks up the pace again. It's a magical time in nature that sadly mostly passes us by today.

This needn't be the case. Whatever we think about the English climate, much like our summers, our winters are uniquely temperate and mostly safe for expeditions and forays beyond the car parks and village greens towards the estuaries and coastal paths. And what a spectacle awaits. Apart from migrant waders and geese, winter is the time to see thousands of seal pups being born, and to look out for waxwings feeding on berry-laden trees. And then there's picking sloes for sloe gin and finding mistletoe clumps in the bare-leaf tree canopy.

But it's not all seal pups and plump berries. There's nothing like some bad weather for storm watching, and the English coast provides one of the most dramatic viewing platforms upon which to see nature in all its dramatic glory. So wrap up warm and head outdoors. Remember, there is no bad weather, just bad clothing.

18 Best for...
OSTARA – SPRING EQUINOX

The March equinox has a dramatic effect on low tides as the subsolar point leaves the southern hemisphere and crosses the celestial equator. The moon's pull drags back waters to their absolute lowest in the days following the equinox, making this an incredible time to explore the rarely accessible coastal shallows for shellfish, sunken wrecks and fossils.

The English climate warms quickly from this point on, but not too far past an average of 18°C (64°F). The bluebells that carpet ancient woodlands in March start to die back by April, as the air fills with the scents of wild garlic and hawthorn blossom.

It's a truly wonderful moment when this equinox combines with warm weather and low-pressure breezes. Nature literally sings its heart out as March moves into April.

This is the best time to wild camp, with the sun setting after 8.30pm and rising with the dawn chorus just before 5am.

Among the wonders of spring are listening out for the bubbling song of curlews, the booming call of bitterns at Sussex's Rye Harbour, or the night noise of male natterjack toads around Lincolnshire's Saltfleetby; walking through coastal bluebell woodlands; catching a glimpse of the male hen harrier's spring sky dance at Essex's Wallasea Island; whale watching and looking out for the first migrating ospreys from Africa; or seeing mad March boxing hares at Norfolk's Upton Broad and Marshes.

Old Harry Rocks

South East
Fingringhoe Wick Nature Reserve (migrant nightingales start to sing) – *Essex*
Reculver Country Park (sand martins arrive to nest in cliffs) – *Kent*
Blue House Farm Nature Reserve (mad March boxing hares) – *Essex*

South West
Duckpool (wild flowering beach) – *North Cornwall*
Chesil Beach (nesting little terns) – *Dorset*
Helford (nesting herons; heronry) – *South Cornwall*

North East
Spurn, River Humber (thousand of swallows and house martins arrive from Africa) – *Yorkshire*
Cowbar Nab, Staithes (nesting kittiwakes on rock ledges) – *Yorkshire*
Flamborough Cliffs (nesting puffins) – *Yorkshire*

North West
Red Rocks Marsh (call of the male natterjack) – *Cheshire*
Heysham Nature Reserve (butterflies) – *Lancashire*
Festival Park, Liverpool (spring flowers) – *Cheshire*

COAST PATH

Lee Bay, Ilfracombe

PART 2

THE
COAST
PATH

Peppercombe

THE COAST PATH

This book has three objectives:

1 To record the story that made the coast path a reality; define it, make it, applaud it.
2 To celebrate the architects and workers who built the England Coast Path – the longest coast path in the world. But most importantly...
3 To guide you to 1,000 places around the 3,000 miles of coast – spaced an average of about 3 miles apart – sometimes more, sometimes less.

WHERE ARE THE 1,000 AMAZING PLACES AROUND THE COAST?

Warm up with a cuppa on a tidal estuary under a cherry tree or skinny dip in the surf under moonlight; watch dolphins breach in an azure bay or pick up 50 million-year-old fossils on a Jurassic beach; gaze at the Milky Way from a hill fort crag or shelter in a beach cave during a summer storm; sleep in a cliff top lighthouse or wild camp on a mattress of samphire and sand; climb rope ladders down to secret beaches or amble up a rock face to a fabled castle.

A STATEMENT OF FACTS

Some 12,000 people, 3,000 miles and £2 per metre, has created a pipeline for 23,000 businesses around the coast that needed a lift, a lifeline or some good old-fashioned custom: coffee houses, cafes, B&Bs, hotels, farm shops, museums, council-run car parks, ice-cream stalls, cottages for rent, campsites and ready-made tents.

THE ENGLAND COAST PATH STORY

An English tale. Thousands of people coming together to create something communal: a tribal legacy; a sacred and safe passage. Launched and opened at the London 2012 Olympics in Weymouth, the England Coast Path is not only 'Made in England' but 'Made *of* England'.

Abbotsbury

Afternoon Teas & Parking

Where parking fees have crept up to £7 or £8 per car, it's sometimes better value to make use of the ECP tea section and invest in a cuppa.

A cream tea will rarely cost more than £8 or £9 in the poshest coastal tearoom, hotel or beachside restaurant. The upside of investing a crisp £10 with a private business is it makes their day, keeps their business ticking over, and best of all you often get free parking and access to sea views and beach fronts that would otherwise be inaccessible.

Pubs, B&Bs, Restaurants, Cafes & Campsites

Food and drink are the fuels that power outdoor adventure.

Carrying water and a packed lunch is great; but combining a coast path visit with a treat moment at a pub, cafe or sleeping overnight is magical.

A word on the pubs, coffee houses and hotels. They are not always included because they are the best or even the cheapest along the ECP. Many offer unique tidal or river access. Sometimes that access justifies paying £5 for a rank coffee or £10 for a cold pie, because it comes with free parking and wonderful views. Maybe even a stroll along a beach stretch only currently accessible to clients.

Seafood

Food sourced from the sea is inevitably going to feature in a book about the coast. Many of the restaurants and bars around our shores specialise in fresh fish and seafood.

That's not to say the eateries, oyster bars, cafes and restaurants are not for vegans, vegetarians or meat eaters. Almost all the restaurants listed in this book cater very well for all diets and tastes. It's partly why they're in here. They also source local produce and in the main have made a commitment to sustainable foods from both the sea and land.

Abbotsbury, St Catherine's Chapel

Directions & parking

Most of the directions to the wild places are linked to official car parks. There's a cost to that – usually from £4 upwards. It may be a price worth paying.

Churches

A significant number of entries in this list of 1,000 places are churches.

There are two reasons:

1 Church wardens and parishioners seem so welcoming most of the time.
2 Churches are built on the places our pagan and non-pagan ancestors considered most sacred – usually high ground where fresh water (springs, waterfalls and rivers) meet the tides.

Irrespective of your faith, atheism or religion, churches retain something of the old values and life-sustaining beauty associated with the most precious locations around the coast.

Stars

Dark skies are best at the coast. A dark sky is like a canary in a cage. When it's non-existent, we are surrounded by urban and city sprawl. Artificial light pollution dims the ability of terrestrial light to reach the back of our retinas.

When we're in a truly wild area, the light from the night skies shines and sparkles on a cloudless evening like a Christmas tree. The further we get from street lights and residential areas, the better the skies, the better our vision. The closer we get to nature, the better the skies. The more use we make of our vision.

The best dark skies in England, unsurprisingly are around the coast.

It's an irony in some ways: a lit city or town is awash with dark corners and shadows, where neither natural nor artificial light can reach.

The coast is divided up into Dark Sky areas graded from 1 to 5. 1 is the best. That will be somewhere that is truly star struck.

The List

Once on the England Coast Path, each of the 1,000 places listed here is an average of 3½

Orford Ness

miles apart. That's equivalent to about a 2 hr
walk (a morning or afternoon round trip). Try it.

The more places you tick off the list, the more
they will deliver on your particular wants and
needs.

Disability

If for any reason accessibility is an issue, this list
of 1,000 places includes literally hundreds of
places for you to enjoy too. Depending on your
disability, this enjoyment may come from the
sights, the smells or the sounds. Maybe all three.
The rush of cold air on arms, shoulders or feet.

There's nothing inherently magical or mystical
about any of these places. It's just nature.
Wonderful enough – but still magic. Let it fill your
nostrils and ears, dance over your open mouth
and then bounce off your skin in all its colours,
shades and flavours. Because it's who and what
we are. It's where we're going and where we
came from.

The Senses

The coast path described in this book is not a
journey in itself. This is not a traditional walking,
cycling or nature guide. This is something closer
to a journey through the five senses.

Our senses are often dulled by either urban
living, domesticity or routine; or a combination
of all three. We really only make proper use of
one of our senses: sight.

Two of the other four senses are underused.
We underuse smell and touch.

The other two are drowned by pollution.
Hearing is constantly polluted by noise. We
sometimes use earphones and music to drown
the noise but these can detach us from reality.
The final polluted sense is taste. It's mostly
drowned by a combination of overeating and
overstimulation by sugars and salts.

Nature is a respite from all of that. It's a
balance. A combination of resetting the overused
senses, and reigniting the underused ones.

Shoebury East Beach

SO FOR THE UNDERUSED SENSES TRY:

1 SECRET SWIMS AND HIDDEN BEACHES...

Touch: Feel the sea breeze on your face. Dip your feet in rock pools. Sit on a riverbank and gently stroke the grass with your palm. Or even better, strip off and float on water so the tide runs over your body. If it's winter, buy a £250 wetsuit and float in ice. Feel hot sand under your feet. Or rest your the toes on a shell bank. Sink your feet into warm estuary mud.

2 WATERSIDE WOODLAND

Smell: Enter a coastal pine forest and inhale the fumes. Walk through the dense, broadleaf trees of an ancient English wood when it's raining. Smell the tree bark and the garlic around the roots. Walk from the wood out on to the dunes and fill your nostrils and lungs with the scent of salty, fresh air.

FOR THE OVER-SENSED TASTE BUDS AND NOISE-WEARY EARS TRY:

1 WILD CAMPS AND FORAGING

Taste: Forage for leaves and fruit along the hedgerows. If you can find a safe water source, drink from the holy wells and springs that feed into the tidal edges of the sands and rocks.

2 WONDERFUL WILDLIFE

Hear: Listen out for the crows over the castle ruins; the buzzards mewing around the church fields; the trickle of water from the brook that runs along the old path. The wind in the canopy of the great elms; the fat bee around the mauve flowers; the rustling blackbird in the autumn leaves.

Then there's our sight. Just like the other four senses, this is an opportunity to touch something deep within ourselves that resonates with a past.

ANCIENT, SACRED AND NIGHT SKIES

Sight: Look down from the top of a hill fort over a sandy bay. Sit on the estuary and watch the tide rise and fall around the creeks and rivers. Notice the changing landcapes; the beacons on the horizon. Catch a fleeting glimpse of the merlin swooping over the marshes or a seal as it pops its head up briefly. Watch dolphins and porpoises breach offshore on the bay. Watch the stars at night. See a shooting star from the corner of your eye. Marvel at your ability to see at night in the wildest, darkest places. See the foxes' eyes illuminated by the full moon, and bats dipping over water at dusk. Spot a fossil on a beach.

Sixth sense: A combination of all these senses... Even if they are encountered with your children and ice creams at the beach, or cod, chips and tartar sauce at the estuary bar overlooking Portsmouth Harbour and the gulls on mud flats. Think about what you experienced and enjoyed and what you want to return to. There are more than 1,000 places in this book. They don't begin to scratch the surface. There is an infinite number of places, sights, sounds, smells, noises and sensations to experience.

What is England?

You have in your hands a rough guide to something remarkable and free.

It's not just a geographic place. It's not even just a spiritual and mystical place. It's also somewhere to escape. It's somewhere to be curious. It's somewhere that can be whatever you want it to be. Whether you're English, Welsh, Cornish, Russian, Haitian, Canadian or just plain bored.

Something quick about being English. I was born in Essex, England. So I declare an interest in the country. When I was at university they told us that 'Englishman' was a myth. A nasty little myth, they said. A sense of entitlement or belonging that demeaned visitors and immigrants by defining a national culture according to something that others couldn't aspire to, even if they wanted to.

I'm not sure that's true. In fact ... I feel the 'character' of the places in every airport lounge or bus stop I arrive at in every country around the world. I feel the 'regional character' at every service station I refuel at across America or Germany or Turkey. I feel it, but I can't define it. Any more than I can explain to you why I prefer Goa over Glastonbury, Suffolk over Norfolk, Lancashire over Cumbria, or why I'd rather spend a month holidaying in Essex than south Devon.

Whatever 'Englishness' is ... this book is about England. This is of England. The England Coast Path. You can decide what that means to you.

KEY TO SYMBOLS

These symbols appear alongside location titles as a guide to the habitat, geology or theme of a place:

Beach or coast

Woodland

Mother nature

Ancient and sacred

Good for dark skies

Accommodation

Restaurant or cafe

KEY TO ABBREVIATIONS

This is a guide to the directional abbreviations used within the location texts:

N – north	**L** – left	**Rez** – reservoir
S – south	**FP** – footpath	**BW** – bridleway
W – west	**Ln** – lane	**ECP** – England
E – east	**Rd** – road	Coast Path
R – right	**Dr** – drive	

Wandsworth Park, London

THAMES SOUTH BANK

WILD THINGS TO DO BEFORE YOU DIE:

LISTEN to bitterns calling over 100 acres of disused reservoir.

HUG an oak tree at Kew Gardens.

RUB your fingers through the sands of Gabriel's Beach.

HIRE a kayak at Shadwell Basin.

LOOK for sparrowhawks hunting feral pigeons.

LISTEN for squawking parakeets in Wandsworth Park.

TAKE the river cruise out to Greenwich.

WATCH the sunrise over the Tower from London Bridge.

Teddington Lock keeper's cabin

Teddington Lock, River Thames

Tidal limit of the Thames. Complex of three locks in the London Borough of Richmond.

➤ **Find** where the river path meets Riverside Dr in Richmond, TW10 7RP. Just before the parked cars, follow the hard FP 390 yards down to the Thames. The Teddington Lock Footbridge can be used to cross to the other side of the river.

51.43009, -0.32211

Obelisk, Richmond, River Thames

Now sadly eroded and defaced, this small obelisk lies on the Old Meridian Line that ran through the King's Observatory in Old Deer Park. The clocks in the Houses of Parliament used to be set in time with this Old Meridian until Greenwich Mean Time took over as the timekeeping benchmark in the 1880s.

➤ **Find** Pools on the Park in Old Deer Park, Twickenham Rd, Richmond, TW9 2SF. From the public car park, walk across the park 600 yards to the obelisk, which is in the middle of the grassy area 325 yards back from the river woodland.

51.464492, -0.314617

Kew Gardens, Kew, River Thames

Vast wood by the River Thames, part of one of the largest botanical garden collections in the world.

➤ **Find** Kew Gardens station, Station Approach, Kew, TW9 3BZ. Park entrance is a 440-yard walk. Also walk 1.2 miles along the riverbank from the obelisk (turn R if facing the river). www.kew.org

51.47922, -0.29559

Leg O Mutton, River Thames

Good place to see bats – over the disused rez, along ½-mile stretch of river front. Also known as Lonsdale Rd Reservoir.
➤ **Find** where Gerard Rd meets Lonsdale Rd in Barnes. From the parking lay-by and facing the river, walk R along the FP 435 yards until you are between the rez and the river.

51.483972, -0.247702

WWT London Wetland Centre, River Thames

Watch bitterns, parakeets, sparrowhawks and sand martins. A wetland over 100 acres of disused rezs on a loop in the Thames. Hides, plus a cafe, daily tours and specialist talks.
➤ **Find** the Wetland Information Centre, off Queen Elizabeth Walk, Barnes, SW13 8AB. Walk through the car park to explore the river and lagoons on all sides.
www.wwt.org.uk/wetland-centres/london/

51.47653, -0.23532

THE SHIP, MORTLAKE, RIVER THAMES

Pub beside an old cobbled ramp down to the stony foreshore. Overlooks the London Boat Race finishing line. Best at high tide when the waters lap up to the road.
10 Thames Bank, London, SW14 7QR
www.greeneking-pubs.co.uk

Wetland centre in West London

Wandsworth Park

THE DUKE'S HEAD, PUTNEY, RIVER THAMES

This Putney pub sits at the start of the Oxford and Cambridge University Boat Race.

8 Lower Richmond Rd, Putney, SW15 1JN
www.dukeshead putney.com

Wandsworth Park, Wandsworth, River Thames

Avenue of trees riverside and cycling on the river wall. Moorings. The 8ha park has 350 species of tree.

➤ **Find** Wandsworth Park, in Putney Bridge Rd, London, SW15 2PA. Past the pay-and-display parking signs, turn L into the park and down towards the small harbour at Wandsworth Riverside 275 yards away.
www.wandsworth.gov.uk/parks

51.46263, -0.20422

St Mary's Church, Battersea, River Thames

Beautiful riverside church. Famous as the last resting place of an American military officer who in 1780 during the American Revolutionary War defected to the British. He led the British army in battle against the very men he had once commanded.

➤ **Find** Battersea Church Rd, Battersea, SW11 3NA.
www.stmarysbattersea.org.uk

51.47665, -0.17538

Battersea Park

London peace pagoda in Battersea Park

FIUME RESTAURANT, BATTERSEA, RIVER THAMES

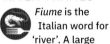 *Fiume* is the Italian word for 'river'. A large Mediterranean piazza-style terrace sits right on the bank of the waterside. With unrivalled views of the Thames.

Battersea Power Station, Circus West Village, Battersea, SW8 5BN
www.fiume-restaurant .co.uk

RIVERSIDE CAFE, LAMBETH PIER, RIVER THAMES

By the water with views of Big Ben on the other side of the river. Hot food and drinks.

Lambeth Palace Rd, Lambeth, SE1 7SG
Facebook: Riverside Cafe Lambeth Pier

The London Peace Pagoda, Battersea, River Thames

Symbolic architecture in a serene location, with views over Chelsea Embankment. One of 80 peace pagodas around the world, it tells a story through a series of gilt-bronze statues. It was presented to Londoners by the founder of a Japanese Buddhist movement.

➤ **Find** Battersea Park overground station 220 yards from the Queens Circus/Queenstown Rd entrance, London, SW8 4NE. Follow the car park inside the park along the lake and then turn R and keep straight 700 yards all the way to the river and pagoda.

51.481980, -0.159067

Gabriel's Beach, Southwark, River Thames

One of the few places past Tilbury where you can find proper sand at low tide. Somewhere to either get on to the water, shore or just to look across.

➤ **Find** Blackfriars overground station. Walk across the bridge to the S side of the river and turn R to find beach 440 yards away.

51.508464, -0.108914

Ernie's Beach, Gabriel's Wharf

THE CUTTY SARK, GREENWICH, RIVER THAMES

Pub claiming to offer the best fresh fish dishes in Greenwich. Try the Greenwich seafood pot for a treat.

4–6 Ballast Quay, London, SE10 9PD
www.cuttysarkse10.co.uk

THE ANGEL, SOUTHWARK, RIVER THAMES

Pub with good-priced ales. Best river views of Tower Bridge are upstairs.

101 Bermondsey Wall E, London, SE16 4NB
www.pubpeople.com

London Bridge, Southwark, River Thames

Watch sunrise over the greatest river city in the world.
This bridge is the river link between the City of London and Southwark.
➤ **Find** London Bridge station, SE1 9RA. Bridge is a 5-min walk. It can take 60 mins to cross with a camera in your hand on a clear dawn, winter or summer.

51.506890, -0.088229

Gallions Hill, Greenwich, River Thames

Great views down to bracken-laden shoreline of Old Wooden Slipway. Park surrounding the area and access to the riverfront.
➤ **Find** the cycle path on Linton Mead, Thamesmead, Greenwich, SE28 8DZ, off the A2040, just past the Thamesmead shopping centre. Follow the path 330 yards to the Thames FP and turn L at the river. Follow the FP 1.2 miles and then turn L away from the river into the park just before the blocks of flats. The hill is 440 yards on the R side of the park.

51.502066, 0.09141

THE MAYFLOWER PUB, ROTHERHITHE, RIVER THAMES

The oldest pub on the River Thames. Enjoy a candlelit restaurant on the decked jetty. You may spot the original 1620 mooring point of the Pilgrim Fathers' *Mayflower* ship. Indoors, while warming yourself by the open fire, imagine who may have been sitting in your seat 400 years ago!

117 Rotherhithe St, London, SE16 4NF
www.mayflowerpub.co.uk

ST CHRISTOPHER'S INN GREENWICH HOSTEL, GREENWICH, RIVER THAMES

Backpacker hostel right next to Greenwich station. Good access for Greenwich Park and river FP. Prices include breakfast.

189 Greenwich High Rd, London, SE10 8JA
www.st-christophers. co.uk/london/greenwich-hostel/

THE OLD THAMESIDE INN, SOUTHWARK, RIVER THAMES

Pub a short stroll from Clink St, Borough Market, Winchester Walk and London Bridge station.

Pickfords Wharf, 1 Clink St, London, SE1 9DG
www.nicholsonspubs.co.uk

Erith Yacht Club, Erith, River Thames

Creeks and waterside on the London/Kent border. The club has a bar with river views. Open on Thursday evenings and Sunday afternoons. Guests are made welcome.

➤ **Find** the club in Anchor Bay Wharf, Manor Rd, Dartford, Erith, DA8 2AD.
www.erithyachtclub.org.uk

51.47887, -0.19885

Cutty Sark, Greenwich, River Thames

Sea cruises and the birthplace of Henry VIII. The *Cutty Sark* was one of the fastest tea clippers that sailed between London and China. It was named after a witch who wore a short ('cutty') garment ('sark') that she had been given as a child.

➤ **Find** Blackheath overground station and car park at Hurren Cl, Blackheath, London, SE3 9LE. Walk 220 yards N into Blackheath Park. Cross the A2 into Greenwich Park after 550 yards. Keep straight in the park down Blackheath Av, past the Royal Observatory Greenwich. The *Cutty Sark* is beside the River Thames, nearly a mile from the A2 park crossing.
www.rmg.co.uk/cutty-sark

51.48303, -0.00960

London South Bank

St Margaret's Bay

KENT

WILD THINGS TO DO BEFORE YOU DIE:

EXPLORE Dungeness' stone desert.
STAND beside an Indian princess.
PADDLE Kingsgate Bay sea arch.
SWIM Sheerness with only butterflies for company.
FORAGE for wild cabbage at the Warren.
WATCH common seals at Horrid Hill.
EXPLORE secret caves at Botany Bay.
WILD camp the ruins of a crumbling fort.
WATCH bird murmurations over Elmley Marsh.
KAYAK Pegwell Bay's Shell Ness.
WALK 'The Street's offshore strip.
WATCH cormorants dive for fish.
FIND underground tunnels at Grain.
LISTEN to nightingales over Sondland.

Dartford Marshes, River Darent

A green lung between the Dartford Thames Crossing and London. Walk the bank where the River Darent meets the Thames while watching the ships flow silently in and out of England's largest city.

➤ **Find** and take the exit for junction 1a of the M25 to take the A206 towards Crayford and Erith for 1 mile. Turn at 2nd roundabout into Joyce Green Ln. Although there's a gate across the road, it's usually open to traffic. Follow the FP 1½ miles to the water's edge, then keep going around the River Darent as it meets the Thames.

51.474575, 0.230137

Pocahontas Memorial, Gravesend

A memorial to the heroic Indian princess. Pocahontas really did come to London after converting to Christianity and marrying an Englishman. Her grave is believed to be here somewhere in St George's Church. A life-size bronze statue honours her memory.

➤ **Find** Stone St next to Railway Dry Cleaners in Gravesend town centre. Walk S to St Georges Church, Church St, DA11 0DN, where the memorial is in the garden. The ferry port 400ft away runs daily services to Tilbury, Essex, for a few pounds.

51.444106, 0.36808C

Cliffe Forte, Cliffe, River Thames

Stunning fort at a narrow in the Thames, and gateway to Cliffe Pools. Increasingly difficult to access because of erosion, which makes it a great place to wild camp. Best attempted either at low tide in boots or by kayak from Coalhouse Fort on the other side of the Thames, Essex. Getting there is an adventure in itself and takes at least 60 mins on foot.

➤ **Find** the end of Salt Ln, ME3 7SU, ½ mile E of The Cliffe Cafe, Buckland Rd, Rochester, ME3 7SR. Pass through the large metal gate into RSPB Cliffe Pools, and follow the FP along the L edge of the pool all the way to Cliffe Creek, where the FP forks L towards the fort. If this access is overgrown or collapsed, try the long walk round to the SW entrance by passing through the gravel works entrance, higher up Salt Ln and then walking up High Creek FP.

51.463509, 0.45536⁰

London Stone, Isle of Grain, River Thames

A beautiful creek and sand delta where a stone marker signals the end of London's control over the tidal Thames. There is no FP access to the beach, but swimmers and pack rafters sometimes cross Yantlet Creek at low tide from the FP W side of the creek (currents and foreign objects do pose a hazard, and there is a danger marked on OS just S and E of the London Stone).

➤ **Find** the public house at Allhallows-on-Sea. Walk N 500 yards to coast path. Facing the Thames, turn E and walk 1 mile to Yantlet Creek

51.472830, 0.67334.

THE LODGE GUEST HOUSE, MEDWAY ESTUARY

 Cheap as chips. 14 bedrooms. Breakfast from 6am. And off-road parking.

Chapel Rd, Isle of Grain, Rochester, ME3 0BZ
www.thelodgeisleof grain.com

Chetney Hill, Iwade

Small island connected to Chetney Marshes by a land bridge. In the 18th century, there were plans to build a holding 'hospital' here to quarantine potential plague carriers arriving from overseas. FP and byway access into and around the island and adjoining creek known as 'The Shade'.

➤ **Find** the FP N at Raspberry Hill Ln, Iwade, ME9 8SN. Walk N 1 mile to island. For access to the land bridge, walk anti-clockwise around the island, along the greenway.

51.394689, 0.705881

Egypt Bay Beach, Thames Estuary

Secluded sandbank beach off Dagnam Saltings.

➤ **Find** and exit the A228 roundabout, ½ mile E of High Halstow, on to Fenn St and follow directions for Allhallows and St Mary Hoo. After 1½ miles, turn L into Shakespeare Farm Rd, Rochester, ME3 8RS, and follow lane to the end. From here, pick up the FP that leads down to sea wall less than 1 mile away, or 20 mins, with small, secluded beaches to be discovered L or R.

51.475663, 0.617182

Grain Fort, Isle of Grain, Medway Estuary

'Urban explorers' tackle the series of tunnels under this derelict fort site jutting E into the mouth of the Medway Estuary. The 19th-century ruin has a small wood a few hundred yards S along the coastal path or bridleway.

➤ **Find** the FPs along the shore and around the fort and park from the end of High St, Isle of Grain, Rochester, ME3 0BS.

51.457049, 0.720050

Isle of Grain

THE SHIP INN, ROCHESTER, RIVER MEDWAY

Home-made food, good prices and views over the river from tables and benches outside. Mostly quiet.

Upnor Rd, Rochester, ME2 4UY
Facebook: @theshiptavernlowerupnor

RIVERSIDE COUNTRY PARK CAFE, GILLINGHAM, RIVER MEDWAY

Cafe and adventure playground by the river.

333 Lower Rainham Rd, Gillingham, ME7 2XH
Facebook: @cafefocusriverside

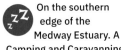

OVERSHAW CARAVAN PARK, RAINHAM, OTTERHAM CREEK

On the southern edge of the Medway Estuary. A Camping and Caravanning Club-certificated site for tents and caravans

136 Horsham Ln, Rainham, Gillingham, ME8 7XB
www.overshorecaravanparkupchurch.co.uk

Cockham Wood Fort, River Medway

Explore the 17th-century ruin and wonderful wooded shore at low tide. Stunning views over Hoo Marsh to the E, and St Mary's Island to the S, across the river. Best in early spring when the red brick is framed by green leaves and wild flowers in full bloom. The abandoned artillery fort was built to protect Chatham Dock Yard from Dutch raids.

➤ **Find** the car park in Upnor Rd, Rochester, ME2 4XB and, facing the river, turn L towards Medway Yacht Club. Walk down on to the foreshore beside the FP and keep walking E 330 yards until you see the fort. Best walked when the tide is on its way out.

51.412354, 0.551125

Holborough Marshes, Snodland, River Medway

Reed beds, marsh and brackish pools meet freshwater springs. Good for reed buntings, warblers, and nightingales.

➤ **Find** Snodland Railway Station, walk E along the High St to the stunning All Saints Church, High St, Wouldham, Rochester, ME1 3TD, beside the River Medway. There was once an ancient crossing as part of the Pilgrim's Way. After exploring the river, walk around the front of the church into the road called Church Field and follow it N for 330 yards as its FP leads out and around the marshes.

51.336480, 0.452356

Battle of the Medway Stone, River Medway

Emotive memorial stone N of Burham Marsh. Set in 1997, it commemorates the Battle of the Medway, when the English tribes were led by Caratacus. Walk ⅔ mile E on the Pilgrim's Way river path to the remote Mary's Church. Look out for kingfishers hunting among the reed beds.

➤ **Find** St Mary's Church, Old Church Rd, Burham, Rochester, ME1 3XY. Facing the church, walk on the FP down its left-hand side and follow it to the river. Turn R at the water and walk 710 yards to the stone, which is set back from the bank.

51.330486, 0.45313416

Baty's Marsh, River Medway

Watch graceful cormorants skilfully dive for fish beside the marina, on Wickham Reach, close to the Medway M2 bridge crossing.

➤ **Find** All Saints Church, High St, Wouldham, Rochester, ME1 3TD, by the River Medway. Facing the church, turn R along High St and then immediately L on to the FP after 44 yards. At the river, turn R and walk 2½ miles along its length, under the M2 bridge, to Baty's, which is the name of marsh just past the marina.

51.375752, 0.483839

Grain Fort

QUEEN
PHILLIPPA B&B,
QUEENBOROUGH
CREEK, RIVER
SWALE

Hotel next to the coast path. Breakfast ingredients sourced from local farm shops. Mixture of single, double and family rooms.

High St, Queenborough,
ME11 5AQ
www.queenphillippa.com

THE GARDEN
CAFE, SHEERNESS,
SWALE/THAMES
ESTUARY

Beachside cafe beside Shellness car park.

The Garden Cafe,
Shellness Rd, Sheerness,
ME12 4RH
01795 511 480

Horrid Hill, Medway Estuary

Fascinating island in the Medway Estuary, off Sharp's Green Bay. It is linked to the mainland by a man-made causeway. Warships, containing French prisoners of war, moored here during the Napoleonic Wars. It's common to see seals feeding at high tide.

➤ **Find** Riverside Country Park Cafe (see page 68). The car park next door looks out on to the estuary marshes. Walk across the car park to the shore 100 yards away. Turn L and follow the path 110 yards through the trees and on to the spit.

51.390095, 0.602071

St Margaret of Antioch Church, River Medway

Beautiful 8th-century Saxon church next to a small creek and harbour on the river. Church contains a fresco of the crucifixion of St Andrew.

➤ **Find** the Medway coast road, Raspberry Hill Ln, Lower Halstow, Sittingbourne, ME9 7PN. From the large shoreside lay-by, facing the sea, walk L 1.8 miles to St Margaret of Antioch Church, Lower Halstow, Sittingbourne, ME9 7PN. The harbour is next door, by the FP. Nice place for a rest.

51.375361, 0.671173

Shellness Beach, Thames Estuary

Long, isolated stretch of shell beach (naturist) at the hamlet of Shellness.

➤ **Find** the car park next to the 90-degree bend near the end of Shellness Rd, Leysdown-on-Sea, Sheerness, ME12 4RP. Keep walking along the unmade road 460 yards past the cottages on to the beach that stretches out in front of you.

51.372481, 0.950152

Princes Drive, Sandwich

THE SHIP INN, CONYER, CONYER CREEK

 Majestic views of the creek, marina and marshes across to the Swale. The Ship Inn is at the end of Conyer Creek, a tidal inlet that separates the mainland from the Isle of Sheppey. Sailing barges were made here. The pub used to be a baker's shop, built in 1642, with a blacksmiths alongside.

Conyer, Sittingbourne, ME9 9HR
Facebook: Ship Inn Conyer

THE SHIPWRIGHTS ARMS, FAVERSHAM, SWALE ESTUARY

An old pirates' and smugglers' inn next to Testers boatyard and creek.

Hollowshore, Faversham, ME13 7TU
www.theshipwrights athollowshore.co.uk

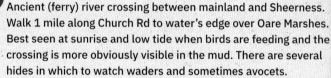

Elmley Marshes

Cloud-like murmurations gather in the winter skies at dusk as thousands of birds arrive to roost here. Explore the moat-like creek that may or may not be man-made. There are several crossings into the circle and a FP crosses the outer SW flank on its way to the bridleway as it circles N. Look out for hares.

➤ **Find** Ferry Rd at its junction with Sheppey Way, Minster on Sea, Sheerness, ME12 3RN, just off the A2500. Follow Ferry Rd to its dead end, past the turning area. At the water, turn L on foot and keep walking along the shore FP for 2.1 miles to Elmley Marshes and the narrow creeks.

51.370585, 0.774305

Ford Crossing, River Swale

Ancient (ferry) river crossing between mainland and Sheerness. Walk 1 mile along Church Rd to water's edge over Oare Marshes. Best seen at sunrise and low tide when birds are feeding and the crossing is more obviously visible in the mud. There are several hides in which to watch waders and sometimes avocets.

➤ **Find** the end of Church Rd, Faversham, ME13 0QD. Just before the water's edge is a car park. Walk out on to the crossing a few yards from the Saxon Shore Way FP. Walk L to explore Oare Marshes and the gaping Oare Creek.

51.345912, 0.889333

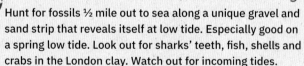

The Street, Whitstable, Swale Estuary

Hunt for fossils ½ mile out to sea along a unique gravel and sand strip that reveals itself at low tide. Especially good on a spring low tide. Look out for sharks' teeth, fish, shells and crabs in the London clay. Watch out for incoming tides.

➤ **Find** the grass promenade above the beach off Marine Pde, Whitstable, CT5 2AJ. Facing the sea, turn L and keep walking to the beach huts, where you'll start to see the sand spit emerge another 220 yards on as the tide goes out.

51.366133, 1.035635

THE SPORTSMAN, SEASALTER, SWALE ESTUARY

Stunning. Located on the old coastal road between Whitstable and Faversham. Fruit and veg from a small kitchen garden. Try the oysters.

Faversham Rd, Seasalter, Whitstable, CT5 4BP
www.thesportsman
seasalter.co.uk

CRAB & WINKLE, WHITSTABLE, SWALE ESTUARY

Remarkable sunsets over the English Channel. Local fish are sold in the restaurant and fish market.

South Quay, The Harbour, Whitstable, CT5 1AB
www.crabandwinkle
restaurant.co.uk

THE HAMPTON INN, HERNE BAY

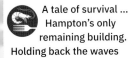

A tale of survival ... Hampton's only remaining building. Holding back the waves as we went to press.

72 Western Espl, Herne Bay, CT6 8DL
www.hamptoninn
hernebay.co.uk

Minni's Bay, Birchington

Long, sandy beach that doesn't attract the larger crowds of neighbouring Margate. Best to swim in summer a few hours before dusk.

➤ **Find** Minnis Bay Car Park, off Darynton Av, Birchington, CT7 9QP. Walk between the beach huts. Facing the water, turn R and walk along the beach.

51.377731, 1.276476

Reculver Towers, Herne Bay

Church ruin with enormous towers next to the beach. Nice for photos and a mooch around the shore.

➤ **Find** The King Ethelbert Inn (see page 72) next to the shoreside car park. The fort is 110 yards on the R.

51.379539, 1.199780

Botany Bay

White cliffs and steps down to the sandy beach, secret caves and uniquely beautiful turquoise/green waters. Keep walking N (L facing the water) for quieter beaches. Take care of tides.

➤ **Find** the outdoor bowls clubs in Eastern Espl, Margate, CT9 2JJ. Facing the green, follow the road R for about 220 yards and turn the bend L. After 66 yards, bear L down the hill towards the Hodges Gap Promenade. Turn R at the shoreside towards the car park with sea views. Facing the water, leave here on foot to the R along the coast path. Keep walking 1⅓ miles, past the glorious Palm Bay, around the long nose spit of Foreness Point to arrive at Botany Bay steps. Once on the beach, keep walking L at low tide to discover the caves.

51.3893, 1.4352

Saxon Shore

Kingsgate Bay

Epic sea arch. Cool tides, wet sand.

➤ **Find** Joss Bay Car Park in N Foreland Hill, Broadstairs, CT10 3PG. Facing the sea, walk 730 yards R along the ECP to the steps down to Kingsgate. As the tide goes out, walk 380 yards across the bay to Bay Sea Arch.

51.1007, 1.2446

Westgate Bay, Westgate-on-Sea

Dramatic low tide, sand walk along the bay beneath the esplanade. Explore the history of the town's two churches in the town: Saint Saviour's Parish Church and Christ Church United Reform Church.

➤ **Find** St Mildred's Bay Car Park, Old Boundary Rd, Westbrook, Margate, Westgate-on-Sea, CT8 8PR. Walk 50 yards N to the shore and then 1 mile W along the ECP to the bay.

51.382296, 1.330497

South Foreland Lighthouse and South Foreland Low Lighthouse, St Margaret's Bay

Watch seabirds circle below from Fan, Crab and Langdon bays. Take care below or over crumbling cliffs. Just to the N are tree-lined chalk cliffs.

➤ **Find** Margaret's Bay Parking, off Bay Hill, St Margaret's Bay, Dover, CT15 6DX. Walk 1 mile SW on the ECP.

51.140347, 1.371183

St Margaret's Bay

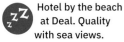

Joss Bay

This wild stretch of sand and chalk coastline gets cooled by southwesterlies in summer. A favourite with windsurfers and kite surfers. Look for sea urchin and sponge fossils.
➤ **Find** Joss Bay Car Park (see Kingsgate Bay, opposite).

51.37390, 1.4500

Shellness, Pegwell Bay

Stunning dune pasture peppered with butterflies, birds and the sound of nightingales in spring. The most remote part of Pegwell Bay and Sandwich is at this shellbank (or ness) at the head of Sandwich Flats. Try to get out there on a low tide with lots of time, or kayak. Sea urchin and starfish fossils are quite common here. The FP ends with a view back to mainland across the River Stour and over Stoneless marsh and woods and the boarded groins.
➤ Park at St George's and walk N along the beach path 2 miles.

51.312259, 1.370008

Walmer & Deal Castles, Deal, Strait of Dover

The resting place of the Duke of Wellington, the hero of Waterloo, who died here in 1852. Take a tour around the gardens and enjoy a cuppa after a swim in the sandy bay.
➤ **Find** the beachside car park in Kingsdown Rd, Walmer, Deal, CT14 7LH. Facing the sea, the castle is 110 yards to the R. www.english-heritage.org.uk

51.200992, 1.402308

St Margaret's Bay, Strait of Dover

Sweeping sand and shingle bay at St Margaret's for swimming. Find fossils around the beach, chalk cliffs or inside some of the boulder-sized stones. Peaceful views and easy parking.
➤ **Find** the end of Bay Hill, at the foot of the St Margaret's Bay Cliffs, Dover, CT15 6DX. Facing the water, turn R and walk 440 yards along the promenade and beach.

51.156847, 1.392964

Dover Castle, Dover, Strait of Dover

England's most important harbour for thousands of years, and the shortest crossing to the Continent. Best views are ½ mile E of the castle grounds towards Fox Hill Down, on the coast FP after the visitor centre and cafe.
➤ **Find** parking on Foxhill Down off Upper Rd, Guston, Dover, CT16 1JA. Spectacular views. Facing the water, walk R 0.6 miles down to Dover Harbour and then R up towards the castle.

51.129524, 1.323919

THE CLIFFTOP CAFE, EAST WEAR BAY

 Walkers' pit stop with panoramic views over to France on a clear day.

111A Old Dover Rd,
Capel-le-Ferne,
Folkestone, CT18 7HT
01303 255 588

THE PILOT INN, LYDD-ON-SEA, ROMNEY MARSH

 Traditional fish and chips served with smuggling tales from Romney Marsh. The inn is said to be built from the timbers of a Spanish vessel wrecked here in 1633.

Battery Rd, Lydd-on-Sea,
Romney Marsh, TN29 9NJ
www.thepilotdungeness
.co.uk

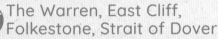

Samphire Hoe, Strait of Dover

Towering chalk cliffs over waterside meadows. Good for butterflies that feed on hundreds of species of wild flower. Corals, ammonites and sharks' teeth fossils within the chalk and rock.
➤ **Find** the information centre and cafe at the end of Samphire Rd (under the tunnel), Dover, CT17 9FL.

51.10480, 1.27553

The Warren, East Cliff, Folkestone, Strait of Dover

Wooded cliffs fall down to sand and gravel beaches. Rare flowers and plant species include wild cabbage. Many fossils around the foreshore and clay-sandstone cliffs.
➤ **Find** The Pavilion in Wear Bay Rd, Folkestone, CT19 6BL. From the car park, face the sea and turn L. Walk ½ mile along the coast path and cliffs.

51.08590, 1.20292

Folkestone Harbour Arm, Folkestone, Strait of Dover

Bustling and historic edge of the harbour, where you can eat, drink and explore.
➤ **Find** the car park in Harbour Approach Rd, Folkestone, CT20 1QQ. The harbour is in front of you.

51.07718, 1.19159

Folkestone

Samphire Hoe

Seapoint Canoe Centre, Hythe, English Channel

Where the beach and sea (almost) meet the Royal Military Canal. Separated by the canoe centre and a small park. Lovely place to explore with the kids, and/or combine with a beach swim and a canal walk. Visit the canoe centre to find out more about lessons and trips.

➤ **Find** Sea Point Car Park, Princes Pde, Hythe, CT21 6AQ, and you have arrived.

51.071069, 1.121598

St Mary's Bay, Dymchurch, English Channel

Miles of secluded beach and promenade to walk and swim just S of Dymchurch.

➤ **Find** the shoreside car park off Dymchurch Rd, Romney Marsh, TN29 0RE. Facing the water, turn R and just keep walking the sand at low tide or use the FP – at least 550 yards.

51.005742, 0.978941

Dungeness, Romney Marsh

Phenomenal pebble beach that serves as a navigational beacon for migrating birds. Visit in spring and autumn to see swallows, swifts and martins coming and going. Many places to stargaze and forage. Water is usually cold and always deep, which makes it better on a hot summer day unless you're wetsuited up. Explore the Denge beach and open pits S of Dungeness Rd, and also the northern areas to the rear of the old coastguard homes.

➤ **Find** the Romney Hythe & Dymchurch Railway, at Dungeness Station, Dungeness Rd, Romney Marsh, TN29 9NA. From the back of the Old Dungeness Lighthouse follow the FP NNW inland to explore the vast wilds. Alternatively, walk the other way towards the pebble shore.

50.931641, 0.944549

Camber Sands

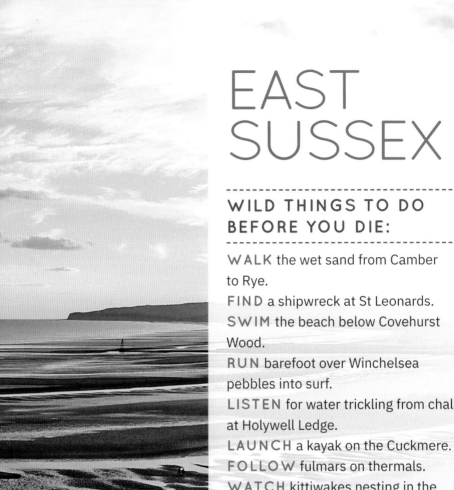

EAST SUSSEX

WILD THINGS TO DO BEFORE YOU DIE:

WALK the wet sand from Camber to Rye.
FIND a shipwreck at St Leonards.
SWIM the beach below Covehurst Wood.
RUN barefoot over Winchelsea pebbles into surf.
LISTEN for water trickling from chalk at Holywell Ledge.
LAUNCH a kayak on the Cuckmere.
FOLLOW fulmars on thermals.
WATCH kittiwakes nesting in the Seven Sisters.
WILD camp around Cliff End.
FIND dino footprints on Bexhill's low tide.
GO rock pooling on Cuckmere Estuary.
EXPLORE Hastings Castle's histories.
SWIM with seals at Normans Bay.
SAVOUR the Beachy Head magic.
MAKE a wish at the Tower Slopes.

Camber, English Channel

Wooded dunes lead down to the most dramatic beach on the SE coast. Best visited on a winter's low tide at sunset. Apart from the surreal peace and light, the parking is cheaper. The crowds vanish after September when the warm westerlies keep the evenings clement. Favourite spot for wind and kite surfers. The tides can be dangerous. Take the low-tide beach to walk W barefoot to Rye Harbour; it's a little more than 1 mile return.

➤ Find the turn for Camber Rd off the A259 at East Gulderford. Continue 2½ miles down Camber Rd to find the parking sign for cars and buses and turn R to the foot of the dunes. Beach is a 5-min walk over the top. There's a toilet block, too. More parking less than ½ mile further on, with cafes.

50.930820, 0.790032

Rye Harbour, River Rother

Tranquil path on the banks of the River Rother. Leads out to Rye Bay and the beaches, along a working harbour that oozes charm and shabby chic. Salt lagoons blend into the coast, grazing marsh and flooded gravel pits. Good for birds. Some of the birdwatching hides have wheelchair access. Information centre in the car park at Rye Harbour.

➤ Find the car park in Harbour Rd, Rye, TN31 7TY. FP opposite the entrance runs along the River Rother for 3,700ft out to the breakwater and sands 10 mins away.

50.936840, 0.762592

Camber Sands

Rye Harbour

Winchelsea Beach, Rye Bay

Magical shingle beach that exposes sand and clay at low tide. Take a 1-mile beach stroll W to the equally enchanting Royal Military Canal Path. The canal path is well worth the 4-mile walk inland to 'new' Winchelsea town. The 'old town' was washed away by the huge flood and storm of 1287 that destroyed and reshaped much of the south coast.

➤ **Find** the A259 bend at Winchelsea and turn off on to Sea Rd. Follow for 1¾ miles through the Rye Bay Caravan Park and eventually past Winchelsea Beach Cafe (see left). There is parking along the beach sea wall just after the cafe.

50.906209, 0.720104

Cliff End, English Channel

Shingle beach for swimming and fossil hunting.

➤ **Find** St Nicholas Church, Pett Level Rd, Hastings, TN35 4EH. A FP runs past the church to the beach. Facing the sea, turn R and walk along the beach ¼ mile to the cliffs.

50.881344, 0.678116

Covehurst Wood, English Channel

Rocky nudist beach that is usually deserted. A long, tricky hike from the top. Care needed, especially in winter. Once on the beach at low tide, consider walking 2 miles W towards Hastings Old Town and coming back via the FP over Ecclesbourne Glen.

➤ **Find** the Fishermen's Museum, Rock-A-Nore Rd, Hastings, TN34 3DW and, facing the sea, turn L to walk along either the beach at low tide or the coast path slightly inland to Covehurst Wood 1½ miles. (Alternatively, park at Fairlight off the Firelight Rd, Hastings, TN35 5EP in the Country Park car park and walk down to the beach by crossing the road and following the narrow, windy FPs.)

50.862971, 0.627667

Hastings from East Hill

Coffee by the sea...
Smoothies and
other sweet stuff
on Hastings Pier. Owned
by a circus-act couple
with a passion for coffee.
A classy pier double act.

East Kiosk 1,
1–10 White Rock, Hastings
Pier, TN34 1JU
Facebook: @billycancoffee

East Hill, Hastings, English Channel

Ancient settlement for star watching and coast views.
> **Find** Barley Ln Car Park, Barley Ln, Hastings, TN35 5NX. Walk
SW through Ecclesbourne Glen to the ECP. Once off the path, walk
another 400 yards to where the hill meets the wooded cliff edge.

50.859729, 0.601850

Hastings Castle, View Point, English Channel

Special view of Hastings from the castle ruin. Bit of a climb,
but worth it. Take the FP up towards West Hill Cafe and lookout
point, then back down to the beach for a swim or cuppa.
> **Find** The West Hill Cafe, Castle Hill Rd, Hastings, TN34 3RD,
with stunning views over the town before dropping down to the
castle and lookout by keeping the cafe on your L.

50.856113, 0.584968

St Leonards-on-Sea, English Channel

Glorious blue waters. The tide goes out a long, long way
revealing sand banks and remnants of a sunken wood.
An old shipwreck becomes visible on the lowest tides.
> **Find** the old port road, next to the T.S. Hastings Sea Cadets
Corps, Cinque Ports Way, St Leonards-on-Sea, TN38 0FD. Follow
the road on foot along the waterside beach huts, past the old boat
and down to the sand. The best beach is just W of Bulverhythe.
Toilets and parking around West Marina.

50.850373, 0.535739 & 50.849073, 0.527577

1 Bexhill-on-Sea & Cooden, English Channel

Dinosaur footprints can sometimes be found on the beach at Bexhill. Best visited after a storm and high tides. Go to Bexhill Museum for dinosaur bones and footprints, bug specimens and a lot of natural history.

➤ **Find** Bexhill Station, Bexhill-on-Sea, TN40 1EB and follow Sea Rd S to the beach. Facing the water, turn R on to De La Warr Pde and follow the dead-end road ¾ mile to where there's a children's playground. From here, drop down on to the beach and walk the last 0.6 miles.

50.84360, 0.50536

Bexhill

2 Normans Bay, Bexhill-on-Sea, English Channel

Pebble beach for a solitary swim, with the odd seal for company.

➤ **Find** your way towards Bexhill-on-Sea (above), but after walking down Sea Rd to the beach, turn R instead of L. Also seafront parking at De La Warr Pavilion, Marina, Bexhill-on-Sea, TN40 1DP.

50.823727, 0.389404

3 The Beachings, Pevensey, English Channel

Tiny dune harbour for small boats and swimmers.

➤ **Find** Ocean View Bakery, 7 Eastbourne Rd, Pevensey Bay, Pevensey, BN24 6EJ, and the large beachside car park in Sea Rd behind it. Facing the sea, walk R along the beach for ⅓ mile to find the small beach green next to Be-Rad Watersports | Kitesurf & Stand Up Paddleboard School, 19 Val Prinseps Rd, Pevensey Bay, Pevensey, BN24 6JD.

50.808498, 0.347601

Sovereign Harbour & Beach, Eastbourne, English Channel

Beach views and swimming from the shingle spit next to Eastbourne's Sovereign Harbour. Good food and drink around the boats afterwards.

➤ **Find** Harbour Reach Cafe off King William Pde, Eastbourne, BN23 6EQ. Facing the sea, turn L and walk ⅓ mile along the shore. There you'll find a 2nd beachside car park closer to the harbour at BN23 6RT.

50.788101, 0.331035

Wish Tower Slopes, Eastbourne, English Channel

Make a wish at the tower. Gardens lead down to a lovely beach for a swim. Lifeboat museum just across the green.

➤ **Find** Eastbourne Lifeboat Museum in the old boathouse, King Edwards Pde, Eastbourne, BN21 4BY. The sloped Wish Tower is a few yards to the R if facing the beach.

50.761089, 0.286188

Holywell Ledge & The Pound, Eastbourne, English Channel

Holywell takes its name from the freshwater spring that seeps from the chalk cliffs into the sea. Anyone can drink from the mug and chain provided. The special status of this wooded beach is evident from the tumuli and sacred mounts peppered around the surrounding hills and paths. The foreshore is protected by a rock and shingle spit, known as Holywell Ledge.

➤ **Find** The Kiosk where the S Downs Way and Foyle Way meet at Dukes Dr, Eastbourne, BN20 7XL. Walk 110 yards to the R along Dukes St, if facing away from the kiosk, and turn R into the narrow lane past the school and public toilets. Follow the FP all the way down to the chalk cliff.

50.750305, 0.269180

The Seven Sisters

Belle Tout, Beachy Head, English Channel

Lighthouse and ancient burial ground flanked by tree cover to the N. Explore the bridleway that loops around the Horseshoe Plantation and tumulus. There are three car parks around this old, sacred site.

➤ **Find** the small car park at Beachy Head Rd, Eastbourne, BN20 0AD. Walk 600 yards W along the ECP to the lighthouse.

50.738415, 0.214414

Falling Sands, Beachy Head, English Channel

Chalky cliffs over blue water. Avoid low-tide swims as there are too many rocks. Wonderful shelter and hiding places back from the cliff top, along the S Downs Way NE.

➤ **Find** parking at the Beachy Head Countryside Centre, Beachy Head Rd, Eastbourne, BN20 7YA. Cross the road and find any of the FPs down towards the cliff edge. Once facing the sea, turn L along the FP 275 yards to find the steps and path down on to the beach.

50.740730, 0.262044

Birling Gap, English Channel

Incredible views and hazardous tides. Beach is best when the water is going out. Long stretches of deserted shingle N of here, towards Seven Sisters, but much caution is needed to explore. Mistimed walks can have fatal consequences if the tide traps you against the cliffs. Fossils can be found here, too.

➤ **Find** the NT Birling Gap and the Seven Sisters, Beachy Head Rd, Eastbourne, BN20 0AB and walk towards the shore for the cafe on the cliffs and a steel staircase down the crumbling chalk to the beach. Facing the sea from the cliff top, walk ⅔ mile R for Seven Sisters (see below).

50.74245, 0.20045

Seven Sisters Cliffs/Baily's Hill Tumuli (alternative name: Crowlink Round Barrow), English Channel

Watch colonies of kittiwakes and fulmars along cliff top views. Access to the beach, but care needed climbing down and in case of getting trapped by incoming tide. Water is cold, so put your brave face on or come with wetsuits.

➤ **Find** St Mary the Virgin Church, Crowlink Ln, Friston, Eastbourne, BN20 0AU. Follow the lane ⅓ mile S to where it forks L and becomes a narrow FP after the cattle grid and sign that says 'Private Rd'. The path leads to the cliff top known as Flagstaff Point. From here, turn L to Baily's Hill, ⅓ mile away. Walk R 1½ miles for Cuckmere River (see page 86).

50.748450,0.188663

Newhaven Harbour

Cuckmere River

 ## Cuckmere River

Kayakers, walkers, cyclists and anglers meet at this natural mecca of fresh water and tides. Either follow the FPs inland along Cuckmere River or explore the beaches either side of the estuary for one of the most iconic views in England. Rock pooling at low tide. Take care not to get trapped by the incoming tide.

➤ **Find** parking at Cuckmere Valley Canoe Club, Seven Sisters Canoe Centre, Seven Sisters Country Park, Seaford, BN25 4AD. Walk back towards the A259 and then turn R on to either the river FP or the S Downs Way. Follow for 1.2 miles to where the river meets the sea at Cuckmere Haven. There are literally hours of fun to be had exploring the beach and navigating the various paths up and down the river's many sides and cuts. For incredible inland views, walk 1 mile on the W side of the river path N to the White Horse (50.788368, 0.142548) by crossing the road bridge across the river at The Cuckmere Inn, Exceat Bridge, Cuckmere Haven, Seaford, BN25 4AB. The canoe club offers equipment hire.

50.759595, 0.151838

Seaford Beach, Seaford Bay

Steep, stony beach.

➤ **Find** Newhaven and Seaford Sailing Club, Club House, Marine Pde, Seaford, BN25 2QR, 440ft from the seafront car park and toilets (BN25 2QR), and a 6-min walk from Bishopstone Station. Keep walking ⅔ mile along Marine Pde, past the sailing club and Buckle campsite, towards the quieter parts of Seaford Bay and the Mill Creek bridge, before running out of beach at River Ouse's E bank, and the port of Newhaven.

50.774051, 0.088438

MARTELLO KIOSK, SEAFORD BAY

Right next to Seaford Museum, looking over the beach. Locally famous for its cakes.

34 Espl, Seaford, BN25 1JJ

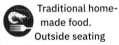
THE HOPE INN, NEWHAVEN, RIVER OUSE

Traditional home-made food. Outside seating beside Newhaven harbour and river.

West Pier, Newhaven, BN9 9DN
Facebook: The Hope Inn

Castle Hill, Newhaven, English Channel

Cliff top views over Seaford, from the W shore of Newhaven harbour. Best in spring when the place is awash with yellow buttercups, butterflies and birdsong. Giant ammonites can be found in the chalk lumps around the beach and harbour mouth.

➤ **Find** The Hope Inn (see opposite) and keep driving towards the harbour wall. Explore the beach and Westside Breakwater to the front, Newhaven Fort and wooded fort hill to the rear, and secluded beach walks under the cliffs to the W.

50.781554, 0.049765

Mill Creek, Newhaven, English Channel

Explore the creek down to the East Pier beach. Walks around Newhaven Harbour after lunch provide a chance to look for fossils in chalk. Good place for large ammonites.

➤ **Find** the car park off the A259, Worthing, BN25 2TW, and walk down Mill Drove towards the beach.

50.785372, 0.063480

Peacehaven Heights, Peacehaven, English Channel

Sacred site and super sea views over Friars' Bay to the W. This SW-facing ridge blows cold in winter.

➤ **Find** Newhaven Beach (see above) and walk 1 mile W on the ECP.

50.783723, 0.028580

Newhaven

WEST SUSSEX

WILD THINGS TO DO BEFORE YOU DIE:

FORAGE for shrimps at West Wittering Beach.

SKINNY dip at East Head Spit at dawn ... and then again at dusk.

WALK the tree-lined waters of Fishbourne Channel.

STAR watch from The Spit.

SWIM the high water at Elmer.

WALLOW in the shallows of Pilsey Island.

FIND giant shell fossils at Bognor.

STAND above the serpent-like Great Deep watching mackerel shoals.

LAUNCH a kayak on to Chichester Harbour from Bosham Church.

WATCH marsh harriers hunt over Broad Rife.

LOOK out for common seals at Horse.

SEE the terns nest at Pagham.

GO dad crabbing with the kids at Will Quay.

Shoreham-by-Sea

Beacon Hill Tumuli, Brighton

Lovely 2-mile 'undercliff' walk from Brighton Marina to Saltdean Lido. Best visited at midday when the sun reflects off the white chalk in a dazzling warm glow. Popular swimming spot. Old English inns beachside for budget stays. The cliff walk lies below a sacred hill. Walk up the old salt track on to the hill by crossing the beach road. (Parking at 50.802634, -0.055435)

➤ **Find** the White Horse Hotel, High St, Brighton, BN2 7HR, and walk N on High St past Costa Coffee. After 730ft and passing The Black Horse Pub on the L, turn L into Nevill Rd. After 670ft, turn R into Sheep Walk and follow the path ⅓ mile on to Beacon Hill. Afterwards, retrace your tracks and drop down on to the beach and undercliff from the White Horse, turning R while looking out to sea.

50.807805, -0.065476

Brighton Pier, English Channel

Iconic pier that's best appreciated at sunset. The Old Pier (50.818987, -0.151842), a few hundred yards W, was last used in the 1970s. Brighton's second-most famous landmark is the naturist beach. Consider sandals or water shoes when taking a dip – the pebbles are crippling.

➤ **Find** the Brighton Fishing Museum, 201 Kings Rd Arches, Brighton, BN1 1NB, next to the Shellfish and Oyster Bar. The pier is to the L.

50.815388, -0.137100

The Canal Wharf, Portslade

Walk the vast wharf attached to Shoreham Harbour by beach or FP. Hove Lagoon at the end of the harbour is a fun place to watch people learning watersports.

➤ **Find** parking beside King Alfred Leisure Centre, Kingsway, Hove, BN3 2WW. Walk on the ECP 1 mile W to the wharf.

50.829117, -0.215533

Murmuration over the ruins of Brighton and Hove's West Pier

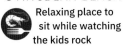

OVINGDEAN CAFE, BRIGHTON, OVINGDEAN BEACH

Relaxing place to sit while watching the kids rock pooling at low tide.

Undercliff Walk, Brighton, BN2 7AF
Facebook: @ovingdeancafe

THE BRIDGE INN, SHOREHAM-BY-SEA, RIVER ADUR

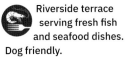

Riverside terrace serving fresh fish and seafood dishes. Dog friendly.

87 High St, Shoreham-by-Sea, BN43 5DE
www.bridgeshoreham.co.uk

HIGH BEACH GUEST HOUSE, WORTHING BEACH, ENGLISH CHANNEL

B&B next to the beach.

201 Brighton Rd, Worthing, BN11 2EX
01903 236 389

COAST CAFE DES ARTISTES, WORTHING BEACH, ENGLISH CHANNEL

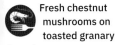

Fresh chestnut mushrooms on toasted granary bread or sausage sandwiches. Lovely. Beach views at the quiet eastern end of Worthing's fine 5-mile beach.

Beach Pde, Worthing, BN11 2ES
www.coastworthing.co.uk

Shoreham Fort & Dunes, River Adur

Formidable fort at the entrance to Shoreham harbour and the River Adur. Explore after a swim.

➤ **Find** Shoreham Fort Car Park, 2 Forthaven, Shoreham-by-Sea, BN43 5HY. Walk on to the harbour and follow it clockwise past the harbour wall and then turn R along the beach.

50.826576, -0.251378

Lancing Beach Green, English Channel

Home to Brighton kite surfers who launch from the shingle beach. Much fun can be had sitting on the beach watching experts and rookies alike skim over the waves. Move a little E or W for shallow and sheltered swims.

➤ **Find** the beachside restaurant Perch, beside the large public car park. Walk W (to the R facing the sea) 2,700ft along the shore.

50.820004, -0.321067

Goring Greensward, Goring-by-Sea, English Channel

Restful beach area separated from Goring central by a strip of woodland. This western section of Marine Dr is something like a communal green. It's not necessarily quieter than other parts, but it has a peacefulness about it ... somewhere to relax and swim in a safe, open and green environment.

➤ **Find** parking on Marine Dr, Worthing, BN12 4XQ.

50.803954, -0.431598

Marine Crescent, Goring-by-Sea

A classic English sea scene reminiscent of bygone eras, but strangely modern. Manicured green that leads up to white beach huts and down to shingle beach.

➤ **Find** Worthing Pier, Marine Pde, Worthing, BN11 3PX. Walk 2 miles W along the ECP to the beach and fields.

50.805923, -0.415357

Littlehampton Fort, River Arun

Fort ruin that in its 19th-century pomp was the cutting edge of military innovation. Still impressive on the dunes of the River Arun. Walk N on the riverbank FP past the marinas and wharves (with the golf club on your L), before looping back after ⅔ mile for a lovely wooded walk back to the beach at Climping. Return to the fort ⅘ mile along the beach.

➤ **Find** the public car park beside the West Beach Cafe, Rope Walk, Littlehampton, BN17 5DL. Next to cafe and disabled parking bays is a short path that leads up to the fort and then on to the dunes and down to the beach.

50.800960, -0.544005

Goring Greensward, Goring-by-Sea

Elmer Beach, Bognor Regis, English Channel

Secluded beach with towering man-made sea breakers that look like islands. Fun place to explore at low tide. High water is better for a swim.

➤ **Find** The Cabin pub, 167–169 Elmer Rd, Bognor Regis, PO22 6JA, where there is occasionally paid-for beach parking made available in the car park. A better option is coming in from Baird's Farm Shop and Cafe on the A259, W of Littlehampton. Turn into Climping St at the farm car park and follow the dead-end road all the way to the bottom. From there, leave the car and walk R, when facing the sea and Climping Beach the 1 mile to Elmer, with quiet beaches along the way.

50.791474, -0.599542

Bognor Regis, English Channel

Enormous fossil shells are found along the beaches. Eagle-eyed fossil hunters also find insect and plant remains. Gets busy in summer.

➤ **Find** Aldwick Boat Park, Marine Dr W, Bognor Regis, PO21 2FZ, and Fish Ln. Once on the beach, walk in either direction – towards the beach huts (and Aldwick Beach Cafe) or the houses. Reasonable-priced parking at The Rock Gardens, Bognor Regis, PO21 2LE.

50.77960, -0.69369

THE LOBSTER POT, FELPHAM BEACH, ENGLISH CHANNEL

Beautiful. Tables and chairs on the promenade and stone beach. Lots of seafood options, but other traditional dishes too.

Canning Rd, Bognor Regis, PO22 7AF
Facebook: The Lobster Pot

CRAB & LOBSTER, PAGHAM HARBOUR

Down a tiny lane. Food sourced from Selsey fishermen and local dairy farmers. Emphasis on fresh fish, crab and lobster. Also traditional English and Mediterranean dishes. Rooms with harbour views.

Mill Ln, Sidlesham, Chichester, PO20 7NB
www.crab-lobster.co.uk

Pagham Harbour, English Channel

Shoreside FP circles the harbour's 5-mile perimeter from the edge of Pagham Village on the NE shore, to Norton Priory in the SW. The walk from Pagham Lagoon to Sidlesham Quay for pub refreshments is a 2-mile taster.

> **Find** St Thomas à Becket Church, Church Ln, Pagham, Bognor Regis, PO21 4NU (parking opposite). Walk out of the car park (facing the church) and turn R. Keep walking 7 mins until you reach the R fork and large metal gate with a Pagham Harbour sign. Walk around the gate on to the FP and harbour.

50.772909, -0.761133

Church Sands, Pagham Harbour, English Channel & Broad Rife Creek

Stunning chapel overlooking Pagham Harbour and Broad Rife creek. Wide beach and swims at high tide but beware currents. One of the most remote places on the West Sussex shore for night-time star watching.

> **Find** St Wilfrid's Church, Rectory Ln, Selsey, Chichester, PO20 9DT. N gate leads to church, second gate (E) leads down to creek.

50.75416, -0.76352

Broad Rife Sands, Pagham Harbour, English Channel

Sandy spit sheltering Pagham Harbour.

> **Find** St Wilfrid's Church, Rectory Ln, Selsey, Chichester, PO20 9DT. Facing the water, turn R and follow the path down to the beach. At the beach, turn L and keep walking at low tide. Beware incoming tides.

50.75355, -0.75558

Chichester Harbour

TURNSTILES, CHURCH NORTON, THE SOLENT

Beachfront holiday home for six with views over the Solent.

161 E Beach Rd, Selsey, Chichester, PO20 9BS
www.selseyholiday
home.co.uk

SEA MIST, SELSEY BEACH, ENGLISH CHANNEL

Bedrooms 100 yards from the shore, with sea views.

West St, Selsey, PO20 9AH

Selsey Beach, English Channel

Wonderful beach at the end of Mill House Ln.

➤ **Find** the little beach kiosk that's usually in the car park in Marine Gardens, Selsey, Chichester, PO20 0LJ. Try to time your visit with an outgoing tide. Walk NW (R if facing the sea) for ⅔ mile for the quieter undeveloped foreshore and beaches. Keep walking past the campsite for the E shore of Broad Rife.

50.732497, -0.807376

Broad Rife

Watch waders and raptors feed over an inland tidal lagoon. The broad fills with water on each tide. Sea wall FP circles most of the water. A very long day is needed to properly explore the beach inlets and sea wall paths.

➤ **Find** parking at Billy's on the Beach, Bracklesham Ln, Bracklesham Bay, Chichester, PO20 8JH. Get on to the beach and walk L (facing the sea) for 1¼ miles, past the holiday homes. There is also a FP S of the marshes from Earnley Church, 3 Church Cottages, Earnley, Chichester, PO20 7JL.

50.747337, -0.828074

Bracklesham Bay, English Channel

Stony beach full of fossils. Look out for ray and sharks' teeth, corals and shells. Often best after stormy windy tides. Although this is a resort town, the bay is rarely busy.

➤ **Find** the car park at Billy's on the Beach (see opposite), then walk R along the beach.

50.761495, -0.863012

Ferring

BILLY'S ON THE BEACH, BRACKLESHAM BAY

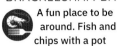

A fun place to be around. Fish and chips with a pot of tea, calamari with a glass of wine, a slab of carrot cake and a good cappuccino or seafood platter and prosecco. You want it, they seem to have it. Dog friendly.

Bracklesham Ln, Bracklesham Bay, Chichester, PO20 8JH
www.billysonthebeach .co.uk

THE QUARTERDECK CAFE, ITCHENOR SHIPYARD, CHICHESTER HARBOUR

Set inside a wonderful boatyard. Good, varied menu.

Itchenor Shipyard, Chichester, PO20 7AE
www.quarterdeckcafe .co.uk

THE SHIP INN, ITCHENOR, CHICHESTER HARBOUR

At the heart of the beautiful sailing village of Itchenor. Popular with walkers and cyclists – 200 yards from the harbour. Self-catering accommodation in a three-bed cottage or two-bedroom apartment.

The Street, Itchenor, Chichester, PO20 7AH
www.theshipinnitchenor .co.uk

Thorney Island

West Wittering Beach, English Channel

Pools of water glimmer across the foreshore at low tide. Children love to play and look for crabs and shrimps. The better beach and dunes are near the windsurfing club. Toilets and cafe.
➤ **Find** Beach Cafe and parking. Walk either way for secluded beaches, some of which are dog friendly.

50.775062, -0.909676

East Head Spit, West Wittering, English Channel

Throw off the clothes. A vast stretch of isolated beach and dunes to explore. Walk the spit head at low tide to appreciate the peaceful beauty of the sandy expanse. Views across Chichester Harbour, Isle of Wight and Hayling Island. The coast walk from spit hinge to Ella Nore, just N of West Wittering, is wonderful. It's a 2-mile round trip. Cafe and toilet block.
➤ **Find** the ice-cream hut and parking along the FP at West Wittering, Chichester, PO20 8AT. Walk 0.8 miles to the head tip, but it's not that far before you'll start to feel alone.

50.781883, -0.916127

Horse Pond, Chichester Harbour

Marshy ridge overlooking Chichester Harbour where thousands of waders feed all year. One of the best places on the south coast to see common seals, which, ironically, are much rarer than the commoner grey seal.
➤ **Find** the car park in Orchard Ln, Chichester, PO20 7AE, next to the Ship Inn in The Street. Head back to The Street and walk N down to Chichester Harbour. FP follows the Chichester Channel N, R and L. Take the L turn through the boatyards and past the beautiful The Quarterdeck Cafe (see left). Horse Pond is 1 mile further on along the shore.

50.802553, -0.885641

Emsworth

SCUTTLEBUTT CAFE, BIRDHAM POOL MARINA

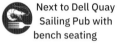 Cafe next to the marina.

The Causeway, Birdham Pool, PO20 7BG
Facebook: @scuttlebuttcafe

CROWN & ANCHOR, APPLEDRAM, FISHBOURNE CHANNEL

Next to Dell Quay Sailing Pub with bench seating waterside.

Dell Quay Rd, Appledram, PO20 7EE
www.crownandanchor chichester.com

BOSHAM, BOSHAM BAY

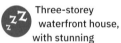 Three-storey waterfront house, with stunning bay views. Good base for sailing, walking and cycling.

Shore Rd, Bosham, Chichester, PO18 8QL
www.bosham-letting.co.uk

Westlands Copse, Fishbourne Channel

Wooded foreshore on Fishbourne Channel. Walk around the working jetties and harbour, which was once an ancient port and settlement.

➤ **Find** the same parking as Horse Pond (see 95), but turn R instead of L at the bottom of The Street, into Chandlers Reach and follow the FP for ⅔ mile to a wooded copse at the end of Spinney Ln. Keep walking for the shipyard and marina at Birdham Pool.

50.802734, -0.855085

Dell Quay, Fishbourne Channel

Walk N of the quay towards Chichester for the best tidal views.

➤ **Find** the Crown & Anchor (see left). Alternatively, visit Church of St Mary the Virgin in the village of Appledram, Chichester, PO20 7EF, off Appledram Ln S.

50.822025, -0.812756

Bosham Quay & Church, Bosham, Bosham Bay

Saxon church next to the navigable part of Chichester Harbour. Depicted in the Bayeux Tapestry as this was the ancestral home of King Harold. Several places to launch kayaks or canoes on Bosham Channel a few hours before high tide, from which to explore Colner and Cutmill creeks.

➤ **Find** the large car park opposite Bosham Walk Art & Crafts Centre, Bosham Walk, Bosham Ln, Bosham, Chichester, PO18 8HX. Facing the art centre, turn S towards Shore Rd and the estuary. Turn R at the water and walk 440 yards around Bosham Quay and to Holy Trinity Church, The Vicarage, Bosham Ln, Bosham, PO18 8HX.

50.829036, -0.860512

Will Quay, Emsworth

Cobnor Point, Bosham Channel

Tiny gravel and sand beach by Bosham Deeps. Northerly views over West Itchenor and W to Thorney Island. Walk the entire coastal finger on its 5-mile FP. Occasional paths and roads inland can be used as a short cut back to any point.

➤ **Find** the FP at the bend and loop in Childham Ln, Chichester, PO18 8TD. Next to the sign that says 'No Public Access', follow the FP to the shore path. It will steer you L (E) towards the shore path that turns S along the Bosham Channel for 1 mile, past the various piers, hards (roads leading down to the foreshore) and the Cobnor Activity Centre.

50.811573, -0.876669

West Thorney Church & hard, Thorney Channel

Waterside church beside a hard into the Thorney Channel. An important settlement and fishing area for thousands of years. Explore the path around the island in both directions.

➤ **Find** the road bend where Prinsted Ln, Emsworth, PO10 8HS meets the tide. From here, follow the incredible shore FP along the Thorney Channel. Find the church and yacht club after 2 miles.

50.816624, -0.908384

Pilsey Island, Thorney Channel

Breathtaking sands; treacherous tides. Wallow in warm water at shallow low tide, from the spit. Incredible birdlife. FP round Longmere Point providing access to the Pilsey Sands and the deep known as Stocker's Lake at the mouth of the harbour.

➤ Same directions as above but walk on another mile.

50.799510, -0.908589

Great Deep, Thorney Channel

Serpent-like channel severs the S of the island from the N. Three tracks cross the deep water. 1) Thorny Rd down the centre; 2) a FP on the E island edge; 3) a FP on the W island edge. Fascinating and powerful at all times of the tide.

➤ **Find** Emsworth Yacht Harbour, Thorney Rd, Emsworth, PO10 8BP and park at the entrance car park. Walk past the 'Harbour Office' sign and keep walking straight to the waterside path. Turn L at the water and follow the path ¾ mile to the Great Deep.

50.831238, -0.929950

Will Quay, Emsworth, Slipper Mill Pond

Viewing gallery from FP peninsula across the tidal Mill Pond from a recently constructed marina. Crabbing for kids.

➤ Same directions as above, but on reaching the water, turn R instead of L. The Quay point is 220 yards away.

50.842811, -0.932967

HAMPSHIRE

WILD THINGS TO DO BEFORE YOU DIE:

FIND crocodile fossils at Taddiford Gap.

DISCOVER rare septarian nodules in a cliff shore.

PLUNGE into a tidal oasis beside woodland.

FORAGE for sea purslane around Langstone Harbour.

WALK a beach along the New Forest boundary.

TRAMP a river over Bunny Meadows.

KEEP quiet ... about the field operations training centre for SAS and SBS at Fort Gilkicker.

EXPLORE a church beside a Roman fort.

CATCH crabs in the Milton Locks pools.

LOSE yourself in the night sky beside a Solent lighthouse.

FIND human skeletons washed up from Burrow Island prison fort ruin.

WATCH merlins and hunt for goldfinches.

SEE terns fish over Hook Lane shingle.

LAUNCH a kayak at Nore Barn Woods.

Langstone Harbour

EMSWORTH SAILING CLUB, CHICHESTER HARBOUR

Enjoy a bar meal in a sailing club with a busy bar. Welcoming to visitors. Carveries and snacks with best views around the harbour.

55 Bath Rd, Emsworth, PO10 7ES
www.emsworthsc.org.uk

SALT SHACK CAFE, CHICHESTER HARBOUR

BBQ breakfasts, home-made soups and afternoon teas. Terrace overlooking Northney Marina and Chichester Harbour on Hayling Island's N shore. Vegan and vegetarian options. Barista coffees.

Northney Marina Club, Northney Rd, Hayling Island, PO11 0NH
www.saltshackcafe.co.uk

Emsworth Beach, Chichester Harbour

Quiet shingle beach within a short walk of Emsworth Harbour. Don't miss walking the length of the beautiful Slipper Mill Pond just behind Emsworth Sailing Club. Much to eat and drink around the harbour.

➤ **Find** Emsworth Yacht Harbour and walk 1 mile W around the harbour and then S around Slipper Mill Pond Promenade to the beach.

50.842430, -0.943900

Nore Barn Woods, Chichester Harbour

Woodland beach with harbour views. Good as kayak landing point. Take the path behind the wood to explore Warblington Church.

➤ **Find** the end of Warblington Rd, Emsworth, PO10 7JX, where it meets a small beach on the old Solent Way. Facing the water, turn R, passing over the small bridge across the creek then beat L off the FP towards the beach path and keep walking 600ft past Nore Barn Woods.

50.841259, -0.955400

Warblington Castle and St Thomas à Becket C of E Church, Chichester Harbour

Path down to a church and castle ruin to old Emsworth Harbour. The Sweare Deep and Emsworth Channel once made this site very important to trade. It's now rather quiet and beautiful.

➤ **Find** the public toilet next to The Ship Inn, Langstone Rd, Langstone, Havant, PO9 1RD, and walk E 1 mile on ECP to church.

50.843698, -0.966053

Quay & Bridleway, Langstone Harbour

Treacherous tidal bridleway best seen at low tide. One of the original tracks on to Hayling Island before Langstone Bridge was built.

➤ **Find** The Ship Inn. Perfect place to enjoy a rest and drink before exploring the foreshore. Bridleway leads from St Nicholas Chapel, Langstone High St, Havant, PO9 1SL and across the water.

50.835569, -0.974528

Hayling Harbour

A public FP runs through this private sailing club. Lovely place to sit, walk and watch the marine community either side of high tide. Good for birds.

➤ **Find** Ruby's Tearoom, 6b Elm Grove, Hayling Island, PO11 9ES opposite the public car park. Facing Ruby's, turn R along Sea Grove Av and then L into Selsmore Rd. After 0.4 mile keep walking straight at the bend into Salterns Ln. Follow the lane to Wilson's Boatyard, Marine Walk, Hayling Island, PO11 9PG. Follow the FP to the shore and walk clockwise around the water.

50.789517, -0.958373

Empty shells, a telltale sign of a forage location

Hayling Island

Black Point & Sandy Point, Hayling Harbour

Sand, shingle and mud spit at the mouth of the harbour. Like most of these estuary sandbanks, low tide provides best access and views. Swim at high tide as currents are usually at their weakest, but much care still needed. Sailing club is popular but private.

➤ Car park looking over the beach, 118–104 Southwood Rd, Hayling Island, PO11 9QF. Facing the water, turn L and walk along the beach 1½ miles to the point and creek and Mengeham Rithe.

50.786982, -0.937859

Gunner Point, Hayling Island, the Solent

Sinah Common's sandy point is a vast sandbank that spans more than 1 mile offshore. The old common above Hayling Bay was turned into a links golf course during the 1890s and was played by golfing greats such as Harry Vardon and James Braid. FP access around the shore.

➤ **Find** Ferryboat Inn public car park at Sinah Beach, Ferry Rd, Hayling Island, PO11 0DG. Once on to the beach, facing the water walk L (S) ¾ mile past Hayling Ferry Sailing Club.

50.785018, -1.021483

Stoke Common, Langstone Harbour

Patchwork of ancient and commercial oyster beds that have been reoccupied by vast flocks of birds. Although the common was farmed in ancient times, in the 19th century it reverted to commercial lagoons and traps created by the South of England Oyster Company. Now council-owned and enjoyed by ornithologists.

➤ **Find** the end of Victoria Rd, Hayling Island, PO11 0LG, then take to foot along the Hayling Bill Trail through the shingle car park and walk 330 yards to Stoke Common and another 0.6 miles to the island's end at the ruin of the old Langstone bridge.

50.824466, -0.983160

Short-eared owl at Farlington Marshes

Farlington Marshes

Watch avocets feed over this salt marsh harbour fed by the Broom Channel. Short-eared owls hunt around the most southerly parts of the marsh before dusk. There are several brackish ponds that attract thousands of seabirds during high tide. A 2-mile coast path explores the most secluded parts of the marsh. Cold in winter, heavenly cool in summer.

➤ **Find** Farlington Marshes car park on the SE edge of the roundabout on the A2030 under the Havant bypass. With your back to the A27, walk forwards on to the path and follow it L along the line of the A27 before turning R after a few hundred yards on to the Solent Way. The path loops all the way around the marsh 3.4 miles to Bendhampton and the wonderful tidal woodlands at Broadmarsh Coastal Park, Harts Farm Way, Havant, PO9 1HS.

50.829365, -1.034584

Milton Locks & Eastley Lake, Langstone Harbour

A salt lake trapped inside Langstone Harbour. A beautiful retreat from Portsmouth's urban mass. Youngsters net fish and crabs between sea purslane, sea aster and common saltmarsh-grass.

➤ **Find** the Thatched House Public House, Milton Locks, Portsmouth, Southsea, PO4 8LT, next to Milton Locks Nature Reserve, for ale and chips. Lake is L along the foreshore from the pub garden.

50.795027, -1.038573

Fort Cumberland, Southsea, East Solent mouth

Strange pentagonal fort used during the Napoleonic wars. Often closed to the public, but the most impressive thing about this site is its scale and beachside location. Explore Southsea Marina at the back of the fort. Nice contrast between old and new.

➤ **Find** the playground at 46 Fort Cumberland Rd, Portsmouth, Southsea, PO4 9LQ, and the large car park opposite. Walk across the scrub common to the fort 330 yards away and then on to Ferry Rd and the marinas, marsh and sandy beaches on either side. Pick up the Hayling Island Ferry at the wonderful sandy spit at Eastnet Landing, just past RNLI Portsmouth Lifeboat Station, Ferry Rd, Portsmouth, Southsea, PO4 9LY.

50.787904, -1.031650

SALT CAFE, PORTCHESTER, PORTSMOUTH HARBOUR

 Cafe in yachting marina next to Wicor Lake.

Cranleigh Rd, Portchester, Fareham, PO16 9DR
www.saltcafe.co.uk

Portchester Castle & St Mary Church, Portchester, Portsmouth Harbour

Coastal fort built by Romans in AD285. Used in the 19th century to jail thousands of French prisoners. Restricted opening times and entrance charges apply. An avenue of trees along Hospital Ln leads towards the back of the castle. The waterside church, St Mary's, was made from Isle of Wight stone in the 1120s.

➤ **Find** parking next to Portchester Sailing Club, Waterside Ln, Castle St, Portchester, PO16 9QN, and walk around the jetties, castle and church.

50.835968, -1.117033

Portchester Castle, Hampshire

Portsmouth

SALT CAFE, PORTCHESTER, PORTSMOUTH HARBOUR

Cafe in yachting marina next to Wicor Lake.

Cranleigh Rd, Portchester, Fareham, PO16 9DR
www.saltcafe.co.uk

CAMS MILL, PORTCHESTER, WALLINGTON RIVER

Converted mill at the tidal limit of the river. Large outdoor seating area with river views. Plenty of parking. Great for meals, snacks, breakfasts or even just a drink.

Cams Hall Estate, Cams Hill, Portchester, Fareham, PO16 8AA
www.camsmill.co.uk

Wicor Path, Portsmouth Harbour

Tree-lined shore around Portsmouth Harbour's Wicor Lake. Stop over at Wicor Marine Yacht Haven for a cuppa by the waterside.
➤ **Find** parking at Wicor Recreation Ground, 106 Cranleigh Rd, Portchester, Fareham, PO16 9BY. Walk out of the car park and turn L and then R down the Wicor Lake jetty and Wicor Marine Yacht Haven. At the water, turn L again. The shore path leads to Porchester Castle 1½ miles away.

50.838835, -1.141664

Fareham Creek Trail, Fareham Marina

Tree-lined path with views over the water to Fareham Marina. Walk S, around the edge of Cams Hall Golf Course, to the small shingle beaches at Cams Bay.
➤ **Find** the car park for Wicor Path (see above), but turn R instead of L across the football pitches along the FP. Keep walking along the sea wall for 2 miles to the bend in the river.

50.848324, -1.175822

Fort James, Burrow Island, the Solent

Human skeletons that sometimes wash up here are thought to be the remains of prisoners-of-war who died on the island fort. The fort can be reached at low tide by a sand bar that links to Priddy's Hard. Beware incoming tides and MoD access.
➤ **Find** public car park by the waterside at Hardway Sailing Club, 103 Priory Rd, Gosport, PO12 4LF. Looking out to the water, turn R and follow the shore at low tide for almost 1 mile past the Explosion Museum of Naval Firepower, and out on to the island.

BAY SIDE CABIN, STOKES BAY, THE SOLENT

Seaside cafe and restaurant, with waterside views across the Solent. Full English, veggie or Mediterranean breakfasts.

Stokes Bay Rd, Alverstoke, Gosport, PO12 2QT
www.baysidecabin.co.uk

THE SHACK, LEE-ON-THE-SOLENT, THE SOLENT

Rock cakes and tea from a little hut on the beach. Look across to the Isle of Wight.

Lee-on-the-Solent, PO13 9YP
Facebook: "The shack"
Hill Head Beach

The sands and mud are constantly shifting so much care is needed as sinking sand can trap unwary visitors and lead to fatalities. Consider kayaking on to the island.

50.803383, -1.120756

Fort Gilkicker, the Solent

Allegedly the field operations training centre for the SAS and SBS. Neighbouring Fort Monckton means history buffs get two forts in the ⅔ mile walk to the Foryon Lake footbridge.

➤ **Find** Gosport Lifeboat Station, Lifeboat Ln, Stokes Bay, Gosport, PO12 2TR, next to the beachside car park. Facing the water, turn L and walk ½ mile along the sand or coast path to Fort Gilkicker. Keep walking another 750 yards to see Fort Monckton.

50.773654, -1.141753

Browndown, the Solent

Military area. Stay away when red flags are out.

➤ **Find** beachside car park at Marine Pde E, Lee-on-the-Solent, PO13 9BJ. Facing the water, turn L and walk 220 yards along the beach and dunes.

50.78835, -1.18544

The Solent, Lepe

Shingle beach most famous for isolation. Walk E along the beach to find fossilised mammal remains around Stansore Point on so-called 'elephant bed' site.

➤ **Find** parking off Lepe Rd, SO45 1AD.

50.784591, -1.360619

Titchfield Haven

Titchfield Haven, River Meon

Stunning septarian nodules are occasionally found along this cliff shore W of the tiny harbour. Brownwich and Chilling cliffs are also good for shell fossils, but most are found on the foreshore washed out of the sand and gravel. Walk up to Seahouse (50.827049, -1.267181) for a secluded swim. Explore the marina and bird hides around Titchfield Haven. Views across to the Isle of Wight.

> **Find** parking all along the beachside of Cliff Rd, Fareham, PO14 3JT. Facing the water, walk back along the sands L (SE) to explore the hides and sands either side of the road.

50.819042, -1.248995

Hook Lane bridle path near Titchfield Common

River Hamble, Fawley

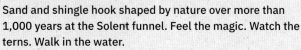

Hook Lane, River Hamble

Sand and shingle hook shaped by nature over more than 1,000 years at the Solent funnel. Feel the magic. Watch the terns. Walk in the water.

➤ **Find** the harbour car park in Shore Rd, Warsash, Southampton, SO31 9FR. Exit the car park on foot S (L if facing the water) along the Solent Way FP, past Strawberry Field and Warmish Maritime Academy. Upon leaving the coast path, the 1-mile trail winds all the way back and on to the sandy hook.

50.845138, -1.307702

Bunny Meadows, River Hamble

Epic walkway that bisects marsh, pools, lake and marina, along a length of the River Hamble. Several marshy strips spread out like fingers down to the waterside. Walk the longer and thickest on Brook Av to get a flavour of what these tree-lined creeks looked like before the axe. Keep walking on to Brooklands Park (50.878996, -1.296365) for more examples of an ancient wooded shore.

➤ **Find** the Hook with Warsash Local Nature Reserve car park, 15 Passage Ln, Fareham, Warsash, Southampton, SO31 9FR. Take the FP N past the loos, not the tidal FP, for ⅓ mile into the middle of the marsh. Keep walking another 2 miles along the glorious path to Swanwick Marina for a cafe and pub. There's a car park there, too.

50.860546, -1.308411

Tide Mill, St Mary's Church & Bartley Water, Eling

St Mary's Church is surrounded by park, trees and river. Visit the toll bridge and mill centre at Eling Bridge, a 2-min walk away.

➤ **Find** the car park at Tide Mill, off Eling Hill, Eling, Southampton, SO40 9HF. Walk down on to Mills Bridge. The church is in the opposite direction up the hill towards King Rufus pub, gallery and tearoom.

50.910551, -1.479453

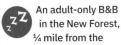

LEYLAND COUNTRY HOUSE, LYMINGTON, LYMINGTON RIVER

An adult-only B&B in the New Forest, ¼ mile from the tidal range of the river.

Undershore Rd, Lymington, SO41 5QA
www.leylandcountry
house.com

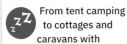

THE SHIP INN, LYMINGTON, LYMINGTON RIVER

Al fresco dining by the marina. Caters for people who want a cuppa, lunch or dinners. Vegan menu too. Kids enjoy crabbing around the marina.

Quay Rd, Lymington, SO41 3AY
www.theship
lymington.co.uk

HURST VIEW, LYMINGTON, THE SOLENT

From tent camping to cottages and caravans with views over the Solent. Less than ½ mile from the coast path.

Lower Pennington Ln, Lymington, SO41 8AL
www.hurstview
leisure.co.uk

Allwoods Copse, the Solent

Wood meets tidal beach on the edge of the New Forest. It's. Just. Stunning.

➤ **Find** The Lookout cafe and beachside car parking (see page 109). Facing the sea, turn L along the beach and keep walking 1.2 miles along the stunning coast to the wooded shores and secluded beaches.

50.794835, -1.335668

Beaulieu River West

One of the most isolated and inaccessible pieces of coastline on the English shore. Kayak or boat only. Take a BBQ.

➤ **Find** Lepe Car Park, Exbury, Southampton, SO45 1AD. Sea kayak across the Beaulieu River estuary to the beach and marshes on the W side of the river for stargazing.

50.774917, -1.394094

Otters Hill Copse, Lymington, Plummers Water

Picnic beside the breathtaking beach and river bridge across Plummers Water at the end of lane. The wooded shore is fed by springs and a vast lake created by stream.

➤ **Find** the end of Tanners Ln, Lymington, SO41 5SP. Consider walking the shore 1 mile to Shotts Ln and then back via the Solent Way ECP.

50.7556451, -1.4885893

Beaulieu River

Hurst Spit near Milford on Sea

Hurst Castle, Christchurch Bay

Brilliant white lighthouse and circular stone tower protecting the Solent and almost touching the Isle of Wight at Cliff End. Walk the beach N for crabbing and paddling in the Sturt Pond.

➤ **Find** public parking opposite the Gun Inn (see left). Walk across the boatyard to Keyhaven River Warden's Office, where a ferry to Hurst Castle runs in the summer. Walk R along the tidal path and follow the water all the way into Salt Grass Ln and then on to the beach ¾ mile away. From here, turn L on the beach and walk another 1⅓ miles to the castle and Hurst Point Lighthouse set on the sandy hook.

50.706611, -1.550657

Taddiford Gap, Lymington, Christchurch Bay

Find crocodile, shark and mammal fossils as well as sharks' teeth, gastropods and other remains all along the beach. Secluded swimming at Barton-on-Sea beside the golf course and stony beach. Views of the Needles. Wait for the tide to go out to enjoy the sands.

➤ **Find** the car park off the B3058, 175 yards E of Barton-on-Sea Golf Course, Milford Rd, Barton-on-Sea, New Milton, BH25 5PP. A FP leads 405 yards down from the car park to the beach. Turn R at the water for Barton-on-Sea beach 1.2 miles away or turn L for Milford on Sea just under a mile away.

50.729664, -1.631588

ISLE OF WIGHT

WILD THINGS TO DO BEFORE YOU DIE:

SWIM the wooded shore of Old Castle Point.

EXPLORE a dinosaur graveyard at Yaverland.

WALLOW in tidal pools around a paradise beach.

SHOOT red squirrels with a camera lens at Bouldnor Forest.

CLIMB down a rock cliff to swim at Watershoot Bay.

RIDE the dramatic Needles cliff lift.

DISCOVER Sheela Na Gig, a pagan idol carved into a church's gateway by mischievous stonemasons.

VISIT lifeboats to learn about the island's unique tidal range.

FIND where geology gets groovy with colour at Whitecliff Bay; the rock pools at Freshwater Bay; and the best island views at Fort Redoubt.

The Solent

Old Castle Point, the Solent

Tree-lined shore on the N of the island with great views across the Solent. Walk through Spring Hill.

➤ **Find** Shoreside Cafe, Espl, East Cowes, PO32 6AD, 220 yards R as you look out to sea. Keep walking R until the beach opens up at the shelter by the trees. From here, continue on the beach another ¼ mile to the point.

50.766361, -1.277577

Barton Wood, Osborne Bay

Wooded shore on Osborne Bay facing Hampshire and Portsmouth. Walk S towards boat launch at Barton Hard, which is next to a small beach.

➤ Follow the direction for Old Castle Point (see above) and keep walking around the shore another 2 miles as the tide is going out.

50.750501, -1.246977

Woodside Beach, the Solent

A paradise beach. Secret, silent and secluded at the end of a tree-lined FP. Tidal pools form in the sandbanks at low tide. Shade or shelter in the tree canopy that hangs over the shoreline.

➤ **Find** the five-way junction at Woodside Rd, Wootton Bridge, Ryde, PO33 4JW. From here, take the FP on the L a few yards after the junction. The FP leads ¼ mile down to Woodside Beach through the trees.

50.739506, -1.222427

Fishbourne

THE DUCK, APPLEY, THE SOLENT

Cafe and bar, with views over Ryde Canoe Lake and the coast. Good for watching urban waterfowl.

Appley Rise, Ryde, PO33 1LE
www.theduckiow.co.uk

DELL CAFE, SEAVIEW, THE SOLENT

Family-run cafe on the sea wall with views over Portsmouth, Southampton and Ryde Sands to the pier. Puckpool Park with its historic Napoleonic Fort is to the rear.

Puckpool Sands, Seaview, PO34 5AR
www.dellcafe.com

Woodside Beach

Firestone Copse, Old Mill Pond

Vast woodland camp on the non-tidal Old Mill Pond. Picnics by the creek are wonderful in summer. Great for cycle trails. Good shelter and respite from tidal excursions.

➤ **Find** the small car park at Firestone Copse, Firestone Copse Rd, Havenstreet and Ashey, Ryde, PO33 4DJ. After entering the car park lane, follow the FPs R to Blackbridge Brook ½ mile away and then turn R and follow the stream up to at the tidal pond. Lots of woodland to explore.

50.715945, -1.218501

Holy Cross Church, Binstead, the Solent

A pagan idol, known as a Sheela Na Gig, is carved into the churchyard's stone gateway. Also many interesting burial stones. Walk through trees to the shore and beach at Binstead Hard. Good place to launch a kayak.

➤ From St Thomas' St Car Park, 17 St Thomas St, Ryde, PO33 2DL, get down on to the beach. Turn L while looking out to sea and walk 1 mile to Binstead Hard. There's a FP leading up from the foreshore to the church in Church Rd, Ryde, PO33 3SY.

50.732087, -1.186626

Ryde East Sands, the Solent

Vast sand spit that reaches more than 1 mile offshore. Walk E of the Ryde Pier at low tide. The beach is best viewed through the tree-gilded frame of Appley Park. St Cecilia's Abbey and the open-air water pool are both worth a visit.

➤ **Find** parking at Appley Park Playground, Garden Walk, Ryde, PO33 1QX. Walk through the park 330 yards past Appley Tower. Try the Dell Cafe (see left) at the end of a bay for a cuppa.

50.726823, -1.137519

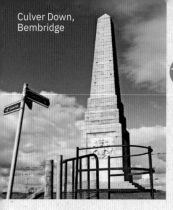
Culver Down, Bembridge

Nodes Point, the Solent

Sensational swim around a collective of tidal bay, rock, shingle and sand spit, under the shadow of wooded shore. Visit at low tide and wait for the waters to lap in, just S of Seagrove Bay. Wonderful 800-year-old Old St Helen's Church on the Duver by the shore.

➤ **Find** the NT car park at St Helens Duver, Duver Rd, St Helens, Ryde, PO33 1XY. Turn R along the beach and walk 0.6 miles to the point past the beachside Old St Helen's Church on the Duver, St Helens, Ryde, PO33 1XZ. The church can also be reached from the car park along the road.

50.706120, -1.098366

Bembridge Foreland, the Solent

Sand and rock naze, good for swimming and kayaking. Fossil-rich (50.688312, -1.070565) with snails, clams and other shells. Visit the lifeboat station to learn about the island's tides and nautical history.

➤ **Find** the RNLI Bembridge Lifeboat Station, Ln End Rd, Bembridge, PO35 5TD, and the pay-and-display car park. Facing the water from the car park, turn R and walk 700 yards along the beach to the foreland. Alternatively, go down Fishermans Walk to the beach a bit further down.

50.683284, -1.069875

Bembridge Beach

BAYWATCH ON THE BEACH, DUVER BAY

Seafood restaurant and cafe right on the beach.

St Helens, Ryde, PO33 1XZ
Facebook:
@BaywatchontheBeach

THE DUVER CAFE, BEMBRIDGE HARBOUR

Opens each April. Good base from which to walk to the RSPB reserve at Brading Marshes.

Bembridge Harbour, St Helens, PO33 1YB
Facebook: @duvercafe

THE HARBOUR VIEW, BEMBRIDGE HARBOUR

On the beach and dunes next to Bembridge Sailing Club.

Embankment Rd, Bembridge, PO35 5NR
01983 872 742

THE BEST DRESSED CRAB LTD, BEMBRIDGE HARBOUR

On stilts in the harbour, with mesmerising sea views. Run and supplied by friends and family of local fishermen. Fresh crabs and lobsters are their speciality.

Fishermans Wharf, Embankment Rd, Bembridge, PO35 5NS
www.thebestdressed crabintown.co.uk

Sandown, from Culver Down

Whitecliff Bay

Where geology gets groovy. Colourful mix of chalk, shingles, clays and sand against wooded cliffs. And great for a swim.
➤ **Find** The Culver Haven Inn, on Culver Down Rd, Bembridge, Sandown, PO36 8QT. There's also parking at the end of the road behind the Culver Down Battery. With your back to the battery, walk N towards the FP and then head towards the beach at the holiday park. Keep walking another ⅓ mile past the park's Wonky Cafe on the beachside.

50.67234, -1.09496

Yaverland, English Channel

The island's best fossil site is especially good after stormy seas.
➤ **Find** beachside parking at Yaverland Rd, Sandown, PO36 8QS. Walk down the ramp to the beach and just keep walking as far as you like.

50.66159, -1.13627

Shanklin, English Channel

Wooded gorge falls down to a wonderful beach for swimming and fossil collecting.
➤ **Find** the car park off 43 Littlestairs Rd, Shanklin, PO37 6HS. Walk 110 yards on to the beach.

50.638453, -1.168866

Steel Bay, Shanklin, English Channel

Vast woodland known as The Landslip in the island's SE corner. Cliff top path leads down to rocky beach at Monks Bay (50.598713, -1.182174) that reveals sands at low tide.
➤ **Find** Bonchurch Landslip Car Park, Bonchurch Rd, Shanklin, PO37 6RH. Follow FP towards the shore for about 110 yards, then bear R as it swings down through the trees to the beach 330 yards further on.

50.604533, -1.177923

Watershoot Bay, Ventnor

Inland quarry for ammonites and other molluscs. Vast landmass of trees, rock and cliffs to get lost in. Slide down to the beach for a swim, then back up again for views over Five Rocks (50.588064, -1.308657).

➤ **Find** the lane at Old Blackgang Rd, Niton, Ventnor, PO38 2BY and follow it all the way to the end by the small parking area. Take the narrow winding FPs down through the green scrub to the beach. Care needed on way down.

50.580785, -1.309212

Brighstone Bay, English Channel

Wonderful tidal creek and bridge. Dinosaur bones and ammonites, brachiopods and bivalves along the beach. Swim at Marsh Chine (50.633650, -1.406913).

➤ **Find** roadside parking off the A3055 Military Rd, Ventnor, PO38 2LJ. Walk to the top of the car park and on to the FP around the N of the wooded water known a Whale Chine. Once at the water, turn R and walk 1¾ miles past Atherfield Bay and Shepherds Chine beaches.

50.61642, -1.37180

Freshwater Bay

Compton Bay, English Channel

Decisions, decisions! Find the shipwreck at low tide or go hunting for dino footprints? The bridleways and greenways explore the cliff tops. Rich in views and ancient burial mounds.

➤ **Find** the end of the lane to Compton Farm, Military Rd, Newport, PO30 4HF for a field for parking. Cross the A3055/Military Rd and find the FP on the other side that leads down to the beach. It's narrow and steep so take care.

50.662661, -1.477380

Fossil Forest, Brook Bay

The best waves on the island form here and roll over and expose the fossil footprints and teeth. A perfect storm of fun and fossils.

➤ **Find** car park at Hanover Point, Newport, PO30 4HB, and walk 400 yards S to the rocks and the point.

50.652129, -1.465822

Fort Redoubt, Freshwater Bay

Incredible views over the English Channel. This cliff top fort (now private) is set above caves and coast that mark the western point of Freshwater Bay. A foil for the sandy Compton Beach, this place is steeped in myth and sacred symbols, and is one of the most iconic places on the island. Rock pooling at low tide and some fine walks, but the place to be at sunset is on top. (On another day, walk or drive from here to the E side of the bay and get on to Compton Down to explore the views and tumulus-rich plateau via the Tennyson Trail.)

➤ **Find** the large car park almost opposite the glorious Albion Hotel beside the bay (see left). There's a FP around the front of the hotel to the beach and fort 275 yards away. Alternatively, take the longer FP trail around the top of the hotel, keeping the hotel car park over your L shoulder. The path leads down to Watcombe Bay and the chalk cliffs, with the fort on the L.

50.668488, -1.513925

Earthworks, Watcombe Bay

A natural platform of nodes, earthworks, cliff face and tree-lined down. Views from High Down cliffs and Tennyson Monument are to die for, which is why so many of our ancestors were buried here. Take time to savour the views, and also the wonderful paths.

➤ Follow directions above for Watcombe Bay, but keep walking another 0.6 mile.

50.668833, -1.525586

The Needles, Isle of Wight

BOAT HOUSE, FRESHWATER, THE SOLENT

Cafe bar with seats right on the waterside looking over to the mainland.

Fort Victoria, Westhill Ln, Freshwater, Yarmouth, PO41 0RR
Facebook: @tboathouse

ANCHOR BOATHOUSE HOLIDAY APARTMENTS, FRESHWATER, THE SOLENT

Right on the beach, next to Fort Victoria Country Park.

Westhill Ln, Freshwater, Yarmouth, PO41 0NA
01983 754 718

THE GOSSIPS CAFE, YARMOUTH, THE SOLENT

Next to Yarmouth Pier, beside the beach – proudly claims over the door to be Yarmouth's only waterside cafe.

Pier St, The Square, Yarmouth, PO41 0NS
www.gossipscafe.co.uk

Red squirrel at Fort Victoria Country Park

Alum Bay

Cave & Lookout, Alum Bay

Breathtaking views of The Needles and surrounding cliff top. Cliff lift is an adventure for thrill-seekers. Escape to Alum Bay's peaceful waters if it all gets a bit much.

➤ **Find** The Needles car park over Alum Bay at Totland, Totland Bay, PO39 0JD. Looking out to sea, keep following the coast path L for 0.8 miles.

50.661423, -1.57944

Fort Albert, the Solent

Outstanding Cliff End naze within touching distance of mainland Hampshire across the Solent. Walk and shelter in shoreside trees to the N. A near-perfect mirror to the New Forest shores on the other side.

➤ **Find** Fort Victoria Country Park, Westhill Ln, Freshwater, Yarmouth, PO41 0RR. Facing the brick-arch buildings, walk L and exit the car park on to the tree-lined beach and keep walking ½ mile to the fort. Walk back through the woodland trail/coast path by exiting the beach at Cliff End Battery, Cliff End, Freshwater, PO40 9XA, and turning L at the FP sign in Monks Ln.

50.700266, -1.534496

Bouldnor Forest, Yarmouth, the Solent

Red squirrels and goldcrests in a pine forest surrounded by fossil-rich pebbles and clay heath. Find the small beach for a dip and search for crocodile, turtle and fish remains.

➤ **Find** the car park at Bouldnor Viewpoint, Shalfleet, Yarmouth, PO41 0ND. Leave the car park on Bouldner Rd and walk L ¼ mile. Turn L into Victoria Rd and follow the path all the way down for 0.2 miles to the beach and the vast forest FPs. For courses or events run at the Bouldnor Forest Centre, park in the Forest at the Loading Bay SZ 378 903.

50.708483, -1.481609

Newton Bay & sea wall, the Solent

One of the most secluded beaches on the island looking out across the Solent from woodland shade. It doesn't get better than this (50.726247, -1.421895). Walk to Newton Harbour sea wall for wonderful sunsets and breathtaking views. For those who don't have a boat, the sea wall walk with views across Newton River and marshes of wildlife is just gorgeous. Best when the tide is in and calm.

➤ **Find** the NT car park opposite Newtown Old Town Hall, Newtown, Newport, PO30 4PA. Leave the car park via the N entrance and turn R into Town Ln. Follow the FP for 0.4 miles to the quay. Keeping the quay on the L, take the FP along the sea wall past the hut and boats and out on to the marsh.

50.724440, -1.403511

Gurnard Bay, Cowes, the Solent

Tiny harbour and low-tide beach renowned for insect fossils; more than 200 species have been found.

➤ **Find** The Little Gloster, 31 Marsh Rd, Cowes, PO31 8JQ. With your back to the restaurant, walk L along Marsh Rd 175 yards to the road bend. Bear R down the track towards the beach, with the boats and tiny harbour on your R. The bay is a few yards to your R.

50.75544, -1.33550

Yarmouth

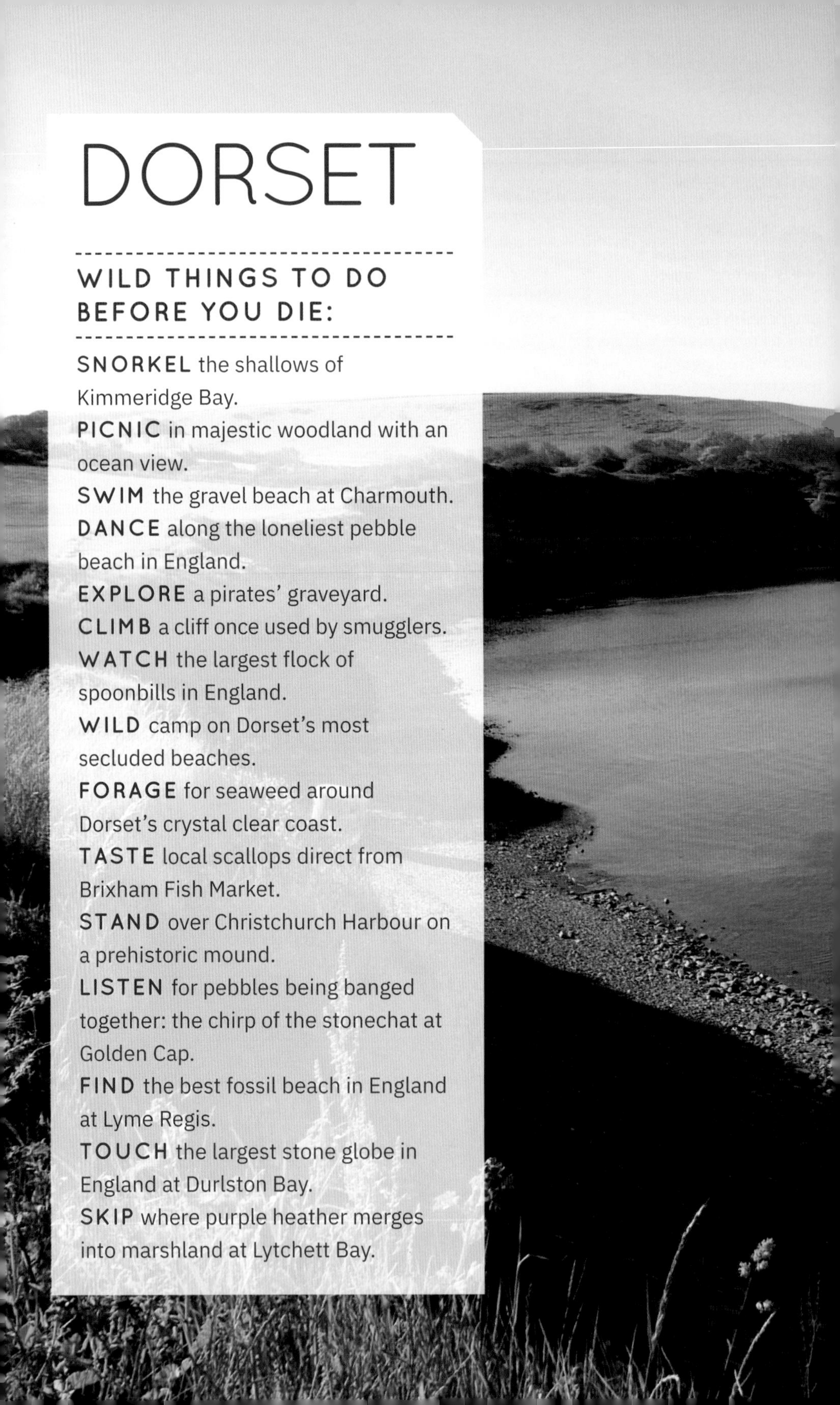

DORSET

WILD THINGS TO DO BEFORE YOU DIE:

SNORKEL the shallows of Kimmeridge Bay.

PICNIC in majestic woodland with an ocean view.

SWIM the gravel beach at Charmouth.

DANCE along the loneliest pebble beach in England.

EXPLORE a pirates' graveyard.

CLIMB a cliff once used by smugglers.

WATCH the largest flock of spoonbills in England.

WILD camp on Dorset's most secluded beaches.

FORAGE for seaweed around Dorset's crystal clear coast.

TASTE local scallops direct from Brixham Fish Market.

STAND over Christchurch Harbour on a prehistoric mound.

LISTEN for pebbles being banged together: the chirp of the stonechat at Golden Cap.

FIND the best fossil beach in England at Lyme Regis.

TOUCH the largest stone globe in England at Durlston Bay.

SKIP where purple heather merges into marshland at Lytchett Bay.

Kimmeridge Bay

THE CLIFF HOUSE, BARTON-ON-SEA, THE SOLENT

Cliff top dining with panoramic views of the Solent. Try the fish pie or an afternoon tea. Seven en suite rooms named after ports and places with a maritime heritage linked to the English coast.

Marine Dr W, Barton-on-Sea, New Milton, BH25 7QL
www.thecliffhouse.co.uk

BEACH HOUSE, MUDEFORD QUAY, ENGLISH CHANNEL

Restaurant on the harbour side of Hengistbury Head sands. Phenomenal views across the harbour, Hengisbury Head and Mudeford Quay. If in season, try the scallops in garlic or fish fillets with asparagus.

The Spit, Bournemouth, Mudeford, BH6 4EN
Facebook: Beach House Mudeford

BRANKSOME BEACH RESTAURANT, POOLE, POOLE BAY

Beside wooded cliffs of Branksome Chine, this seaside restaurant was converted from England's first solarium. Fresh seafood sourced from local catches. Cakes and scones are baked on site.

Pinecliff Rd, Poole, BH13 6LP
www.branksome beach.co.uk

Highcliffe Castle, Highcliffe, English Channel

Spectacular wooded ridge, cliffs and ornate gardens over sand and shingle beach. Views across to Isle of Wight and Mudeford quays. Walk along the shore to Highcliffe Beach.

➤ **Find** the car park at Highcliffe Castle, Highcliffe, Christchurch, BH23 4LD. Or even better, use the car park for Hengistbury Head (see below) and walk R instead of L, 0.8 miles to the Highcliffe foreshore and beach.

50.736640, -1.715569

Hengistbury Head, Highcliffe, English Channel

Vast cliffs over Dorset's most easterly point at the entrance to Christchurch Harbour. Warren Hill and Round Barrow are both riddled with breathtaking walks, prehistoric settlements and burial mounds.

➤ **Find** the beach car park at Highcliffe, Christchurch, BH23 5DF. Looking towards the sea, follow any of the FPs to the L. The most scenic is S and L. Follow the FP for 1½ miles to the head. Keep going, turning L up towards East Cliff to complete a 4-mile circuit of the head. The Beach House offers great seafood and fish from the spit if you have the stamina to keep going.

50.713918, -1.754502

DWT Lytchett Bay/Arc Nature Reserve, Upton

Where heather merges into marshland around a bird-rich bay. A choice of two parts of the reserve to visit in Upton, Poole: 1) At junction of Lytchett Way and Shore Ln, Upton signposted 'Footpath No.12'; 2) Sandy Ln, Upton (just W of Otter Cl). Beach, parking and watersports training area at entrance to the Rock Lea River watersports centre.

➤ **Find** the FP in Border Rd, Poole, BH16 5SA. Walk to reserve from Upton, Hamworthy and Lytchett Minster. A short distance from Moorland Way, bus stop routes 8 and 9, and ¾ mile from Hamworthy station. There's limited off-street parking. Follow the path across the recreation ground shoreside on to Turlin Moor.

50.732112, -2.031120

Brownsea Island, Poole Harbour

Spoonbills, avocets, wildfowl and flocks of waders on a spectacular pine-ringed lagoon. Breeding common terns and Sandwich terns in summer. Red squirrels, sika deer and kingfishers.

➤ **Find** regular ferries on to the island. Brownsea Island Cafe (see right).

50.689844, -1.96172

Studland

BROWNSEA ISLAND CAFE, POOLE HARBOUR

Cuppa by the quay.
Brownsea Island,
2 Farm Cottages,
Poole, BH13 7EE
www.nationaltrust.org.uk

NT KNOLL BEACH CAFE, STUDLAND BAY

Relax around one of the best beaches in Dorset. Warm
drinks or local ciders,
beers and fruit juices.
Studland, BH19 3AH

Studland Heath, Poole Harbour

Stunning beach broken from Bournemouth Bay arc. Today, the breach leaks tidal and fresh water on the ebb and flood to create what we know as Poole Harbour. The heath is a landmass of green and dune that has barely changed in 1,000 years. Like most of the Jurassic Coast, this is not a window into the past. It *is* the past. Little Sea is a tree-lined brackish lake reminiscent of a Sinbad novel; all adventure, marsh and monster. Venture if you dare, otherwise kick off the shoes and walk through the surf and sandy shore south imagining opulence and Eden.

➤ **Find** the Shell Bay NT car park, in Ferry Rd, Studland, Swanage, BH19 3BA. Looking towards the ferry terminal to Bournemouth, turn R down towards the beach and walk for 1½ miles along the glorious Shell Bay. Now turn L on any of the paths towards Little Sea ... and get lost. Wonderful. Alternatively, cross the road at the car park and explore the S, and quietest, side of Poole Harbour.

50.659182, -1.956548

Dancing Ledge, Langton Matravers

Take a dip or paddle in the pool that was blasted out of the rocks 200 years ago so that school children, including Ian Fleming, could swim safely. Landslips make the steep FP down difficult at times. Feel the ruts in the rock; remnants of wheel tracks from man-drawn carts that carried Purbeck limestone out to waiting boats. Listen for nesting peregrine falcons. Puffins feed and nest here, too. Watch rock climbers of all abilities tackle some of S England's most popular climbs. Good fishing or lunch spot.

➤ **Find** Spyway Car Park, Durnford Drove, Langton Matravers, Swanage, BH19 3HG, then walk 1 mile S on the FP to the ECP and the ledge.

50.591344, -2.004654

Swanage Bay Cliffs, Swanage Bay

Listen for burrowing bees while exploring cliff falls and landslips on the beach beyond the groynes at low tide. Beware: the Swanage cliffs are especially prone to collapse since they are made of soft rocks, sandstones and clays (known as Wealden beds). It's even possible to get cut off by a combination of landslide and rising tide. Care is therefore needed when visiting from above or below, so explore landslips from a distance.

➤ **Find** Main Beach Car Park, Information Centre, A351, Swanage, BH19 1PW, then walk E 500 yards to the beach. Walk 1 mile N to New Swanage Bay Beach and cliffs.

50.624091, -1.951962

Kimmeridge Bay

Durlston

Durlston Bay

One of the largest stone globes in the world, perched over the English Channel, Great Globe is a 10ft-wide, 40-tonne Portland stone installed here in 1887.

➤ **Find** the car park at Durlston Country Park, St Catherines Rd, Swanage, BH19 2JL. From here, walk another 330 yards along St Catherines Rd, past the Seventh Wave Cafe & Restaurant for a coffee and cake.

50.595130, -1.951370

Chapman's Pool, St Albam's Head

Natural harbour for swimming tucked into the W-facing armpit of St Albam's Head. Wonderful beach walk down cliffs, but it's a slog back up. Find loads of fossilised ammonites and shells. Take in the view from gardens and the Royal Marines Commando Memorial over the southern bay top.

➤ **Find** Renscombe Car Park, 3 Renscombe Rd, Worth Matravers, Swanage, BH19 3LL. With your back to the road, exit the car park along the FP to the L and follow it ⅔ mile down to the beach. Paths are narrow and steep.

50.593179, -2.063930

Fine Foundation Wild Seas Centre & Kimmeridge Bay

Snorkel trail around the shallows of Kimmeridge Bay. You'll need your own wetsuit to experience the coral wonders of sea anemones, crabs, bass, lobster and seaweed. Check tide times to gain the most reward. Nov–Mar: closed for the winter. Apr–Oct: open every day, including bank holidays, 10.30am–5pm. Some of the cliff paths are steep in places, with slippery rock pools. The Wild Seas Centre is very user-friendly.

➤ **Find** the A351 from Wareham to Corfe Castle and the first turn R to Creech. Follow the road to the top of a steep hill and round a hairpin bend signposted to 'Church Knowle'. About 2 miles on, turn R to Kimmeridge. Drive through the village to the toll booth. Find parking and toilets at Purbeck Marine Wildlife Reserve, Kimmeridge Bay, Wareham, BH20 5PF. Parking fee payable to Smedmore Estate.

50.609742, -2.129967

Gad Cliff, Brandy Bay

Hardy trees along a sacred platform that has served as a burial ground and lookout for thousands of years above Brandy Bay. Smugglers used this route for centuries to reach cart tracks E and W. More recently taken over by the MoD. Visit on the weekend when the area, including the abandoned village Tyneham, and the beach, is open to the public.

➤ **Find** St Mary's Church, Tyneham, Wareham, BH20 5QN. Keeping the church on your R, take the R turn down the track towards a large car park. Leave here on foot walking S ½ mile, taking the L fork in the FP after the first 220 yards.

50.618720, -2.165772

Hambury Tout Barrows, Oswald's Bay

Sacred site above beach and sand at Oswald's Bay. Explore barrows and views, then look for the ancient tracks down past Dungy Head to Stair Hole and Pinion Rock. Best seen at low tide when rock pools are alive and fossils are easier to find. A detour from Lulworth Cove en route to Durdle Door and calm waters of Man O' War Beach.

➤ **Find** Jurassic Coast Activities, 38 Main Rd, West Lulworth, Wareham, BH20 5RQ on the W bank of Lulworth Cove. From the public car park opposite, and with your back to the centre, walk W along the coast path 660 yards veering off R to look out for the barrow and L for better sea views.

50.622020, -2.261750

SHORE COTTAGE, RINGSTEAD, ENGLISH CHANNEL

zzZ A three-bed family-run cottage, with a garden that runs over the cliff to the shingle beach.

SW Coast Path, Ringstead, Dorchester, DT2 8NG
www.shorecottage
dorset.co.uk

TOP FIELD, EWELEAZE FARM CAMPSITE, OSMINGTON, ENGLISH CHANNEL

zzZ Tent camping in August only. The farm opens up this cliff top field. Fires are allowed. There are also two cottages available to hire all year.

Osmington, Weymouth, DT3 6EG
www.eweleaze.co.uk

Oswald's Bay

Durdle Door, Wareham St Martin

Wonder what it was like to be at Stone Henge 3,000 years ago? Head to Durdle Door: the famous limestone archway is best seen during August when the beach is packed with zealots. It's like a religio/pop concert, and that's no bad thing – it adds to the mystique. Arrive before 5am and leave no later than 3pm.

➤ **Find** Durdle Door Car Park, Wareham, BH20 5PU and walk ⅓ mile W on the FP and then the ECP to Durdle Door beach.

50.621279, -2.276815

Durdle Door, Lulworth

THE LOBSTER POT, PORTLAND, ENGLISH CHANNEL

Great food right next to the famous Portland Bill Lighthouse. Family-run business, famous for fresh locally caught crab and Dorset cream tea. The owners claim to have an almost fanatical obsession with creating the perfect chips!

Portland Bill Rd, Portland, DT5 2JT
www.lobsterpot
restaurantportland.co.uk

King Rock Beach, Holworth, English Channel

Previously one of the best fossil sites until a landslide allowed brambles to grow up and encase the ammonite exposures in impassable thorns. Occasional fossils can be found after landslides and high tides. The best specimens are seen at nearby museums.

➤ **Find** Ringstead Bay Car Park, Osmington, Dorchester, DT2 8NG, then walk 1 mile E on the pebble beach to the rocky point after high tide.

50.627521, -2.327640

Osmington Mills, English Channel

Fabulous tree-lined cliffs and rock ledges, many of which have been used historically as natural docks for landing goods. Ammonites along foreshore or set into the rocks. Cafe, pub, parking and toilets. Swim and low-tide rock pooling. Nearby camping at Rosewall Camping.

➤ **Find** the Smugglers Inn, Osmington Mills, Weymouth, DT3 6HF, and the public car park and toilets opposite. Stunning views. With your back to the sea, turn R immediately after the Smugglers Inn on to the coast path and walk it. Alternatively, walk down from the car park on the L side, facing the sea, to the beach via the narrow, steep FPs that pass by the Mills Cafe. The R side path from the car park offers lovely beach walks but be wary of incoming high tides.

50.63391, -2.37571

THE COVE HOUSE INN, PORTLAND, ENGLISH CHANNEL

Right beside Chesil Beach with views over Portland. Locally caught fish and seafood include Portland crab and seared scallops. Freshly ground coffee.

91 Chiswell, Portland, DT5 1AW
https://thecovehouse
inn.co.uk

Church Ope Cove

Church Ope Cove, Portland, English Channel

Iconic pirates' graveyard in the shadow of a 13th-century castle ruin (no access, but good for photos). Steep pebble path though trees to a stone cove circled by beach huts. Full of fossils and calm. Difficult access because of the rocks.

➤ **Find** Portland Museum, 217 Wakeham, Easton, Portland, DT5 1HS. The museum has a car park 88 yards along Pennsylvania Rd, on the R, under trees. Walk back to the museum and turn R into Church Ope Rd. Follow the lane all the way to Rufus Castle and the coast path 220 yards away. Turn R along the path and walk another 110 yards to get down on to the cove. Walk back into the trees to explore the ruin of Portland's first parish church, St Andrews Church.

50.53731, -2.42884

Chesil Beach, Wyke Regis, English Channel

Named 'Dead Man's Bay' by Thomas Hardy, Chesil Beach is one of England's most remarkable natural wonders. The shingle beach is 18 miles long, 600ft wide and 50ft high. See little terns in April – the second-rarest breeding sea bird in the UK, with fewer than 2,000 breeding pairs. The best way to see the birds is from the *Fleet Explorer* and there are special tern-watching trips running as well.

➤ **Find** the Fine Foundation Chesil Beach Centre, Portland Beach Rd, Portland, DT4 9XE and the pay-and-display car park. The boardwalk next to the Centre provides easy access to the beach. From here, it's possible to walk 8 miles along the beach to Abbotsbury Swannery, New Barn Rd, Abbotsbury, DT3 4JG, on the site of an old monastery. Take care of rising tides and exposure.

50.57843, -2.46975

Chesil Beach

St Catherine's Chapel, Abbotsbury

EAST FLEET FARM TOURING PARK & CAMPING SHOP, CHICKERELL, FLEET LAGOON

Campsite for tents and caravans on a 20-acre organic farm, beside the shores of the vast lagoon overlooking Chesil Beach. There's a decent pub and restaurant.

Fleet Ln, Chickerell, Weymouth, DT3 4DW
www.eastfleet.co.uk

Merchants' Railway, Portland, English Channel

This disused track now used as FP provides incredible views to Portland Harbour and the cliffs of Purbeck. Portland Harbour is very sheltered and therefore an ideal home for the National Sailing Centre. It was also a natural choice as the venue for the sailing in the Olympics of 2012.

➤ **Find** New Ground Car Park, off Yates Rd, Portland, DT15 1LQ, then facing Yates Rd, turn and walk 400 yards E to the prison. From there, walk clockwise on the ECP 700 yards to the top of the hill via steps.

50.562959, -2.440988

Pirates Cove, Wyke Regis, English Channel

Chesil Beach is severed from the mainland by a tidal lagoon, known as The Fleet, part of which includes Pirates Cove. Low-tide access to a fossil-rich beach and safer (but rarely safe) swimming overlooking Chesil Beach.

➤ **Find** Weymouth Camping and Caravan Park, 40 South Rd, Weymouth, DT4 9NR. A FP runs down the R side of the campsite. Follow the path for ¼ mile, with the camp on your L, to where it meets the ECP and beaches L and R.

50.594466, -2.481486

West Bexington Nature Reserve, English Channel

Reedbed and grazing marsh behind the shingle beach. Cetti's warbler, reed bunting and linnet. Watch out for adders in spring.

➤ **Find** The Club House cafe looking out on to the beach. From the beach car park, facing the sea, turn R and walk 330 yards to the reserve. Several FPs lead up from the beach around the pools.

50.678918, -2.672233

MOONFLEET MANOR, WEYMOUTH, ENGLISH CHANNEL

A manor estate linked to a novel about smuggling and the ghost of Colonel 'Blackbeard' Mohune, who is said to still haunt the local churchyard. It's all fiction of course – ahem! – apart from the name of the original owners, the Mohune family. To explore this wonderful piece of coast and estate, choose either an afternoon tea or a luxury night or two in a colonial-feel room. Dog friendly.

Fleet Rd, Weymouth, DT3 4ED
www.moonfleetmanor hotel.co.uk

EYPE HOUSE CARAVAN & CAMPING PARK, EYPE BAY

Tent camping, caravans and pods on the grassy cliffs over the bay.

Mount Ln, Eype, Bridport, DT6 6AL
www.eypehouse.co.uk

WATCH HOUSE CAFE, BRIDPORT, ENGLISH CHANNEL

Fresh fish, pizza and cuppas on the pebble beach at the start of the Chesil Bank. Breakfast and lunch menus.

West Bay, Bridport, DT6 4EN
www.watchhousecafe .co.uk

Path to Burton Bradstock

Burton Bradstock, English Channel

Fossilised shark fins, shells and ammonites. Cliff falls leave the foreshore scattered with finds.

➤ **Find** the Hive Beach Cafe, Beach Rd, Burton Bradstock, Bridport, DT6 4RF. From the beachside car park, walk L a few yards towards the chalk cliffs. Keep going for ¾ mile along the beach to reach the beautiful Cogden Beach.

50.69608, -2.72253

Burton Mere, Burton Bradstock, English Channel

Snorkel rocks and marine life from shingle with sandstone cliffs as a backdrop, at the long N entrance to Chesil Beach (see page 133). Tens of thousands of mackerel and bass breed here in summer.

➤ **Find** Burton Bradstock Hive Beach NT Car Park, Beach Rd, Burton Bradstock, DT6 4RF, then walk down on to the beach. Walk further E for quieter sections of beach.

50.695601, -2.721034

West Cliff, Eype, English Channel

Taste freshly caught bass cooked on a portable stove. Look for fossils and rock pool wildlife while listening to buzzards mewing overhead. An unusual number of different blackbirds (three) sing at dusk around where the cliffs have fallen.

➤ **Find** Eype Beach Car Park, Eype, DT6 6Al, and walk 150 yards S and E to Mouth Ford. Then walk ½ mile E to the cliffs.

50.712824, -2.773041

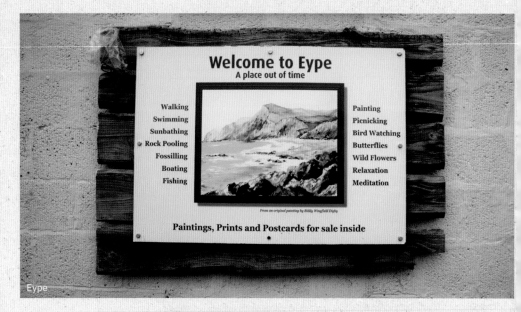

Eype

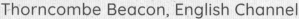

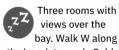
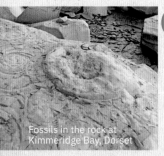

Fossils in the rock at Kimmeridge Bay, Dorset

Thorncombe Beacon, English Channel

Great views of the Jurassic Coast and Portland Bill. Keep climbing W to Golden Cap, nearly 2 miles away.

➤ **Find** Eype's Mouth Car Park at the end of Mount Lane, Bridport, DT6 6AL. Facing the sea, turn R on to the path and walk 1 mile to the beacon.

50.71866, -2.80369

Golden Cap, English Channel

The highest cliff on the S coast is England's only natural World Heritage site. Stunning views above the ruin of St Gabriel's Church. Scoop up ammonites from the beach on the way into Seatown. Listen for the sound of the stonechat, which gets it name from its chirp, which sounds like two pebbles being banged together.

➤ **Find** the Eype House Caravan & Camping Park (see page 135) and keep on to the bottom of the lane to the beach car park. Facing the sea, turn R and walk 1 mile to Golden Cap. Alternatively, walk down on to the beach. Beware incoming tides.

50.72258, -2.84052

Charmouth Beach, English Channel

Gravel beach for swimming and fossils.

➤ **Find** the Charmouth Heritage Coast Centre, Lower Sea Ln, Charmouth, Bridport, DT6 6LL for guided fossil-hunting walks. Looking out to sea, turn L and walk around the tiny beach estuary of the River Char. Cross the river bridge on the ECP. After the bridge, ignore the cliff walk and move on to the beach for up to 1 mile to find the quietest parts and the best finds.

50.73160, -2.88596

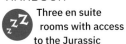
Lyme Regis, English Channel

The fossil capital of England. Even the lamp posts are shaped like ammonites. Fossil shops, tours and museums. Get on down to the beach.

➤ **Find** Charmouth's long-stay car park in Charmouth Rd, Lyme Regis, DT7 3DR, then walk down the wide steps 220 yards towards the concreted coast walk. Turn L and walk another 165 yards to the concrete staircase down on to the beach. Walk on another 220 yards for the better finds. For wheelchair access to the coast path and great views, find Cobb Gate Car Park, Marine Pde, Lyme Regis, DT7 3QD.

50.72957, -2.92715

Chippel Bay, Monmouth Beach, English Channel

Huge ammonites that are easy to see in the rocks. You'll need a hammer, safety glasses and a low tide.

➤ **Find** the RNLI Lyme Regis Lifeboat Station next to fishing trip boats at the Cobb harbour, Lyme Regis, DT7 3JJ. From the large beachside car park, facing the sea, walk R ¾ mile while exploring the beach. Keep walking an extra ¾ mile to reach Pinhay Bay.

50.71955, -2.94310

Charmouth

SOUTH DEVON

WATCH basking sharks at Labrador Bay; dolphins breaching at Berry Head; starling murmurations over the Exe Estuary.

SNORKEL the reef at Pinhay Bay.

SWIM the creeks of the River Erme.

CYCLE the River Exe path.

HUNT the foreshore of Hope's Nose for fossils and seals.

WALK the magical Burgh Island.

LISTEN for the plop of water voles at Slapton Ley.

FORAGE for sea purslane at South Efford Marsh.

EXPLORE the only place in Britain where you can find the tiny Warren crocus.

FIND the oldest human bones ever found in Devon ... and England; peregrines flying over Beer Head; the coastal forest on the sand cove at Rousdon Woods.

Brixham

Pinhay Bay

Reef to snorkel. Deep water and rocks along sweeping cove. Best accessed from Lyme Regis at low tide. Tree-lined cliffs at Ware or Pinhay. Find fish, ammonites and shell fossils on the beach, in rock and chalk.

➤ **Find** Chippel Bay, Monmouth Beach (see page 135). Keep walking along the cliff top 1.4 miles.

50.71294, -2.96478

Charton Undercliff, Rousdon Woods, Lyme Regis, English Channel

Coastal forest on shingle and sand cove. Rock pools at low tide.

➤ **Find** Monmouth Beach Car Park, Lyme Regis, DT7 3JN, and facing the sea walk W (to the R) 3 miles on the ECP.

50.7054, -2.9950

Beer Head, English Channel

Peregrine falcons hunt here. Walk and swim around Chalky Naze, off S Down Common. Ammonites on the beach around Hooken Cliff in sand and chalk. Steep walks down to the beach.

➤ **Find** the Beer Head Caravan Park, Common Hill, Beer, EX12 3AH, and the E Devon Council car park opposite. Great views from here, but walk down towards the beach on to Little Ln and then R along the lane towards the coastal path and steep climbs to the beaches and rocks. Paths down are sometimes lost to erosion so you may need to keep walking S and W to the Beer Head Point and then Hooken Cliff beach.

50.69337, -3.09315

Branscombe Beach

Sidmouth

LOWER HALSDON FARM, EXMOUTH, EXE ESTUARY

B&B on a 110-acre working farm. Views across the estuary. Guests get access to the orchards and woodland. The Exe Estuary Trail and ECP passes the farm entrance.

Mudbank Ln, Exmouth, EX8 3EG
www.lowerhalsdon.com

THE LIGHTER INN, TOPSHAM, EXE ESTUARY

English pub on the banks of the estuary. Sit by the log burner in winter or on the large terrace over Topsham Quay in summer.

The Quay, Topsham, EX3 0HZ
www.lighterinn.co.uk

Sidmouth, English Channel

Dinosaur footprints and bones around the wooded cliff face and beach. Fossils sometimes found around fallen boulders. The best views over the bay from an old settlement site on High Peak.

➤ **Find** the Mutter's Moor Car Park in Peak Hill Rd, Sidmouth, EX10 0NW. Either cross the road and follow the FP opposite down to the cliff tops or walk down Peak Hill Rd the ⅓ mile to the cliff top path E (to the R). Access to the site is at low tide from the coastal path.

50.674901, -3.2573269

Exe Estuary

Starling murmurations at dusk and dawn over the Exe Estuary. Best seen from the Topsham side of the River Exe or from the FP under the M5. Also look out for sand martins and avocets.

➤ **Find** the very end of Station Rd at the Lions Rest Eco Park, Exminster, Exeter, EX1 3SA. Facing the Exeter Canal, turn L on to the path and walk 1 mile towards the M5 road bridge. Continue on under the bridge for a longer walk. Less than ⅓ mile from Station Rd a ferry sometimes runs across the River Exe to Topsham with several cafes along the shorefront.

50.686774, -3.477832

St Clement's Church, Powderham, River Exe

Church next to the River Exe. Fields to the E of the church have been eroded by the tide. Good cycle path to Exeter.

➤ **Find** St Clement's Church, 1 Church Rd, Powderham, Exeter, EX6 8JJ. Facing the River Exe, turn L along the FP and walk riverside 1.4 miles for a delightful stop at the Turf Hotel right beside the water.

50.650396, -3.4546013

HUNTERS LODGE CARAVAN AND CAMPING SITE, STAPLAKE BROOK

A 10-acre site for tents and caravans by Staplake Brook, which empties into the River Exe 1,000 yards away. The Exe Estuary Cycle Trail runs through Starcross. A passenger ferry runs to Exmouth in summer.

Starcross, Exeter, EX6 8FL
www.hunterslodge-
camping.co.uk

THE BEECHES BED & BREAKFAST, DAWLISH, RIVER EXE

Family-run B&B 20 mins from the coast path. Sea views from some of the rooms.

15A Old Teignmouth Rd, Dawlish, EX7 0NJ
www.thebeeches
bandb.co.uk

CAFE, ANSTEYS COVE, ENGLISH CHANNEL

Breakfast, snacks and beer beside the pebble beach. Sea kayaks can be hired along the beach.

Anstey's Cove Rd, Torquay, TQ1 3YY
www.ansteyscove.info

The Geoneedle, Exmouth, River Exe

Landmark celebrating 180 million years (or so) of the Triassic, Jurassic and Cretaceous rock formations that make up this unique coastline. The Geoneedle is crafted from the many rocks that form the World Heritage coastline, with a 'Jurassic coast hopscotch' to enable walkers to jump through time from Triassic (red sandstone) to Cretaceous (limestone). Look for the tiny purple and white flowers of the rare bithynian vetch.

➤ **Find** the car park, 339 Queen's Dr, Exmouth, EX8 2DP, then walk E ⅔ mile to the Geoneedle.

50.607159, -3.387115

Dawlish Inner Warren, River Exe

The only place in Britain where you can find the tiny Warren crocus in spring. Stunning sand spit at the mouth of the River Exe. Thousands of birds feed at 'The Warren' and its surrounding mudflats as part of their migratory stopovers. Look out for Sandwich and Arctic terns.

➤ **Find** Warren Golf Club, Dawlish Warren, Beach Rd, Dawlish, EX7 0NF, next to the large public car park and Dawlish Warren Station. Exit the car park at the bottom, heading E with your back to the railway line, towards the public toilets. Keep walking to the beach and then choose whether to walk along the sand or the paths to Dawlish Warren Point 1⅓ miles away. Return along the point's NW shore for a view across the entire natural harbour.

50.605461, -3.435713

Herring Cove, Shaldon, Labrador Bay

This isolated stretch of coast is famous for its Devon sandstone cliffs. Dartmoor ponies chew their way through scrub and woody growth; they're allowed to graze here to protect the grassland from being lost to scrub.

➤ **Find** Labrador Bay Nature Reserve Car Park, A379, Shaldon, Torquay, TQ1 4TP. Facing the water, turn R on to the ECP and walk ⅔ mile to Herring Cove and Mackerel Cove.

50.51457, -3.50995

Oddicombe Beach, Babbacombe Bay

Cliff railway runs overhead in summer. Walk down to swim, then catch the rail back. Look for oval-shaped coral fossils trapped in the sandstone 'breccia' blocks used to make the building walls at the bottom of the cliff railway. The surrounding red-rock breccia cliffs are a kind of sandstone formed 250 million years ago in desert conditions.

➤ **Find** the car park at Watcombe Beach Rd, Torquay, TQ1 4SH, then walk 1¾ miles S on the ECP to the beach.

50.481861, -3.515096

ANSTEY'S COVE BREAKWATER COFFEE SHOP & BISTRO, BRIXHAM BEACH, ENGLISH CHANNEL

Drinks from the Sharpham Vineyard served beside the beach. Fish from Brixham Seafoods and Devon crab from The Blue Sea Food Company.

Berry Head Rd, Brixham, TQ5 9AF
www.breakwater
bistro.co.uk

THE GUARDHOUSE CAFE, BERRY HEAD, ENGLISH CHANNEL

Home-made food, including cream teas. Built in the 19th century, the Berry Head Fort protected a battery of guns on the end of the headland. The guardhouse was used by the troops defending the fortress. The tearoom was built into the guardhouse 100 years ago. Part of the fort tunnel system can still be seen inside.

Berry Head Nature Reserve, Brixham, TQ5 9AW
www.guardhousecafe.com

Hopes Nose, English Channel

A naze from which to watch seals. Popular with anglers. One of the best locations in Devon for fossils found on the foreshore at low tide.

➤ **Find** the costal road along Ilsham Marine Dr, Wellswood, Torquay, TQ1 2PH. At its junction with Thatcher Av, bear L off the road on to the FP and walk ⅓ mile to the end of the rocky peninsula. There's limited parking sometimes in Marine Dr so consider instead finding Babbacombe Cricket Club, Walls Hill Rd, Torquay, TQ1 3LZ, in neighbouring Babbacombe, where there's a public car park (and a lovely beach). With your back to the car park, walk R along Walls Hill Rd and just keep on to Walls Hill and the coast path. Turn R from here and follow the old ECP 1¼ miles back to Ilsham Marine Dr, and on to the Nose.

50.46347, -3.48159

Labrador Bay

Look out for dolphins, basking sharks and nesting peregrines.
➤ **Find** Ness Cove Beach and car park, Shaldon, Teignmouth, TQ14 0DP. Facing the water, turn R on to the coast path and walk 0.6 miles to Smugglers Cove and Labrador Bay.

50.52956, -3.50199

Berry Head, English Channel

Dolphins and seals swim off this Napoleonic fort. It's far enough from Brixham to feel isolated. Wheelchair access.
➤ **Find** Berry Head National Nature Reserve at the end of Gillard Rd, Brixham, TQ5 9AP. From here, walk N along the coast path, detouring R after 275 yards towards The Guardhouse Cafe (see left). Walk on another ¼ mile to the Berry Head Lighthouse and Compass Statue for best views.

50.399763, -3.483598

Berry Head

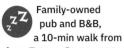
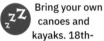
Scabbacombe Sand, English Channel

Steep cliff walk down to a naturist beach. A whole cove for rock pooling, crabbing and snorkelling.

➤ **Find** the Man Sands NT car park in Woodhuish Ln, Kingswear, Dartmouth, TQ6 0EF. Keep heading S ½ mile for another tiny car park on the R. From the car park, follow Scabbacombe Ln as it winds its way 0.6 miles to the coast path and tiny beach.

50.357720, -3.521141

Duncannon Beach, Ashprington, River Dart

Church FP to beach via a wooded lane.

➤ **Find** St David's Church at the Nern end of the village, Ashprington, Totnes, TQ9 7UP. With your back to the church entrance, walk L and then first R into the small lane with a FP sign. Walk 1⅓ miles along the FP, past Sharpham Wood at the bottom of the lane, to the waterside spot on the River Dart.

50.4048, -3.6343

Great Copse, Old Mill Creek

Woodland and mud sand beach on Old Mill Creek overlooking the edge of Dartmouth and the harbour.

➤ **Find** the river bay at the Ham playground, at the end of Ham Ln, Dittisham, Dartmouth, TQ6 0HB. From here, walk along the beach FP to The Ferry Boat Inn (see opposite), 330 yards away. Turn R at the Inn into Manor St and walk with your back to the river for 330 yards, before turning L on to the tiny lane at the bend. This FP winds its way inland for ½ mile to Fire Beacon Hill (50.373837, -3.601008). From here, follow the FP another 1 mile, back down to the coast to Mill Creek and the wooded copse.

50.360958, -3.592056

Compass Cove, Dartmouth

Touch or collect chicken of the woods fungi that grow around the base of large oaks on the cove's W face. The dark sand and shingle beach is surrounded by shade. Access is often restricted because of landslips so even more care than normal is needed around this bit of coast.

➤ **Find** Western Combe Cove (see opposite), then walk 1 mile N on the ECP to the cove.

50.333783, -3.56855

Dartmouth

THE FERRY BOAT INN, DITTISHAM, RIVER DART

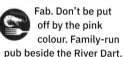

Fab. Don't be put off by the pink colour. Family-run pub beside the River Dart.

Manor St, Dittisham, Dartmouth, TQ6 0EX
www.ferryboatinn
dittisham.pub

THE VENUS CAFE, BLACKPOOL SANDS, ENGLISH CHANNEL

Cuppa and kayak hire on a wonderful beach.

Blackpool Sands, Blackpool, Dartmouth, TQ6 0QR
www.lovingthebeach.co.uk

Dartmouth Castle, Dartmouth, Dart Estuary

Coastal fort guarding the Dart Estuary and the strategic port of Dartmouth. Tearoom and coastal church, too.

> Find the corner at Redcap Ln, Dartmouth, TQ6 0JR, and walk between the two car parks on the E-facing and -pointing bridleway. Follow the lane 1.2 miles on Castle Rd to the edge of the river and the castle. Explore Deadmans Cove, Sugary Cove and Castle Cove. There is a small car park here (Castle Rd, Dartmouth, TQ6 0JN), but it's often busy and the walk (or cycle) from Redcap Ln is lovely. Consider walking on another 1 mile along the coastal roads and the B3205 to Dartford's centre.

50.34203, -3.56829

Western Combe Cove, Ashprington, English Channel

Beautiful S-facing beach, steps and cove. Several larger coves including neighbouring Forest Cove. Best walked at low tide.

> Find the Redcap Ln car park (see Dartmouth Castle), but walk through the lower car park on to the Serly FP. After ⅓ mile, the FP bears L. Continue on the final ⅓ mile to Combe Point and Shinglehill and Willow coves.

50.3264, -3.5728

Landcombe Cove, English Channel

Diversion 220 yards from coast path. This place is less busy than other Sern shores. But it's a cove with a stream.

➤ **Find** The Venus Cafe (see page 145). Walk through the large public car park, away from the cafe, on to the beach after the tide has gone out. Keep walking ⅓ mile to the cove. If the tide comes in, walk back on the incredibly beautiful coast path walk, crossing the road at 50.315261, -3.619009. Be wary of walking back on the A379. Although it's less than ⅓ mile, there is no pavement, and the road can be busy throughout the year.

50.3142, -3.6159

Slapton Ley

Filled by the River Gara, this fascinating freshwater lake straddles coast and country, with Widdecombe Ley less than 1 mile S. A wonderful walk or drive with water either side. Listen out for the plop of water voles and the wedged ripples of 'saw ya'. Kayak trips sometimes available. Neighbouring shore beach is stony.

➤ **Find** the Slapton Sands Memorial Car Park, beside the beach, off the A379, Kingsbridge, TQ7 2QW. Either cross on to the beach or walk along the road into Sands Rd to explore the lake. Slapton Sands Camping & Caravanning Club Site (see left) is a 10-min walk from here.

50.277063, -3.649410

Mattiscombe Sands, English Channel

A sandy treasure. Take the long walk to Start Point for some of the best Devonshire views.

➤ **Find** Start Point Car Park, Stokenham, Kingsbridge, TQ7 2ET and walk S (with the gate to the lighthouse on your L) towards the bay 765 yards away.

50.220301, -3.659617

THE LIME COFFEE CO, SLAPTON SANDS, ENGLISH CHANNEL

On the beach at Strete Gate. The cafe takes its name from the limestone quarries and kilns that once lined the coastline. Award-winning pasties and fine coffee.

Strete Gate, TQ6 0RR
Facebook:
@Limecoffeecompany

SLAPTON SANDS CAMPING & CARAVANNING CLUB SITE, SLAPTON SANDS, ENGLISH CHANNEL

Sea views and beach access. Tent and caravan pitches within walking distance of the ECP.

Sands Rd, Middlegrounds, Kingsbridge, TQ7 2QW
www.campingand
caravanningclub.co.uk

Slapton Sands

River Avon

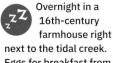

NT Overbeck's Sharpitor Museum, Salcombe Harbour

Best in autumn when parts of the garden fill with the smell of flowering ginger lilies and sea air. Otto Overbeck's museum and garden are filled with nautical exhibitions of model sailing ships and photographs of boats and shipwrecks. The subtropical garden has incredible estuary views.

➤ **Find** the car park at Overbeck's, Sharpitor, Salcombe, TQ8 8LW).

50.223152, -3.784031

Mill Bay, Salcombe, Salcombe Harbour

The cream of Salcombe is its harbour. Bask in the sunshine and river traffic in the late afternoon. It's a lovely place in which to cool your heels under the trees or to go for a swim. Walk to Wickham Common for views over the water to the wonderfully named Stinke Cove.

➤ **Find** parking with sea views at the hairpin in the road at E Portlemouth, Salcombe, TQ8 8FD. Follow the FP down and bear L ⅔ mile through the trees to the beach.

50.229035, -3.766134

Frogmore Creek, Kingsbridge Estuary

The incredible Kingsbridge Estuary. Wooded and utterly solitary.

➤ **Find** the Ashburton Arms, Charleton Way, W Charleton, Kingsbridge, TQ7 2AH. Facing the pub from the main road, walk R 150 yards and turn R on to the FP beside the rows of houses. Keep walking S and L for ⅔ mile until you reach the creek. Turn L and follow the FP all the way to Frogmore. Find the Springfield Farm Shop (tearoom and butchers), Kingsbridge, TQ7 2AR.

50.263612, -3.737221

Slapton Ley

Kingsbridge Estuary

Hallsands, Start Bay

Listen to the colony of breeding kittiwakes that nest on the cliffs and ruined buildings. The fishing village was wiped out by storms in 1917. Strete Undercliffe nearby went at the end of the 18th century. What remains is 1½ miles of beach coves and pools.
➤ **Find** the car park near 5 Prospect House, Kingsbridge, TQ7 2EY. Walk 300 yards E along the road to the beach and then walk S a few yards.

50.240050, -3.658702

Gammon Head, East Portlemouth

Touch the jagged stone of this mica schist and look for the white quartz that runs through the rock, still pulsing with energy. The rare six-banded nomad bee *Nomada sexfasciata* has been seen here on flowers. There are lovely views over Elender Cove.
➤ **Find** East Prawle Car Park, Kingsbridge, TQ7 2BX. Walk downhill to the ECP, turn R and walk 1 mile along the ECP to Maceley Cliffs and Cove. Gammon Head is the rocky point that separates them; the cove to the E and the cliffs to the N.

50.207954, -3.726449

Bolberry Down, Malborough

Hear the sound of male sika deer in rutting season. Experience cliff top views from 150 yards above sea level. Listen, too, for skylarks, meadow pipits and the rare Dartford warbler.
➤ **Find** the public car park (50.231545, -3.838786) close to Oceans Restaurant (TQ7 3DY), then walk NW ½ mile on the ECP.

50.231902, -3.845113

Bolt Tail Hill Fort, Bigbury Bay

Wild and open naze from which to watch sunset over Bigbury Bay and the SW coast. Bracken lines the paths that once trailed through forest. Some of the fort banking is still on view, but most has been eroded and lost. Slip down to Hope Cove for swimming, rock pools and sand.

➤ **Find** The Sun Bay Hotel & Restaurant, Hope Cove, Kingsbridge, TQ7 3HH. From the public car park, walk down and then L towards the beach ramp. Climb the staircase and follow the FP through the woods and around the cliff top to the naze 765 yards away.

50.24229, -3.86655

South Efford Marsh, Avon Estuary

Tread quietly over salt marsh next to the River Avon to catch a glimpse of an otter. Alternatively, look out for their fun mud slides, droppings or maybe even a tiny, muddy footprint. Lots of curlews, ducks and little egrets. Foragers look out for sea purslane, glasswort and sea spurry.

➤ **Find** the Fisherman's Rest, Fore St, Aveton Gifford, Kingsbridge, TQ7 4JL, and the public car park across the roundabout. Cross Tidal Rd, and continue on to the River Avon bridge, passing over two sections of the Avon. After the 2nd crossing, take the first R on to the Avon Estuary Walk. The 1½-mile path leads to the water's edge at Stiddicombe Creek via the marshes.

50.306579, -3.839571

THE OYSTER SHACK, BIGBURY, RIVER AVON

Check tide times. The Shack was once just an oyster farm by the river, to which oyster lovers would come with a packed lunch and buy oysters to go with it. The menu and shack have both since grown. All ingredients are caught, foraged and sourced from the area.

Milburn Orchard Farm, Stakes Hill, Bigbury, TQ7 4BE

www.oystershack.co.uk

Bigbury-on-Sea

Burgh Island

Burgh Island Fort, River Avon

Take the low-tide path out to wonderful Burgh Island at the mouth of the River Avon. There's usually tractor access when the tide is in. Former chapel set on an island peak at its centre reached by FPs. Wonderful views over Warren Point to N and Avon mouth to SE. Rock pooling and kayaking.

➤ **Find** parking next to Venus Cafe, Warren Rd, Bigbury-on-Sea, Kingsbridge, TQ7 4AZ. Walk to the island at low tide.

50.279518, -3.900286

Aylestone Brook, Rive Erme

Swim in Aylestone Brook where it forks with the River Erme at the end of a tiny wooded lane through Tor Wood. There's a bridleway on the other side of the river from Orthseton Wood up towards Holbeton.

➤ **Find** the church next to The Dolphin Inn, Kingston, Kingsbridge, TQ7 4QE. With your back to the church gate, turn L and walk 110 yards before taking the first lane R. Walk on for 1 mile to the brook down an increasingly narrowing path to the edge of the River Erme.

50.322851, -3.935087

Erme Mouth, River Erme

Low-tide FP across the River Erme surrounded by fast water and wonderful wet sands.

➤ **Find** Schoolhouse Devon, Mothecombe, Plymouth, PL8 1LB. Walk down through the car park keeping the restaurant on the R-hand side. The beach and water are 250 yards away.

50.311851, -3.947625

THE SWAN INN, NOSS MAYO, NOSS CREEK

Return to Noss Creek to the E at the Swann Inn.

Pillory Hill, Noss Mayo, PL8 1EE
www.swaninnnossmayo.com

ONE OLD COASTGUARDS, WEMBURY, RIVER YEALM

Georgian coastguard cottage right by the river, with steps down to the water from across the path.

1 Old Coastguard Cottages, Wembury, PL9 0EJ
07738 342 850

THE EDDYSTONE INN, HEYBROOK BAY

The menu changes regularly, but favourites are Asian noodle broth with sea bass, and oven-roasted fillet of hake. Just a few yards off the ECP.

Heybrook Dr, Heybrook Bay, PL9 0BN
www.eddystoneinn.co.uk

THE OLD PUMP HOUSE, LOPWELL DAM, RIVER TAVY

Home-made cakes and hot drinks where the tide meets the fresh water. Walk the tidal ford at low tide into woodland paths on the other side.

Lopwell Dam, Plymouth, PL6 7BZ
www.swlakestrust.org.uk

Church Of St Peter The Poor Fisherman, Stoke Bay

Medieval church ruin on the cliffs over Stoke Bay.
➤ **Find** Stoke Car Park, off the Stoke Rd, Plymouth PL8 1JG. Follow the FP towards the sea away from the road, and then bear L as it loops up and around the cliff top towards the church, and in front of the caravan park to the church and church cove 1 mile away.

50.3005111, -4.0174631

Newton Wood, River Yealm

Wonderful birdwatching on the River Yealm and the banks of Shortaflete Creek, N of Newton Ferrers.
➤ **Find** the Ferry Service launch (Easter–mid-Sep), next to The Harbour Office, Yealm Rd, Newton Ferrers, PL8 1BN. From here, with your back to the pier, walk L, following the coast road and then the FP along 1 mile of glorious views over the River Yealm. Take a stopover at wooded Shortaflete Creek.

50.320589, -4.049101

Saint Werburgh's Church, Wembury beach, Wembury Bay

Stunning church and graveyard by the beach.
➤ **Find** The Old Mill Cafe, Church Rd, Wembury, PL9 0HP. The church is next to the large public car park overlooking Wembury beach. Facing the sea, walk L 1½ miles along the coast path to Red Cove, the mouth of the River Yealm. NB no graveyard access for wheelchairs.

50.317207, -4.084982

Aylestone Brook, River Plym

The oldest human bones ever found in England are 140,000 years old. They were discovered here in a cave. Visit the city museum to find out more about the bones. Ask the harbour office about launching a kayak.
➤ **Find** Royal Western Yacht Club, in the car park at Queen Anne's Battery, Plymouth, PL4 0TW. Facing the marina, walk R to explore Sutton Harbour or to cross the marina on to the other side. Walk L along the coast path for a view of the industrial wharves.

50.363782, -4.124407

Warleigh Point, Plymouth, River Plym

An ancient oak wood less than 3 miles from town centre. Best in spring for wild flowers and silver-washed fritillary butterflies.
➤ **Find** Warleigh Point Nature Reserve where there's limited roadside parking on Station Rd, Tamerton Foliot, PL5 4LD. Follow the path to the L of the metal gate and the bridge over the railway line into Warleigh Wood.

50.426546, -4.183534

Marazion

SOUTH CORNWALL

WILD THINGS TO DO BEFORE YOU DIE:

WALK to the magical island home of Jack and the Beanstalk.

SWIM among ancient oaks at Fal-Ruan.

SNORKEL at the Freathy Grotto.

TASTE local oysters at St Mylor shore.

MARVEL at the starlings over Marazion Marshes.

LOOK for rare orchids at Rame Church or dolphins off Mullion Island.

STAR watch over Dodman Point.

GRAZE with Dartmoor ponies at Rame Head.

SIT by the standing stones at Kemyel Cliff.

WATCH nesting cormorants at Ropehaven.

FIND seabirds and seals at Looe Island.

EXPLORE the beach caves of Mullion Cove.

SIT in the church on the Tamar marshes.

HIRE a boat at Mylor Creek.

THE TAMAR INN, CALSTOCK, RIVER TAMAR

An old drinking hole for smugglers and highwaymen on the riverside.

The Quay, Calstock,
PL18 9QA
www.tamarinn.co.uk

THE EDGCUMBE TEA ROOM, SALTASH, RIVER TAMAR

Cornish 'jam-first' cream tea by the river surrounded by garden and orchard. There's a restored sailing barge moored at the quay. Dog friendly.

Cotehele House, Saltash,
PL12 6TA
www.nationaltrust.org.uk

St Indract's Chapel, Halton Quay, River Tamar

A tiny chapel with wonderful views beside the tidal River Tamar on Halton Quay. Services are still held here.

➤ **Find** Halton Quay, St Dominick, Plymouth, PL12 6SL. Parking on the shore.

50.4677202, -4.2369135

Landulph Church, Tamar Estuary

Church on one of the largest areas of mudflats with a large wintering population of avocets.

➤ **Find** Landulph Church 1¼ miles N of Saltash, at PL12 6NG. A wooded FP leads from the church down to the water's edge 1,400ft away. Turn L at the water, as the winding path follows the river N almost 1½ miles to the quay and pub at Cargreen. Walk back to the church on the inland FP if you can find it, to make a circle.

50.431433, -4.210514

Dandy Hole, River Lynher

Kayak access only. Beautiful little beach on the River Lynher. Larger boats sometimes overnight here.

➤ **Find** access to the water from the road by the park at Wacker Quay, Antony, Torpoint, PL11 3AH, right next to the A374. If you don't have a boat, access the riverbank on the other side from the 1-mile FP that leads NE to the river from Blessed Virgin Mary, Sheviock, Cornwall, PL11 3EH.

50.3768632, -4.2759739

Tamar Estuary

EDDYSTONE CAFE, WHITSAND BAY, ENGLISH CHANNEL

 A cuppa on one of the best surfing beaches in S Cornwall, at the bottom of Tregonhawke Cliff. Occasional BBQs and activities.

Tregonhawke Cliff, Millbrook, Torpoint, PL10 1JX
www.eddystonecafe.com

SEATON BEACH CAFE, RIVER SEATON

 Kind, attentive people, they provide doggie towels to pooches when they come out of the sea. Caters for every diet, from vegan to gluten free. Great place to paddle when it's hot.

Looe Hill, Seaton, Torpoint, PL11 3JQ
www.seatonbeach cafe.com

BLACK ROCK BEACH CAFE & BISTRO, MILLENDREATH, ENGLISH CHANNEL

 Not just teas ... draught Cornish lager (Korev) Cornish ale (Tribute) and Cornish cider (Cornish Orchards). Cocktail menu too. A grade-2 Dark Sky area. Dog friendly.

May Ln, Millendreath, Looe, PL13 1PE
www.millendreath.co.uk

Seaton

Penlee Battery, English Channel

A gunsite ruin that exudes tranquility. Coastal grassland, woods and caves. Look out for bee orchid flowers, whose lower lip resembles the body of a queen bee in colour and shape. After taking in the views, walk W along the cliff to Rame Church.
➤ **Find** the end of Military Rd, Torpoint, PL10 1LB. The FP in the furthest corner leads to the battery 765 yards away.

50.321032, -4.198362

Rame Head, Plymouth Harbour

St Michael's Chapel tops the naze at the widest entrance to Plymouth Harbour. Unbeatable sunset views over Whitsand Bay. The chapel rests on the site of an old hill fort. Dartmoor ponies graze.
➤ **Find** the National Coastwatch Institution at the end of Ramehead Ln, Rame, Torpoint, PL10 1LH. Walk with the Coastwatch building to your L and continue down the FP to St Michael's Chapel and the cliff edge.

50.312464, -4.223250

 ## The Grotto, Freathy, English Channel

Series of coves for snorkelling and swimming around cliffs. Steep cliffs can make getting down tricky. Occasionally closed due to erosion or firing range activity, in which case walk 1 mile L (SE) to Whitsand Bay.
➤ **Find** the Sharrow Point car park on the coast road, Torpoint, PL10 1JW. Cross the road and, looking to the sea, walk L along the coast path looking for paths down.

50.3464, -4.2521

Looe in Cor

 ## Looe Island, English Channel

Breathtaking steep, slippery trail out into a world of offshore
birds and sycamore woodland. Cornwall's largest breeding
colony of great black-backed gull. Grey seals and dolphins.
Boat trips area available if the ⅔ mile trek is flooded at high tide
➤ **Find** the Hannafore Kiosk, Marine Dr, Looe, PL13 2DJ and keep
going until the road ends after 330 yards. Wait anywhere along
here for the tide to go out. Keep walking ⅔ mile if the tide is in to
look out over Samphire Beach.

50.341196, -4.449468

 ## Lansallow Cove, English Channel

The Church of St Ildierna is a little way above the pebble and
sand beach, next to an even smaller Parson's Cove. Some of
the tombstones tell fascinating stories.
➤ **Find** Highertown Farm Campsite, Looe, PL13 2PX. From the
car park opposite (facing the campsite), walk L down the road to
the Church of St Ildierna, 220 yards away. Take the FP L of the
church and follow the lane along the wooded spring for ⅔ mile.

50.3319, -4.578

 ## Great Wood & Manely Wood, Rivers Fowey and Lerryn

Vast wooded naze at a fork in the rivers Fowey and Lerryn.
➤ Walk 1 mile NW along the shore to the incredible St Winnow
Church and campsite next door. Campfires in the orchard. Circle back
along the FP E and then swing back down through the pines and ferns
of Mill Wood to loop along the shore. It's a wonderful 3-mile hike.
➤ **Find** Lerryn River Stores, Fore St, Lerryn, Lostwithiel, PL22 0PT
and the car park looking out across the river. Facing the store,
turn R along the river road for 293 yards before it becomes a FP
through the woods. Walk on another ½ mile into the woods.

50.373998, -4.637929 & 50.379726, -4.63137

St Catherine's Castle, River Fowey

Swim in the cove at the mouth of the River Fowey with wooded walks and ruins. The views are more impressive than the remains of the castle, but worth the climb. Readymoney Cove below is sheltered and fun to explore at low tide for youngsters who can't face the climb up.

> **Find** Readymoney Long Stay Car Park, Tower Park, Fowey, PL23 1DG, 1 mile S of Fowey. Walk away from the road towards the FP along the car park, turning L (S) 400 yards to the cove. Walk anticlockwise around the cove through the woodland and follow the coast path 10 mins to the castle point.

50.3291, -4.6445

Gribbin Daymark, Fowey Estuary

Touch the red-and-white striped daymark (a tower used as a daytime aid to navigation), which was built in 1832 to warn sailors not to mistake St Austell's Bay, with its shallow treacherous waters, for the deep-water harbour of Falmouth 17 miles further on. Inspiration for the horror story *The Birds* came from a farmer being attacked by gulls while in his field close to the daymark. A flag flies when it is open for viewings. Smell the overwhelming scent of wild garlic in elm woodland either side of the daymark after climbing the 109 steps.

> **Find** Menabilly Beach Car Park, Fowey, PL24 2TN, then walk S on the road ⅔ mile to the ECP. Turn R (SW), then walk ½ mile to the tower.

50.317100, -4.673051

Gribbin Head from the Fowey Estuary

Black Head

Black Head, Ropehaven Beach

Cormorants and fulmars nest on incredible tree-lined cliff ledges at Ropehaven. Walk 1 mile S to the natural platform that has historically served as fort and sea defence. Remnants of woodland and scrub.

➤ **Find** the Small Car Park, St Austell, PL26 6BH, over Ropehaven Beach and the trees. Walk towards the sign on the L of the road marked 'Trenarren'. Take the L fork and continue on along the coast path for 1 mile.

50.299276, -4.754854

Dodman Point, English Channel

The most important coastland ridge in Southern England. Vast cliff headland sometimes associated with 'Dead Man' and the Briton 'dodman' mystics – an ancient holy man or woman, wizard, wise woman (aka witch) – who once practised here, rather than the geometrical importance of this point. Stunning pebble beaches on either side. A 1-hr walk, at either Hemmick Beach or Bow Beach. Both are good for snorkelling.

➤ **Find** the NT The Dodman car park, St Austell, PL26 6NY. Leave the car park and turn L on the road, then straight on at the bottom into the FP. Continue S 1.8 miles to the point.

50.219851, -4.803549

Cellar Cove (née Sandheap Point), English Channel

Ropes down to the beach.

➤ **Find** the same car park as that for Dodman Point (see above). Leave the car park and turn R. After a few yards, find the FP L and walk ⅓ mile down to meet the coast path and beach.

50.2316, -4.8144

Pendower Beach, English Channel

Sand and shingle on to Gerrans Bay at the mouth of a freshwater stream that runs across the beach. Shallow sea for safer swims. Loos, parking and ice cream, but often quiet. Walk SE to Nare head for views back over the bay.

➤ **Find** the parking at the end of the lane on the Pendower Rd, Veryan, Truro, TR2 5PE. Walk down to the shore.

50.206324, -4.944019

St Anthony Lighthouse, Roseland Peninsula, Falmouth Harbour

Breathtaking rock peninsular that hooks towards Falmouth, without quite getting there. The gap means the traveller must walk the 40 miles to get around the River Fal and its estuary. It's a 1-mile walk to the headland point and views around St Anthony Lighthouse.

➤ **Find** the end of Military Rd, Truro, TR2 5HA. From the car park cross the road, then walk towards St Anthony Head Battery and, keeping the Battery on your L shoulder, keep walking towards the lighthouse.

50.141077, -5.016105

Towan Beach Rock Pools, Roseland Peninsula, Gerrans Bay

Rock pools, sand. Low-tide lagoon created by an offshore bar.

➤ **Find** NT Porth Workshop, parking in Porth Farm House, St Anthony, Truro, TR2 5EX. Walk past the coffee shop down the FP to the beach.

50.157284, -4.982994

Percuil Quay & Pelyn Creek

Wooded bay on the river. Walk 1 mile N along the shore to Polingey Creek, or walk S around the Percuil Quay to Pelyn Creek for a 1-mile circular trail back to the river.

➤ **Find** the car park at Percuil Boat Yard, Truro, TR2 5ES. Find the FP on the R just past the car park towards the river, and follow it around the shore 1 mile to the creek.

50.169264, -4.999278

St Just In Roseland Church, St Just Creek

Heavenly church on St Just Creek. Best in winter on a misty day at high tide when you'll have it all to yourself. Explore the boatyard and gardens and enjoy a cream tea.

➤ **Find** St Just Church Cafe, St Just in Roseland, Truro, TR2 5HZ. From the car park opposite, walk towards the church and river before turning L and walking 3 miles to St Mawes Castle.

50.1819, -5.0165

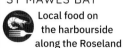

THE WATCH HOUSE, ST MAWES BAY

Local food on the harbourside along the Roseland Peninsula. Lobster from St Mawes Bay or purple sprouting broccoli from the local farm.

1 The Square, St Mawes, Truro, TR2 5DJ
www.watchhouse
stmawes.co.uk

HERON INN, MALPAS, TRESILLIAN RIVER

Stunning woodland and river views. Dine on local vegetables, fish and meat while looking over the Truro and Tresillian rivers where they join the River Fal. There's a ferry service from Malpas to the Roseland Peninsula.

Trenhaile Tce, Malpas, Truro, TR1 1SL
www.heroninnmalpas
.co.uk

PANDORA INN, RESTRONGUET CREEK, RIVER CARNON

Benches by the dock. Eat fish caught from restaurant's own pontoon and by local fishermen. Named after HMS *Pandora*, the naval ship sent to bring back mutineers of Capt Bligh's *Bounty* from Tahiti.

Restronguet Creek, Mylor Bridge, Falmouth, TR11 5ST
www.pandorainn.com

CAFE IN THE PARK, TRURO, RIVER TRURO

Lovely little spot under the trees by Boscawen Park for a cuppa near the river.

Truro, TR1 1QT
www.visittruro.org.uk/food-drink/cafe-park

SWANPOOL BEACH CAFE, SWANPOOL

Near Falmouth, beside a sand and shingle beach. The unique pool was created by a bar of shingle moving over the entrance of a small creek, creating a freshwater lake. Sea water now enters the pool at high tide, creating a brackish lagoon fed from one end by springs and streams and the sea at the other.

Swanpool, Falmouth, TR11 5BB
www.swanpoolbeach.co.uk

Jacka Point, Portloe, Veryan Bay

This spot provides fine views on the approach to the unspoilt fishing village of Portloe and its tiny harbour.

➤ **Find** the car park (Portloe, TR2 5RD), then walk S on the road and ECP 400 yards to the point via the N edge of the village's beach.

50.217258, -4.891135

Carne Beach, Veryan Bay

Touch the shell fossils in the rock towards the middle of the bay at low tide. Trilobite fossils dating from 500 million years ago can also be found, but are rare. Walk 1 mile between Carne and Pendower beaches at low tide.

➤ **Find** the parking at the end of the lane on Pendower Rd, Veryan, Truro, TR2 5PE. Walk down to the shore, then carry on 400 yards E along the sand.

50.206252, -4.935707

Fal-Ruan, Fal Estuary

Snorkel the crystal-clear estuary awash with fish and molluscs. Ancient oaks right down to water's edge. Guided Snorkel Safari provided by Cornwall Wildlife Trust at Porthscatho, Roseland, off Roseland Peninsula.

➤ **Find** the end of the FP that leads to the shore from the back of the church next to The Roseland Inn, Philleigh-in-Roseland, Truro, TR2 5NB. The pub is one of the best in the area. Great food.

50.225261, -4.989482

St Moran Church, River Fal

It's a church near the river. But the road access to the water is stunning.

➤ **Find** St Rumon's church, Ruanlanihorne, Truro, TR2 5NY. Walk down the lane along the church's L side. Turn R at the bottom and continue on for ⅓ mile until the road meets the river at a small quay. Launch a canoe or kayak here and paddle on to St Moran church, St Michael Penkivel, Truro, TR2 4HT.

50.237383, -4.97664C

Pencalenick, River Tresillian

Riverside woodland track. The walk to Kiggon via Tresemple Pond is spectacular. There are no words for the feeling afterwards resting on the bench while looking across the water at St Clement.

➤ **Find** the car park beside St Clement Holy Well, Truro, TR1 1SZ, a few yards from St Clements Parish Church. Looking across the water, turn L and walk along the bridleway 1¼ miles to the wooded naze.

50.268942, -5.00533

St Mylor Churchyard Cross, Mylor Creek

Ancient cross in the churchyard at the head of Mylor Creek and harbour. Visit the shore for 'ethically sourced' oysters. Boat hire available and slipway for kayak launch.

➤ **Find** Fal Oyster Ltd t/a Cornish Native Oysters on Admiralty Quay, Mylor Churchtown, Falmouth, TR11 5UF, and walk across the public car park to Penarrow Rd. The church is a few yards on the R, overlooking the harbour.

50.176635, -5.054553

Church of St Mawnan and St Stephen, Helford Estuary and River

Church path leads down to the Helford Estuary and River.

➤ **Find** the car park on the ECP, Falmouth, TR11 5HY. You have arrived. Turn R while looking out to sea and walk ⅓ mile to Toll Point for views over the estuary.

50.103953, -5.095100

Helford Point, River Helford

Shaded woodland on the river an hour's walk out of Helford. Perfect for hot summer days staying out of the sun while watching fish feed on the surface at high tide. Shingle beach at Bosahan Cove with rock pools to explore.

➤ **Find** the Holy Mackerel Cafe car park in Helston, TR12 6JU. Take the path opposite the cafe and follow it 0.8 miles to the woodbine-lined shore.

50.096026, -5.121677

elford Passage

Helford village on the Helford Estuary

Porthoustock Beach, St Keverne

A quiet beach for relaxing and seaweed foraging. Seals come in with the fish in June and July.
> **Find** Porthoustock Village Hall Car Park, Helston, TR12 6QW, then walk E 200 yards.

50.055889, -5.063857

Giant's Rock, Porthleven, River Helford

Sit on the mysterious Giant's Rock at low tide, just near the entrance of Porthleven Harbour. Also known as the 'Moonstone', this type of garnet-gneiss rock isn't found anywhere else in the UK, and no one knows how it arrived in Cornwall. Although some claim it to be a glacial erratic, the ice sheets never reached Cornwall, hence the folklore and name, Giant's Rock – as in, 'A giant must have carried it there.'
> **Find** First Downs Car Park, Helston, TR13 9ES, and walk 1½ miles NW on the ECP.

50.081641, -5.321502

Mullion Cove, English Channel

Walk the crumbling breakwater harbour pier, which will surely be gone in less than 50 years. It was most famously painted by JMW Turner's maternal relation, Louis Burleigh Bruhl, in 1923. The harbour has been repaired beyond recognition at least twice since its construction in 1898 to help struggling pilchard fishermen land more catch. By the time the NT took ownership in 1945, the harbour walls (made from faulty Victorian blocks and soft serpentine rock) needed replacing. Mullion storms buffeted and damaged the pier, costing the NT more than £1 million in repairs. The NT states that repairs cannot go on forever. Walk it now before it's all gone. Only Bruhl's iconic painting will live on.
> **Find** Porthmellin car park (Coastal Retreat, Mullion, TR12 7EU), then walk 500 yards W along the road to the harbour.

50.014792, -5.25858

THE SHIP INN, PORTHLEVEN HARBOUR

Fish pies, steaks, mussels, crab and the catch of the day from the harbour. Seating over the quay.

Porthleven, Helston, TR13 9JT
www.theshipinnporth leven.co.uk

Mullion Cove

Church Cove, Gunwalloe, English Channel

Ancient church cut into the Lizard cliff perfectly positioned over the W-facing beach. Sheltered by rocks, with coves either side.

➤ **Find** the public car park at Gunwalloe Church Cove Beach, Gunwalloe, Helston, TR12 7QG. Facing the sea, walk L towards the church looking over the bay. Best seen at low tide. Various paths down to the sand next to the golf course.

50.03788, -5.26700

Church Cove

St Michael's Mount, Mount's Bay

A low-tide walk you'll never forget. The castle and island form the setting for the Cornish legend of Jack the Giant Killer. In winter, walk to the R along the beach to Marazion Marshes to watch flocks of starlings roosting at dusk.

➤ **Find** St Michael's Mount Slipway Car Park (Kings Rd, Marazion, TR17 0EQ). If the tide is in, wait a while at The Godolphin (West End, Marazion, TR17 0EN) while looking across the sea.

50.117122, -5.477102

COCKLESHELL COTTAGE, MARAZION BEACH, ENGLISH CHANNEL

A beach hideaway with spectacular sea views to St Michael's Mount.

Cliff House, Chapel St, Marazion, TR17 0AE
www.cockleshellcottage.co.uk

St Michael's Mount

Kemyel Cliff, English Channel

Sacred high grounds from Point Spaniard to Kemyel Rock down to Lamorna Cove. Indicated by several standing stones. Freshwater springs riddle the area and leach into the sea. Small conifer plantation slopes down to the sea (50.064453, -5.550536). Fungus in summer and autumn. Lamorna Cove Beach for snorkelling and kayak launch.

➤ **Find** Lamorna Cove Cafe, Lamorna, Penzance, TR19 6XJ. Walk across the beach and up on to the ECP. Continue on for ⅔ mile past Kemyel and another 1 mile to the Swingate Standing Stone.

50.066911,- 5.552535 & 50.074541, -5.544292

St Clement Isle, Mousehole, English Channel

Bring binoculars so you can watch seabirds and seals over rooftops, look on to the rocky St Clement Isle ... or else take a kayak out from the harbour.

➤ **Find** Mousehole Car Park, Penzance, TR19 6PS, then walk SW up the hill away from the harbour to look over the isle.

50.081820, -5.532773

Porthgwarra Cove, St Levan, English Channel

Snorkel a bay full of seaweed and sealife: seals, spider crabs and sand eels. At low tide, look for caves. Also explore the wooden remains of crates that fishermen once used to keep fish fresh for market before taking them by horse and cart to Newlyn. The crates, known as 'ullies', were covered by the high tide and can still be seen on the E side of the cove.

➤ **Find** the car park at Porthgwarra Cove, Penzance, TR19 6JR, then walk SE 100 yards on the ECP.

50.034939, -5.672970

Treryn Dinas, English Channel

Stunning views of beaches from Logan Rock and Porthcurno from the cliff fort. Climb down to Pedn Vounder Beach at low tide for view and access to a magical sand island and salt pools. Near Treen.

➤ **Find** the car park next to Treen Local Produce Cafe and Shop, Treen Hill, St Buryan, TR19 6LF. Follow the signposts to Treen Farm Campsite, 220 yards away along the bridleway, then bear L and carry on 330 yards down the path to the beach and cliffs.

50.041983, -5.636885

Porthtowan

NORTH CORNWALL

WILD THINGS TO DO BEFORE YOU DIE:

SWIM around a church with a fantastic story.

EXPLORE Merlin's mythical cave.

WILD camp the coves around Bosigran Castle.

SNORKEL the clear waters below Rusey Cliff.

CLIMB down ropes on to Beacon Cove.

FIND the submerged forest at Portreath.

CANOE camp the bass-rich waters of Little Petheric Creek.

EXPLORE the tin mines at Chapel Porth.

PICNIC at an Iron Age castle over Beacon Cove.

WATCH basking sharks at Godrevy Point and the flood tide over Strangles sands.

LOOK for choughs at Porth Nanven.

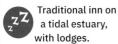

THE OLD QUAY HOUSE, HAYLE, HAYLE ESTUARY

 Traditional inn on a tidal estuary, with lodges. Breakfast served in the estuary-view restaurant. Dog and child friendly, with a playground.

Griggs Quay, Hayle, TR27 6JG
www.quayhouse
hayle.co.uk

Meineke, Land's End, English Channel/Atlantic Ocean

Feel the 'otherworldly' nature of this place. It's unmistakable – much like The Lizard. The offshore beacon is a reminder that wild places come with a safety warning, which is perhaps why the magic is partly obscured by too many people and the trinket shops behind. Walk for 30 mins in either direction to find fewer people and more nature.

➤ **Find** Land's End Car Park, Penzance, TR19 7AA, then walk W 300 yards to the hotel, where there is a telescope and view of Meineke.

50.069007, -5.717132

Porth Nanven, Cot Valley, Atlantic Ocean

Sand and shingle cove that's best swum and explored at low tide. Look out for choughs. There's an annual swim from Priests' Cove to Brisons islets.

➤ **Find** Porth Nanven car park on the coast path, Penzance, TR19 7NP. The beach is a few yards away. Some tricky climbs in places so care is needed.

50.119240, -5.700679

Kenidjack Cliff Castle, Atlantic Ocean

Better than Land's End, and fewer people. Cliff top fort on edge of Cairn Circle. Walk 1 mile S to Cape Cornwall for lovely bay views. Walk N to swim the tiny sand beach at Portheras Cove.

➤ **Find** NT Cape Cornwall Car Park at Priest's Cove, at the end of the Cape Cornwall Rd, St Just, Penzance, TR19 7NN. Walk away from the sea along the road, turn L on to the FP and walk just under 1 mile to the old castle cliff.

50.134368, -5.702680

Godrevy Point

COVE CAFE, PHILLACK, ST IVES BAY

Cornish cream teas and Cove afternoon teas for two.

80 Riviere Towans, Phillack, Hayle, TR27 5AF
www.covecafehayle.co.uk/

SANDY ACRES CAMPSITE, HAYLE BEACH, ATLANTIC OCEAN

Camping on 170 acres of private towans and dunes with direct access to the beach. Toilets, hot showers, a washing-up area and fresh drinking water.

Hayle, TR27 5BH
www.sandy-acres.co.uk

Bosigran Castle, Atlantic Ocean

Cliff Fort at Castle Rock above Halldrine and Porthmoina coves. No turrets, just a spectacle of ancient time. Walk to Gurnard's Head. Proper wild.

➤ Find Carn Galver Engine House public car park on the B3306, Zennor, Penzance, TR20 8YX. Walk past the R side of the engine house (keeping it to your L) along the FP. Keep going for ⅓ mile until you reach the cliff edge.

50.177403, -5.621953

St Ives Cross, Atlantic Ocean

Beachside, town church overlooking St Ives, hosts a sacred and historic cross.

➤ Find Barnoon Long Stay Car Park, Clodgy View, St Ives, TR26 1JF. Walk to the top of the car park for views over the graveyard. Leave the car park at the bottom entrance and walk down to the beach. Turn R towards the pier. The St Ives Parish Church, 15 St Andrew's St, St Ives, TR26 1AH and Celtic cross are just past the West Pier behind the lifeboat station.

50.212428, -5.479926

Porthkidney Sands Caves, St Ives, Hayle Estuary

Visit in winter to see and listen to the thousands of birds that migrate for the warm air; the dunes never freeze on Britain's most south-westerly estuary. It's often quiet because parking is limited.

➤ Find St Ives railway station (TR26 2BH), then walk S on to the ECP and 2½ miles E to the caves.

50.193538, -5.437093

Carrack Gladden, Carbis Bay

Human remains found around the dunes between the shore and golf course indicate that the area may have once been an ancient burial site. Also, the lost chapel of St Antra may have been based here. Visit at low tide when the sands E of this point stretch more than 1 mile out to the shoreline.

➤ Find Porthkidney Sands Caves (see above) and walk 1 mile W along the beach at low tide to the point. If the tide is in, walk the ECP along the railway FP.

50.198208, -5.455204

St Nicholas Chapel, Atlantic Ocean

If you like a story ... this chapel has a special one. The Atlantic views are awe-inspiring. Beaches on either side of the church for swimming.

➤ Find the mount next to The Island Car Park, Burrow Rd, St Ives, TR26 1SY. The chapel is 110 yards away.

50.218266, -5.477870

BASSET ARMS, PORTREATH BEACH, ATLANTIC OCEAN

An old 'seafarers and miners' pub in a fishing village, 200 yards from the beach.

Tregea Hill, Portreath, Redruth, TR16 4NG
www.thebassetarms-portreath.foodanddrink sites.co.uk

HELL'S MOUTH KITCHEN AND BAR, GWITHIAN, GODREVY COAST

A roadside cafe without a view. But cross the road and ... suck in the scenery of the Hell's Mouth cliffs.

B3301, Gwithian, TR27 5EG

BLUE BAR, PORTHTOWAN BEACH, ATLANTIC OCEAN

Shabby-chic dog-friendly bar on the dunes.

Beach Rd, Porthtowan, Truro, TR4 8AW
www.blue-bar.co.uk

TREVELLAS MANOR FARM CAMPSITE, TREVELLAS PORTH, ATLANTIC OCEAN

Campsite between Perranporth and St Agnes. 15-min walk to the beach.

Trevellas, Crosscombe, St Agnes, TR5 0XP
www.trevellasmanorfarm campsite.co.uk

St Uny's Church, Lelant, Hayle Estuary

Church with a tearoom next door. The old church path leads down to the sea, across the golf course and railway line to dunes, caves and the river estuary at Hayle.

➤ **Find** Lelant Heritage Centre & Cafe, Church Ln, St Ives, TR26 3DY. The church is next door.

50.188702, -5.435953

Godrevy Point, Atlantic Ocean

Watch seals and sunset and, on a good day ... basking sharks. Godrevy beach is a mating site for seals, which give birth to their pups here. Best from May to September.

➤ **Find** Godrevy parking on the ECP, next to the loos. Facing the sea, with the loos to your back, turn R along the FP to the point 330 yards away.

50.2401, -5.3939

Fishing Cove, Navax Point, Atlantic Ocean

Taste line-caught bass cooked on a beach BBQ. The headland is backed by orderly fields of green and the chaotic swim of waves over rock. It's a breathtaking rocky point that opens up into a cove for swimming, and sometimes grey seals. If you see seals, go fishing somewhere else. It's a steep walk down. Naturists favour the cove. Walk to Hell's Mouth Kitchen and Bar for a cuppa if the cafe is open and the fishing fails.

➤ **Find** Hell's Mouth Kitchen and Bar (see left). With the cafe on the L and the sea to the R, continue on ¼ mile to the public car park over the cliffs. From here, looking to the sea, walk L along the path, ⅓ mile to the cove. The Point is 0.8 miles from the car park.

50.237166, -5.372332

Porthtowan

Padstow

Portreath Submerged Forest, Portreath, Atlantic Ocean

Submerged forest that gets exposed after winter storms at low tide. Surfing and body boarding on the N shore beside the pier.
➤ **Find** The Atlantic Cafe Bar, The Seafront, Portreath, TR16 4NN. Walk though the public car park down on to the beach a few yards away. Walk out at low tide.

50.262520, -5.292734

Chapel Porth, St Agnes, Atlantic Ocean

Tin mine tunnels to be explored at low tide. Walk along the beach to see the remains of the Towanroath shaft. Fresh water meets sea at this sacred Chapel Porth. Follow the line of the stream up from the beach along the bridleway to Chapel Combe.
➤ **Find** the NT Chapel Porth car park, St Agnes, TR5 0NS. The beach is a few yards from here.

50.3010, -5.2357

Beacon Cove, Atlantic Ocean

Great views. No access path down, so boat only, unless you can find the ropes that sometimes hang down and on to the beach. Care needed. Below an Iron Age castle.
➤ **Find** Catch Seafood Bar & Grill on the B3276, Mawgan Porth, Newquay, TR8 4BJ. Cross the footbridge across the River Menalhyl and turn R following the course of the ECP at the hairpin bend. Walk 1 mile around the coastline to Beacon Cove.

50.4605, -5.0378

DENNIS COVE CAMPSITE, PADSTOW, RIVER CAMEL

The closest campsite to Padstow on a gentle hill looking over the harbour.

Dennis Ln, Padstow, PL28 8DR
www.denniscovecampsite.co.uk

THE ROCK INN, ROCK, CAMEL ESTUARY

Seafood specialities include Porthilly mussels in marinière sauce, crab and locally caught fresh fish.

The Rock Inn, 6 Beachside, Rock, Wadebridge, PL27 6FD
www.therockinnrock.co.uk

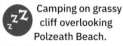

TRISTRAM CAMPING PARK, POLZEATH, CAMEL ESTUARY

Camping on grassy cliff overlooking Polzeath Beach. Cracking Crab Cafe next door for breakfast and lunches.

Tristram Cliff, Polzeath, Wadebridge, PL27 6TD
www.polzeathcamping.co.uk

St Piran's Church remains, Perranzabuloe, Atlantic Ocean

Look for human bones and skeletons that can be found when sand is blown or moved from the remnant of a lost cemetery. The church ruin and oratory is close to St Piran's cross, one of two three-holed crosses in Cornwall; the other is at Wadebridge. St Piran's is the oldest Christian site in Cornwall, founded in the 5th or 6th century.

➤ **Find** Holywell Bay Car Park, Holywell Rd, Newquay, TR8 5DD, and walk 3 miles S on the ECP. At Perran Beach, after ⅓ mile walk E across the dunes to find the church wall remains.

50.366174, -5.134458

Pentire Steps, Bedruthan, Atlantic Ocean

Secret steps to the N end of the beach, but take care.

➤ **Find** the car park off the B3276, at Wadebridge, PL27 7UW. Facing the beach, walk along the cliff top to the N end of the beach ⅔ mile away.

50.486319, -5.033223

Little Petheric Creek & Saint's Way

Schools of bass feed on the surface of the creek on a calm day. The wooded cliffs are somewhere to find plant fossils.

➤ **Find** the bridge at The Old Mill House on the A389, Little Petherick, Padstow, PL27 7QT. Opposite the Mill is a small blue parking sign. Follow the sign and walk past the church, through the car park and on to the creek FP. Follow for ⅓ mile to the woodland or keep walking 1⅓ miles to Padstow on the Camel Trail, beside the River Camel.

50.515744, -4.939682 & 50.524638, -4.939547

St Michael's Porthilly Churchyard Cross, Camel Estuary

Sandy cove marked by an ancient cross in a churchyard on the banks of the Camel Estuary, Porthilly Cove. A short walk from the village of Rock, or a ferry ride from Padstow. Nice views from the churchyard benches.

➤ **Find** Rock Quarry Car Park, on the ECP, Rock, Wadebridge, PL27 6LD. Looking across the river at Padstow, turn L and walk up the beach past the Rock Sailing & Waterski Club. At low tide only, walk around the hard-sand cove ⅓ mile to the church. Alternatively, turn R at Rock Quarry car park and walk 1.1 miles to the stunning views over Daymer Bay at low or high tide from Brea Hill (50.557152, -4.926245), one of the most sacred sites in England.

50.540992, -4.912897

Trebarwith Strand

THE STRAND CAFE, TREBARWITH BEACH, TINTAGEL COAST

 Outdoor benches over the rocky beach. Good place to relax after a morning's rock pooling.

Trebarwith Strand, Tintagel, PL34 0HB
Facebook: @TheStrand
CafeTrebarwith

Daymer Bay

Walk over soft mud and dry dunes between creeks and streams. The sand at low tide is breathtaking. Bass feed on the flood tide. The shallow water is good for swimming but beware rip tides and currents. The bay is the entrance to Cornwall's second longest river, which trails 30 miles into Bodmin Moor.

➤ **Find** Daymer Bay Car Park, ECP, Wadebridge, PL27 6SA, and walk along the beach.

50.559742, -4.928946

St Enodoc Church, Trebetherick, Daymer Bay

Explore the graveyard of this 12th-century church bunkered between sand dunes and the golf course. Until the 19th century, the church was completely buried by sand and was known as 'Sinking Neddy'.

➤ **Find** Daymer Bay Car Park (see above) and walk ½ mile SE over the beach and dunes, keeping Brea Hill (see opposite) on your right shoulder.

50.558107, -4.921694

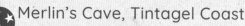

Merlin's Cave, Tintagel Coast

A freshwater well inside a magical cavern under 3 million tonnes of rock. Walk 1 mile to Tintagel Castle and King Arthur Sculpture. Only an open mind for myths and magic is needed to smell the gold. Dreams are made of this.

➤ **Find** the Castle Car Park, 5 Atlantic Rd, Tintagel, PL34 0DD, and walk on to Castle Rd from one of the most epic trails in England. Within less than ⅔ mile, explore the magic of Merlin's Cave, King Arthur Sculpture and Tintagel Castle. Turn L at Tintagel Castle to check out St Materiana's Church, too. Keep walking in either direction for seclusion and rocky views.

50.668236, -4.759280

Widemouth Bay

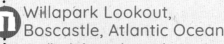

Willapark Lookout, Boscastle, Atlantic Ocean

Headland of an ancient settlement most recently used as a coast watch station. Walk up to St Symphorian Church to explore the graveyard, before returning to Boscastle and Warren Point on the N side of the harbour. Good for fossils.

➤ **Find** The Riverside restaurant, The Bridge, Boscastle, PL35 0HE, on the River Valency. There's a public car park right next door. Follow the river path downhill and cross the arched bridge just past The Museum of Witchcraft and Magic. After crossing the bridge, turn R and uphill away from the river. Walk to the cliffs ⅓ mile away, where you'll find the naze that looks over Boscastle harbour. Walk a little further along the coast path before finally turning L towards the church.

50.689629, -4.704406

Rusey Cliff, Boscastle, Atlantic Ocean

Look for fossil plants and corals. Snorkelling is good on the far L of the beach.

➤ **Find** the car park on the Unnamed Rd, Boscastle, PL35 0HN. Facing the road, turn R and walk 110 yards before turning L on to the greenway path. Follow the path a little way down and then veer off to the R and down to the cliffs and coast path and paths down to the beach.

50.715545, -4.651741

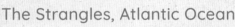

The Strangles, Atlantic Ocean

Accessible at high tide only. The FP is the telltale sign that something wonderful happens here. Watch the sands unravel as the tide recedes like a slow-motion tsunami. It comes back in quite slowly too, but take care. Good for surf and body boards.

➤ **Find** the Haven Beach Shop & Café, Mill Ball Hill, Crackington Haven, EX23 0JG. The public car park is opposite. Walk a few yards down to the beach.

50.74454, -4.63774

Widemouth Bay, Bude Bay

Find fossil molluscs and other shells. Stony at high tide but vast sands as the water goes out to reveal rock pools. It's fun to watch surfers. Swimming possible, but care needed around rips.

➤ **Find** the Freewave Surf Academy off Marine Dr, Widemouth Bay, Bude, EX23 0AD. Walk R and along the vast beach.

50.79127, -4.55726

LIFE'S A BEACH, BUDE BAY

Seafood specials over sand. Beach cafe feel by day; bistro by candlelight at night. Watch the tide come in over the sands to experience the full range of Summerleaze social.

16 Summerleaze Cres, Bude, EX23 8HN
www.lifesabeach.info

Bude cliffs, Bude Bay

It's rare, but the Bude cliffs are home to a 300-million-year-old goldfish-sized sea creature – *Cornuboniscus Budensis*. It has never been found anywhere else in the world. Good luck. Enjoy a river walk out of Bude to the beach and Compass Point. It's quite a climb but worth it if you're staying in Bude.

➤ **Find** Margaret's Rustic Tea Garden, just off the ECP, Bude, EX23 9ED. With the tearoom on the L, follow the road 275 yards to the NT car park. Walk on to the coast path from here, turning L looking to sea. Walk back to Bude along the cliff tops down to Summerleaze Beach and the River Neet estuary. Cross the river estuary at low tide via the bridges. Take a break at the Life's A Beach cafe (see left), and then return to the start.

50.830533, -4.549466

Sandymouth, Atlantic Ocean

Summer surf hire. Vast rock pools to explore at low tide. Rocks fall around the foreshore and expose their fossilised contents, mostly plant remains.

➤ **Find** the Sandymouth Cafe and surf school (see left). Lots of parking to the rear. The beach is a few yards away.

50.861023, -4.557958

Sandymouth Beach near Bude

Morwenstow

THE RUSTIC TEA GARDEN, NORTHCOTT MOUTH

A river runs through it. Delightful tearoom in a tiny river valley, where the stream meanders beside benches and grass down to the beach 110 yards away.

SW Coast Path, Bude, EX23 9EG
Facebook: The Rustic Tea Garden

SANDYMOUTH CAFE, SANDYMOUTH BEACH, ATLANTIC OCEAN

Relaxing family-run cafe serving food and drinks for energetic walkers. Local ingredients.

Stibb, Bude, EX23 9HW
www.sandymouth.com

St Morwenna's Well, Morwenstow

Reopened by Rev Hawker, but since lost to time, all that's left is crumbling cliff and vegetation. At various intervals, a FP is cut back down to the well 400ft below, but it's hazardous and best avoided. It's nice to know it's there though.

➤ Find Rectory Farm Tearooms, Morwenstow, Bude, EX23 9SR, and walk 600 yards E to the coast path and then 300 N to find the well location. There's a small waterfall close to the footbridge to make up for the well's status as sometimes missing, collapsed or hazardous.

50.910687, -4.563973

Marsland Mouth, Welcombe

Taste whelks foraged from the rock pools around the beach and cooked into broth. Look for Alexanders either side of the beach. They were once cultivated as a pot herb, similar to celery, and make a lovely whelk soup cooked over gorse. The first Alexander shoots are found in late autumn and winter. Late-summer seeds can be used to spice your soup.

➤ Find the NT car park at end of the lane for Welcombe Mouth Beach, Bideford, EX39 6HL. Facing the sea, after high tide, walk 600 yards R to the mouth of West Mill Beach. The waterfall can be found up the cliff along the ECP.

50.929264, -4.544054

NORTH DEVON

**WILD THINGS TO DO
BEFORE YOU DIE:**

DIVE the crystal water of Wild Pear
Beach.
SWING by rope down to the bay
at Crook Point Sands.
VISIT a burial ground famous for UFO
sightings.
CANOE the wild edge of the Taw
Estuary at Crow Point.
DANCE around standing stones on
the Lee Bay Cove cliffs.
SHARE paths with mountain goats
on the walk to the Valley of the Rocks.
SWIM the Sandy Mouth at Stibb.
EXPLORE the secluded caves around
Baggy Point.
DISCOVER a waterfall on the
wooded shores of Clovelley.
FIND the triangular rock arch at
Blackchurch; the mythical well linked
to King Arthur; the best viewpoints on
the Devonshire coast at Hangman's
Hill; and the hand-carved tunnels
next to Ilfracombe's shingle beach.

Great Burland Rocks

WRECKER'S RETREAT, HARTLAND QUAY, ATLANTIC OCEAN

Malthouse, stables and haylofts were converted into a hotel and pub at the end of the 19th century. Perfect stop on the path for walkers with dramatic Atlantic views and brutal winds. The name is a reference to the number of ships that have been ruined on the shores.

Hartland Quay Hotel, Hartland Quay, Bideford, EX39 6DU
www.hartlandquay
hotel.co.uk

Marsland Water

Wooded river valley that empties into Marsland Beach with a waterfall. Follow the stream paths a little inland to walk among oak, ash, holly, hazel. Rare butterflies, including pearl-bordered fritillaries, can be seen in summer. There's a stone shelter on the way down to the low-tide dark sand and shingle beach.

➤ **Find** The Old Smithy Inn, Welcombe, Bideford, EX39 6HG. With the pub on your R, follow the road to the three-lane junction. Take the middle lane. At the next crossroads, go straight over, following the sign for Welcome Mouth. There is a small car park on the ECP looking R over the beach. Walk from here, by turning L as you look out to sea along the coast path. Keep walking past the stone building, known as Ronald Duncan's Writing Hut, and the small beach below. As the beach ends, the path hooks inland. Follow this path all the way inland, ignoring the path that turns back to the coast. Keep taking the L path that follows the line of the stream (Mill Lete), and eventually a ford ⅔ mile from the beach.

50.926939, -4.520794

Welcombe Mouth, Atlantic Ocean

Magical meadow glades surrounded by woodland and beach. Waterfalls and pool at the N end of the beach just S of Chiselridge Beach (50.93939972, -4.55010087). Discover more waterfalls S at Marsland Mouth (50.92869948, -4.54698536) and the Old Mill Leat stream. Low-tide dark sand and shingle. The stone shelter, Ronald Duncan's Writing Hut, is near the top of the steps on the way down to the S beach.

➤ **Find** the car park at the end of the lane, Bideford, EX39 6HL.

50.93380, -4.54440

Hartland Point, Hartland, Atlantic Ocean

Look for fin whales between the spectacular views over Lundy Island and S Wales. There are also varied rock formations between Hartland Point and Hartland Quay.

➤ **Find** Hartland Point Car Park (EX39 6AU) and walk 300 yards E to the point.

51.022371, -4.525943

Parish Church of St Nectan and St Nectan's Well, Stoke

Divert inland to the church spire that hangs almost 130ft above the coastline like a beacon – it's the tallest spire in Devon. Look for St Nectan's Well (Stoke) nearby as it has a fascinating story worthy of being kept alive.

➤ **Find** the river FP and walk SE from Dyers Lookout (51.002521, -4.530539) where it leaves the ECP and follow it for 1 mile to the Parish Church of St Nectan, Stoke, EX39 6DU.

50.995486, -4.516411

Speke's Mill Mouth

Speke's Mill Mouth, Hartland Quay Woods, Bideford, Atlantic Ocean

Dramatic waterfall into a plunge pool; sandy bays either side of the falls. Short walk S for views. A 1-hr walk N from here to Hartland Point.

➤ **Find** Wrecker's Retreat (see opposite). Facing the sea, walk L along the coast path ⅓ mile to St Catherine's Tor. Walk on another ⅔ mile for the Mill Mouth and the path inland to Milford for a cuppa at Docton Mill Gardens & Tea Rooms, Hartland, EX39 6EA. Milford is 1.6 miles from the car park.

50.9848, -4.5297

Blackchurch Rock Arch Woods, Bideford Bay

Triangular rock arch on a beach of large pebbles and rock. It's a steep walk down. Walk through Brougham Woods.

➤ **Find** Lower Brownsham Farm Tea Room and the NT car park next door at Brownsham, Lower Brownsham Farm, Hartland, Bideford, EX39 6AN. With your back to the tearoom and facing the car park, take the FP and then follow it as it curves R towards the shore and beach 1.2 miles away. Nearest car park at Brownsham. Walk less than 1 mile E for Brownsham woodlands and Mouthmill beach on the edge of Hartland. Clovelly is just over 1½ miles W along the shore.

51.013740, -4.425993

Clovelly Park, Clovelly Woods, Bideford Bay

Fishing village set into the rocks surrounded by woodland. A waterfall into the sea can sometimes be accessed along the S shore at low tide (be wary of the incoming tide). Otherwise, access is from one of the woodland walks (but there may be an entrance fee), around The Hobby lanes.

➤ **Find** Clovelly Visitors Centre, Clovelly, Bideford, EX39 5TL and walk ⅓ mile to the harbour.

50.9985, -4.3972

Clovelly Park

Clovelly Harbour

The Hobby (Drive), Higher Clovelly

Feel the long and winding road... This woodland walk of substance leads you out of, or into, Clovelly. It can become extremely tiresome if you're already exhausted after a long day's walk, but it's uplifting before lunch with glimpses through the trees of Bideford Bay and Clovelly harbour.

➤ **Find** St Anne's Church, Bucks Mills, EX39 5ND. With the church on your L, continue on the lane another ½ mile to the NT car park on the R. Walk 2⅓ miles W to The Hobby. Take care: it's steep.

50.987352, -4.378008

Bucks Mills Beach, Bideford Bay

Waterfall by Buck's Cross Church. Best seen at low tide. Masses of ancient woodland, beach and cliffs to explore in all directions.

➤ **Find** St Anne's Church, Bucks Mills, EX39 5ND. With the church on your L, continue on the lane another ½ mile to the car park on the R. Make the rest of the way on foot. The beach is ⅓ mile down the lane.

50.9895, -4.3465

Peppercombe Castle, Bideford, Bideford Bay

Hill fort, bothy and beach. The castle seems to have been mostly lost to erosion, which is a good reason to go and explore the tide and shore.

➤ Follow the directions for Bucks Mills Beach (see above). At the sea, turn R along the coast and walk 2 miles to the castle and bothy.

50.993, -4.309

Peppercombe Beach, Bideford Bay

The dark stones here heat up so much in the summer sun that the sand and beach shimmers into a mirage. Swim later in the afternoon as the cold water will have been warmed on the hot pebbles.

➤ **Find** Bucks Mills Car Park (50.98521, -4.34108). The beach is ⅓ mile down the lane.

51.005138, -4.293957

THE BEAVER INN, APPLEDORE, TORRIDGE ESTUARY

Pub where rivers Taw and Torridge join before emptying into the sea. Riverside patio for dining on local fish and organic produce.

Irsha St, Appledore, Bideford, EX39 1RY
www.beaverinn.co.uk

FREMINGTON QUAY CAFE, BARNSTAPLE, RIVER TAW

Locally sourced seafood, bread, meats, fruit and veg. Delightful views over the river.

Fremington Quay, Barnstaple, EX31 2NH
Facebook: Fremington Quay Cafe

Instow Dunes, Instow, River Taw

Combination of stunning dunes and 360-degree views of both the Taw and Torridge estuaries. Keep walking to find the lonely places and one of the best sunset views, over Appledore and Westward Ho!, in north Devon.

➤ **Find** Sandhills Car Park, 8 Sandhills, Instow, EX39 4LF, and walk S 100 yards into the dunes and 100 yards E to the beach on the River Taw.

51.058453, -4.179595

Horsey Island, River Caen

Fish for mullet and bass over marsh and creek. The island's land access is mostly lost because of erosion so consider a kayak or packraft from Velator Quay or walk in from Broad Sands beach (see page 188). The ECP once navigated the island's edge. The FP entrance points are still visible at the SW and NE ends of the island, but have been closed.

➤ **Find** Velator Quay Car Park, Braunton, EX33 2DX. With your back to the road, walk towards the River Caen and ECP, then walk 1 mile S to Horsey Island entrance.

51.079834, -4.173387

Yelland Stone Rows, River Taw

An avenue of nine stones along the Isley Marsh harbour. The last time someone looked in 2018, the two rows were covered in silt and not visible. But don't let that stop you looking. It only takes one storm or high tide to wash the silt away.

Buck's Cross

WATERSIDE COFFEE HOUSE, BRAUNTON, TAW–TORRIDGE ESTUARY

 Raised outdoor benches looking out across the Taw–Torridge estuary.

Chivenor Business Park, Braunton, Barnstaple, EX31 4AY
www.waterside-coffee-house.co.uk

SURFER'S PARADISE, CROYDE BAY CAMPSITE, CROYDE BAY

 Wake up a few yards from sandy beaches.

Croyde, Croyde Bay, EX33 1PP
www.surfparadise.co.uk

PUTSBOROUGH BEACH CAFE, CROYDE, PUTSBOROUGH SANDS

 Cafe and terrace on the beach. Also cottages, touring, but no tents.

Croyde, Braunton, EX33 1LB
www.putsborough.com

➤ **Find** the Biketrail Cycle Hire and Cycle Shop, Fremington Quay, Fremington, EX31 2NH. Facing the sea, turn L on the Tarka Trail and walk across the river bridge. Keep on another 1½ miles from the bridge to reach the marsh. Have a cuppa at the Fremington Quay Cafe (see opposite) upon your return.

51.075438, -4.155061

Crow Point, River Taw

Like a wild scene from a real-life *Pirates of the Caribbean* saga. Pay a toll fee to drive up the path to get next to the beach. Or else walk in.
➤ **Find** Crow Point Car Park off American Rd, Unnamed Rd, Braunton, EX33 2NX. Facing the River Taw, walk R along the FP ½ mile to Crow Point. Best at low tide. Watch out for mud.

51.0667063, -4.1904747

Crow Point

Baggy Point sea caves, Atlantic Ocean

Explore caves and tunnels around the bays either side of Baggy Point. Putsborough Beach is stunning at low tide and good for swims.
➤ **Find** Surf South West, Beach Rd, Croyde, Braunton, EX33 1NZ, next to the public car park. Walk back to Moor Ln, with your back to sea, and turn L. Walk 1.2 miles out of town to Baggy Point along the coast path.

51.1394, -4.2550

Damage Barton 1, 2 & 3, Ilfracombe, Bristol Channel

Three standing stones on the cliff top plateau NW of Lee Bay Cove. Drop down into the cove to explore the stone corridors and beach caves at low tide (51.1994, -4.1815).
Find The Grampus Inn, Ilfracombe, EX34 8LR. Enjoy a pub meal and drink and then ask for directions. The stones are a 1-mile walk from here, past Lee Beach. Parking is tricky.

51.196957, -4.188427

THE SMUGGLERS, ILFRACOMBE HARBOUR

On the harbour front. Not much to look at from the outside. But inside ... great service, clean and good-value food.

The Quay, Ilfracombe, EX34 9EQ
01271 863 620

BEACH COVE COASTAL RETREAT, HELE BAY

Luxury beach hut-inspired accommodation with hot tubs and sea views.

Hele Bay, Ilfracombe, EX34 9QZ
www.darwinescapes.co.uk

LITTLE MEADOW CAMPSITE, WATERMOUTH COVE

Tents, caravans, huts and luxury cottages, about 150 yards from the coast path.

Watermouth, Ilfracombe, EX34 9SJ
www.littlemeadow.co.uk

WATERMOUTH VALLEY CAMPING PARK, WATERMOUTH, BRISTOL CHANNEL

Great views over the bay. Showers and all facilities right next to the coast path. Explore Watermouth Cave.

Watermouth, Ilfracombe, EX34 9SJ
www.watermouthpark.co.uk

Hele Bay

Tunnels Beach, Ilfracombe, Bristol Channel

Hand-carved tunnels next to shingle beach and tidal pools. This Victorian sea-bathing complex is Ilfracombe's most popular beach attraction. Tidal pool three hours before and after low tide. Fees apply.

➤ **Find** Brookdale Car Park at the town centre, Brookdale Av, Ilfracombe, EX34 8AY. The tunnels are only 220 yards away, walking down into town towards the Tourist Information.

51.208523, -4.126966

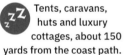 Hillsborough, Hele Bay

Known as the sleeping elephant, because that's what it looks like from Ilfracombe Harbour, with the trunk flat and out to sea. The old hill fort looks over Ilfracombe Harbour.

➤ **Find** the Hele Bay Pub, 39 Beach Rd, Ilfracombe, EX34 9QZ, and the large public car park. Follow the beach road down to the cove and walk along its L edge up and on to the ECP. From here, follow the path as it zigzags around the summit and leads up on to the plateau, some 330 yards back from the cliff face.

51.209587, -4.102976

Broad Sands, Combe Martin Bay

Several hundred steps down to the beach. Series of coves with caves, sheltered swims.

➤ Access and parking can be tricky around Combe Martin, so this is a lovely 1⅓-mile walk. Find the public car park in Castle Hill, Ilfracombe, EX34 9SE. Exit the car park on foot and turn L into Castle Hill and R into Barton Ln, with St Peter's Church on your L. Follow Barton Ln ⅔ mile, across the A399 until the T-junction at Barton Hill. Walk straight ahead into the lane marked Old Coast Rd. The beach is just under ½ mile down this lane, which is part of the ECP.

51.212244, -4.058637

MARTINHOE MANOR, PARRACOMBE, WOODY BAY

Self-catering holiday apartments surrounded by woodland. Ask for one overlooking the bay and the Bristol Channel. Lovely walk down through the trees to the top of the beach.

Parracombe, Barnstaple, EX31 4QX
www.marsdens.co.uk/group-cottages/lynton-lynmouth-exmoor/martinhoe-manor-woody-bay

Wild Pear Beach, Combe Martin Bay

Shingle beaches accessed by eroded steps. Naturists welcome.
➤ See above, except turn R at the T-junction at Barton Hill and keep walking along the coast path to Combe Martin. Once at the bay, walk on another ⅔ mile along the ECP to Wild Pear Beach. Alternatively, find the Combe Martin public car park beside the beach at 1 Hangman Path, Combe Martin, Ilfracombe, EX34 0DN.

51.210964, -4.031533

Little Hangman Hill, Combe Martin Bay

One of the highest points on the Devonshire coast with 360-degree views. Great Hangman, at 1,000ft, is a 1-mile walk along the path.
➤ **Find** the Combe Martin public car park beside the beach at 1 Hangman Path, Combe Martin, Ilfracombe, EX34 0DN. Follow the path to Wild Pear Beach (see above) and walk on another ¼ mile.

51.213610, -4.027386

Trentishoe Settlement & Tumuli, Combe Martin Bay

Famous for UFO sightings and ancient hut circles, the old settlement is on the path at the bottom of a hill. From the top, see the Brecon Beacons to the N and Exmoor to the rear (S). This is magic country.
➤ **Find** the drive to Coastal Path Cottage, Holdstone Down, Combe Martin, Ilfracombe, EX34 0PF. Keeping the cottage on your L, continue on 330 yards, where there is a small car park on the L. Walk towards the shore and the coast path. The settlement's old location is between the car park and coast path. Explore this important headland on all sides. And look out for UFOs!

51.215638, -3.967077

Broad Strand Beach near Combe Martin

MOTHER MELDRUMS TEA GARDENS & RESTAURANT, LYNTON, WRINGCLIFF BAY

Impressive setting at the bottom of the stone face in the Valley of the Rocks. Good food, fruit pies and cream teas.

Garden Lodge Lee Abbey, Lynton, EX35 6JL
Facebook: Mother Meldrums Tea Garden

The Pines, Parracombe, Woody Bay

Smell the perfume of elderflowers on the wild woodland walk to Woody Bay. It's harder and much longer coming up. You've been warned.

➤ **Find** the car park off Berry's Ground Ln (51.221148, -3.897382) and walk 1½ miles down the cobbled track signposted 'Martinhoe Manor' to the beach, passing an ancient limekiln as you go.

51.223962, -3.886072

Crook Point Sands, Lee Bay

Sandy beach … via ropes at the end of a path through a hedge tunnel. Explore neighbouring coves.

➤ **Find** space to park in the lane at Lynton, EX35 6JJ, above Lee Bay. Walk down to the beach. Climb back up to the car park and exit on foot on to the lane and turn R. Walk 330 yards and the ECP should be signposted forking off to the R. Follow the cliff edge another ⅓ mile to reach the point.

51.226163, -3.883874

Valley of the Rocks, Wringcliff Bay

Fossils embedded in rocks where Exmoor meets the sea. Climb down to the beach along the steep, snaking paths patrolled by mountain goats.

➤ **Find** Mother Meldrums Tea Gardens & Restaurant (see left). Facing the sea, the rocks are 330 yards to the L. Loos and parking. Easy access from Lynton.

51.231553, -3.85747(

The Valley of the Rocks

Lee Bay, North Devon

Wester Wood, East Lyn River

River valley trail to beach. The water trail leads back inland 5 miles to Brendon. Enjoy a pub meal and hike back to the beach for a swim.

➤ **Find** the public car park at Watersmeet Rd, Lynmouth, EX35 6EP, beside the river. Facing the river, turn R and walk down to the steel-mesh bridge and cross into Tors Rd. Turn R. Follow the road all the way up to the parking bays and keep on going up along the wooded path. Find the heart of Wester Wood ⅔ mile from the bridge crossed earlier. The wooded river path goes all the way to Brendon 3½ miles away. The Staghunters Inn, 1 Lea Villas, Brendon, Lynton, EX35 6PS is there.

51.224871, -3.816768

Sister's Well, Lynton

Well and spring with a mythical story. Allegedly founded by Joseph of Arimathea, the 'secret disciple'. He has strong links to the Holy Grail and Arthurian legends, based on stories that gained in popularity in the 12th century.

➤ **Find** the car park of the A39, Lynton, EX35 6NQ. Cross the A39 and follow the wooded, gated FP towards the sea, via Sister's Fountain, ⅓ mile.

51.228831, -3.730352

Glenthorne Plantation, Bristol Channel

Rock arch surrounded by cliffs and trees. Explore the Roman fort and beautiful Wingate Combe stream. Access to beach (51.232681, -3.719968).

➤ Same directions as for Sister's Well (see above). The plantation is ⅔ mile away from the car park, past the well. Offshore is a natural rib called Giant's Arch.

51.233270, -3.731846

St Audries Bay

SOUTH SOMERSET

WILD THINGS TO DO BEFORE YOU DIE:

SWIM on a secret beach at the end of the wooded path out of St Beuno's.

CYCLE 10 miles of wooded bridleways that zigzag over Culver Cliff.

KAYAK the shingle headland at the mouth of the River Parrett.

LOOK for peregrines hunting small birds over Brean Down.

CATCH a glimpse of the blue jewel kingfishers along West Huntspill River.

WADE out on to Berrow Beach. But not too far ... the tide goes 1¼ miles out.

EXPLORE one of Alfred the Great's defensive castles by the Washford River.

THE BOTTOM SHIP (FORMERLY THE SHIP INN), PORLOCK WEIR, BRISTOL CHANNEL

Great-value en suite B&B rooms beside Porlock Weir. On the coast path surrounded by Exmoor hills.

Lane Head, Porlock Weir, Minehead, TA24 8PB
www.shipinnporlock
weir.co.uk

KITNORS, BOSSINGTON, BRISTOL CHANNEL

Tearoom in a 500-year-old cottage a few yards from the ECP.

Kitnors, Bossington, TA24 8HQ
www.kitnors.com

TUDOR COTTAGE, BOSSINGTON, PORLOCK BAY

Old 15th-century farmhouse converted to a B&B on the fringes of Exmoor.

Bossington Ln, Bossington, Nr Porlock, TA24 8HQ
01643 862 255

MINEHEAD CAMPING AND CARAVANNING CLUB SITE, MINEHEAD, BRISTOL CHANNEL

Seaview from a campsite for tents and campers. No caravans. Woodland walks

Hill Rd, Minehead, TA24 5LB
www.campingand
caravanningclub.co.uk

Greenaleigh Sand, Minehead, Bristol Channel

Look for porpoises between the roll of water over boulders at high tide in late July. Walk and paddle down in the bay, via the remains of Burgundy Chapel. Hammock in the trees towards the back of the stone beach.

➤ **Find** North Hill Moor Wood Car Park, Hill Rd, Minehead, TQ24 8SJ. Follow the ECP S for a few yards and then take the FP fork (leaving the ECP) down through the Chapel Combe. Keep walking down to the beach via Greenaleigh Farm FP and Greenaleigh Point The wooded walk is just over 1 mile long.

51.223921, -3.50203?

Bossington Hill, Alleford, Bristol Channel

Listen for tawny owls around the trees at the bottom of the hill. The surrounding hills stay lit up in sunshine even on overcast days, and buttercups add to the cheer when they are in full yellow flower.

➤ **Find** the NT Car Park for Bossington, Minehead, TA24 8HQ. Turn L out of the car park on to the road, then follow the ECP L over North Bridge and continue on the FP for 1 mile to Hurlstone Point. Take the ECP NE, and then W, 1 mile up the hill.

51.224352, -3.570311

Western Brockholes Spring, Minehead, Bristol Channel

Listen out for male stonechats calling and chasing females in spring, perched on top of gorse. They sound, as you'd expect, like two stones being knocked together on the beach below. Look out for the birds' red breast and black head. Exmoor has the highest coastline in England. Savour awhile the cliff view ... 800ft above sea level.

➤ **Find** Hill Rd car park, Minehead, TA24 5LB and walk W on the ECP for 3 miles.

51.229254, -3.55003?

Porlock Weir

Selworthy Sand, Selworthy, Bristol Channel

Fish for the first run of mackerel in early June and cook them on a beach BBQ. The beach is best at low tide when lighter sands and rock pools are exposed.

➤ **Find** the NT Car Park for Bossington, Minehead, TA24 8HQ. Walk out of the car park on to the road and turn R. Walk down the lane ½ mile to the beach. Walk around Hurlstone Point after high tide. Avoid getting cut off by the incoming tide.

51.220736, -3.549308

Porlock Weir coastline, Porlock Weir

Walk in a sunken woodland at low tide. Fossilised stumps mark the 6,000-year-old treeline that turned to stone. Also look for bones from Porlock aurochs, the large oxen that grazed here more than 3,000 years ago.

➤ **Find** the car park at Porlock Weir, Minehead, TA24 8PB.

51.218234, -3.624366

Yenworthy Wood, Lynton, Bristol Channel

Walk from Porlock through the trees for a snap of solitude in the wild quiet. Look out for secret paths, ponds and tunnels. It's fun getting lost ... but only before midday. Listen for barking nightjars.

➤ **Find** Porlock Weir Car Park, Minehead, TA24 8PD, and walk 4 miles W on the ECP.

51.229552, -3.708155

St Beuno's Church, Porlock Weir, Bristol Channel

The smallest parish church in England with a woodland path down to the shore.

➤ **Find** The Bottom Ship (see opposite) and public car park that look over the quay. Either walk past the quay and follow the beach round the bend to the base of the wood, or else follow the coast path through the heart of the wood to the beach. Find signposts for the coast path down by the quay beside a staircase. The path includes a 110-yard section of Worthy Toll Rd before it forks off L under the house arch. It's a 1.4-mile walk to the church.

51.225275, -3.656972

Culver Cliff, Bristol Channel

Wooded cliff over 1 mile long above sandy bays. More than 10 miles of bridleway.

➤ **Find** RNLI Gift & Souvenir Shop, Quay St, Minehead, TA24 5UL, and the public car park next door looking over the sea. Walk R facing the sea, past the small roundabout and on to the coast path. The cliff is 0.4 miles away as the path turns into the woodland. Park at Moor Wood and walk the bridleways or Minehead.

51.218282, -3.485900

SMUGGLERS INN, BLUE ANCHOR, BRIDGWATER BAY

A cottage and rooms off the seafront road between Exmoor and the Quantock Hills.

Blue Anchor Bay Rd, Blue Anchor, Minehead, TA24 6JS
www.thesmugglersinn.co.uk

THE MARINA CAFE (& CURIOSITY SHOP), WATCHET HARBOUR

Cafe and ice-cream parlour.

10 The Espl, Watchet, TA23 0AJ
www.watchetmarina.com

CHANTRY TEA GARDENS, KILVE PIL BEACH, BRISTOL CHANNEL

Tearooms ⅓ mile from the beach.

Sea Ln, Bridgwater, TA5 1EG
01278 741 457

THE ANCHOR INN COMBWICH, COMBWICH, RIVER PARRETT

The first pub on the river in a village with wonderful views.

Riverside, Combwich, Bridgwater, TA5 2RA
www.combwichanchor.co.uk

Culver Cliff Sand

Culver Cliff Sand, Minehead, Bristol Channel

Feel polished red pebbles underfoot, beside the elder, oak and tamarisk shore. Walk from here to Greenaleigh Sand if you set off just after high tide. Beware incoming water and eddies. There are so many wooded overhangs and shaded places in which to rest that you'll wonder why you ever chose to leave this place. Look for red-and-white fly agaric mushrooms about birch roots in November.

➤ **Find** Warren Rd Upper Car Park, Minehead, TA24 5SJ, and walk W 2 miles on the ECP. At the woodland, scramble under the branches down the cliffside 50 yards. There are gaps in the trees and it's not too steep, but care is needed when it's muddy.

51.221599, -3.491165

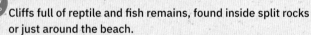

Blue Anchor, Bristol Channel

Cliffs full of reptile and fish remains, found inside split rocks or just around the beach.

➤ **Find** The Blue Anchor, on the B3192, Blue Anchor Bay Rd, Minehead, TA24 6JP. Follow the road on to the seafront parking. Facing the sea, walk R 220 yards down the boat ramp and on to the beach.

51.18330, -3.38522

Crow Covert, Watchet, Bridgwater Bay

Tree-lined shoreline where you can find reptile and ammonite fossils.

➤ **Find** Watchet Harbour Marina, 10 The Espl, Watchet, TA23 0AJ, and the public car park next door. Facing the marina, walk L along Market St and past Watchet Museum, along West St and Cleeve Hill. Turn off the road on to the coast path at the ruin of Daws Castle (see opposite). Walk on another 0.8 miles from the castle, keeping the campsites on your L and the sea on your R.

51.182374, -3.359957

LOWER LAKES, CHILTON

Log cabins and apartments beside a lake. Just ⅓ mile from the River Parrett, N of Bridgwater. Walking and cycling breaks.

Straight Drove, Chilton Trinity, TA5 2BQ
www.lowerlakesltd.co.uk

LABURNUM HOUSE HOTEL, HUNTSPILL RIVER

Budget hotel within ⅔ mile of the coast and right beside the river.

4 Sloway Ln, West Huntspill, TA9 3RJ
www.laburnumhouse hotel.co.uk

Daws Castle, Watchet, Washford River

Hill fort by the Washford River. One of several built by Alfred the Great to defend the coast from Vikings. They are connected by a military road, called the Herepath, which allowed armies to move quickly along the coast.

➤ See directions for Crow Covert (opposite).

51.181389, -3.344167

Watchet Market House Museum, Watchet, Bridgwater Bay

Museum and harbour. Good for crabbing and views over the Bristol Channel.

➤ **Find** parking at Crow Covert (see opposite). Find the museum at 32 Swain St, Watchet, TA23 0AD.

51.182613, -3.330656

Doniford Bay, Bristol Channel

Find white ammonite fossils on the rocks on the foreshore.

➤ **Find** Doniford Beach Train Station, Doniford Rd, Watchet, TA23 0TR. Facing the beach, walk 300 yards along Doniford Rd. Just past the bend is a FP down to the beach. Alternatively, park at Watchet Harbour Marina car park and turn R at the harbour, following the coast path 0.8 miles past the holiday homes.

51.17991, -3.330857

West Wood, Bridgwater Bay

Cold waterfall on to a beach.

➤ **Find** Chantry Tea Gardens, Sea Ln, Bridgwater, TA5 1EG, and keep on 220 yards to the Kilve Pil Beach Car Park. Facing the sea, turn L on to the coast path and walk 2.8 miles to the wood.

51.179872, -3.282251

Kilve Pil

Quantoxhead, Bridgwater Bay

Cliffs and wave-cut platform full of ammonites and reptile remains. Paddle in the running stream and rock pools. The beach is flanked by two churches, ¾ mile apart, both called St Mary's Church, both with FPs down to the shore. They are linked E to W by a woodland FP.

➤ Same directions as West Wood (see page 197), but the rocks here are only ⅓ mile from the Kilve Pil Beach Car Park.

51.19144, -3.23692

Lilstock, Bridgwater Bay

Beach and old boat launch and dock, around the stream that once brought coal from Wales. Whole reptile skeleton fossils and ammonites are sometimes found on the foreshore or in the cliff E towards Hinkley.

➤ **Find** the car park 220 yards from Lilstock Beach, Stringston, Bridgwater, TA5 1SU. Facing the sea, walk R on to the coast path 1½ miles.

51.20476, -3.16133 & 51.200891, -3.186488

Stert Point, River Parrett

Shingle and sand headland at the mouth of the River Parrett. Looks out on to Stert Island in the Bristol Channel, which is a used as a bird roost. The site became an island when it broke away from the headland in 1798. Best visited at low tide.

➤ **Find** the beach car park, Stert Drove, Bridgwater, TA5 2PU. Facing the sea, turn R on to the coast path and walk 2 miles to the point.

51.218203, -3.020998

West Huntspill River

Kingfishers dart about the riverbank along a short inland walk off the coast path to Sloway Ln. Keep walking inland for the best starling murmurations at Avalon Marshes.

➤ **Find** Highbridge & Burnham Station, off Market St, Highbridge, TA9 4AT, and the free parking nearby. Walk back to Market St, turn L and then L again at the roundabout and over the River Brue bridge. Immediately over the bridge, find the riverside FP on the R. Follow this river and coastal path 2¾ miles all the way to the estuary and then along the beach. Turn L at the Huntspill River for the inland path. It's possible to return to Highbridge Station via an inland shortcut along the FPs and roads, via St Peter & All Hallows' Church and Alstone village, which lead back 1½ miles to the river bridge.

51.205737, -3.01373(

Burnham-on-Sea Low Lighthouse, Bristol Channel

Wooden tower – one of three at Turnham and the only one still in use at the time of writing. Built in 1832. Wonderful for photos at sunset. Bridleway from town just past the lighthouse to watch riders down on to the beach.

➤ **Find** Tourist Information Centre, S Espl, Burnham-on-Sea, TA8 1BU, next to the huge public car park. Facing the sea, turn R and walk along the beach and sea wall 1.1 miles.

51.249964, -3.008407

Berrow Beach, Bristol Channel

Unique tide and sands. Banks are constantly shifting as the Bristol Channel has a tidal range of 50ft, second only to the Bay of Fundy, in Canada. Water can go out 1¼ miles at low tide. It's fun to explore, but caution is needed due to off-shore mud and quicksand. An old shipwreck is visible at low water, but mud is exposed as the tide recedes, which is a major hazard.

➤ **Find** Sundowner Cafe Bar, Beachside Holiday Park, Coast Rd, Brean, TA8 2QZ, where there's beach parking in the summer. Facing the sea, turn L and walk 1⅓ miles along the sands.

51.263646, -3.020065

St Mary's Church, Berrow, Bristol Channel

Church separated from the beach and dunes by a links golf course but linked on a bridleway. Makes for a peaceful diversion from the sands. WWII pillbox on the Berrow FP.

➤ **Find** St Mary's Church on Coast Rd, Berrow, Burnham-on-Sea, TA8 2NF. Take the FP to the side of the church down to the coast and turn L or R for the beach. Walk 1.4 miles to the lighthouse.

51.266710, -3.013932

Fiddler's Point, Brean Down, Bristol Channel

Look out for peregrines on the steep walk up to Howe Rock. Incredible views. Keep dogs on a lead in case they chase rabbits and fall over the cliff edge. Toilets and cafe at the fort end.

➤ **Find** Brean Down Parking, Warren Rd, Burnham-on-Sea, TA8 2RS. Facing the sea, walk R along the beach, up on to the cliff and turn L. The down is ½ mile along the top.

51.325734, -3.022928

Brean Down Fort, Brean Down

Headland famous for hill forts and sacred burials. The Roman and Bronze Age and artefacts found here can be seen in the Museum of Somerset, Castle Green, Taunton, TA1 4AA.

➤ **Find** the fort ⅓ mile on from Brean Down (see above).

51.325411, -3.027091

Dog Rose, Brean Down

Mountain goats
at Brean Down

GLOUCESTER & NORTH SOMERSET

WILD THINGS TO DO BEFORE YOU DIE:

SWIM in Clevedon Marine Lake after a high tide.

LISTEN to the flutter of tiny wings as thousands of dunlins flock over Blake's Pools.

COLLECT fossils on the beach next to the lido at Battery Point.

WATCH rabbits on the warren at Wain's Hill.

PICNIC on a wooded hill fort over the Bristol Channel.

FIND rare butterflies around Walborough's grassy slopes.

VISIT the church named after a local girl who was murdered; the Ships' Graveyard at Purton; and the red-and-white cliffs that prop up the Severn Bridge.

Clevedon

UPHILL WHARF CAFE-BAR, WESTON-SUPER-MARE, RIVER AXE

 Popular with cyclists, who ride the way from Weston to Brean.

Uphill Wharf, Weston-super-Mare, BS23 4XR
www.wharfcafebar.co.uk

TIFFANYS RESTAURANT, WESTON-SUPER-MARE, BRISTOL CHANNEL

 Fish and chips to afternoon tea for two on the pier.

Marine Pde, Weston-super-Mare, BS23 1AL
www.grandpier.co.uk

SAND BAY TEA ROOMS, KEWSTOKE, SAND BAY

 Cakes, scones and lunches a few yards from the coast path and beach.

81 Beach Rd, Kewstoke, Weston-super-Mare, BS22 9UQ
www.sandbaytearooms.co.uk

SAND FARM CAMPING & TOURING, KEWSTOKE, SAND BAY

 Tent pitches 165 yards from a long beach.

11 Sand Farm Ln, Kewstoke, Weston-super-Mare, BS22 9UF
Facebook: @SandFarmCamping

Weston-super-Mare

Walborough, Bristol Channel

Grassy slopes full of butterflies in summer. They include the nationally rare Somerset hair grass and honewort. Waders and wildfowl, sea barley and lavender around the salt marsh. Marina and lake camping nearby.

➤ **Find** Uphill Beach, Type 25 Pillbox, Uphill, Weston-super-Mare, BS23 4XY, and the beachside car park. With your back to the sea, walk back up Links Rd ¼ mile to Uphill Marina. Follow the FP around the R edge of the marina along the River Axe waterside path. The marshes are ⅔ mile from the beach.

51.314833, -2.985116

Worlebury Camp/Weston Woods, Bristol Channel

Hill fort on a headland jutting into the mouth of the Bristol Channel. Some pits, rubble and mounds are all that remain of the fort. Ancient trackways (bridleway and multiple FPs) circumnavigate the wooded cliffs and E towards Worlebury Hill and Weston Woods.

➤ **Find** the beachside car park opposite The Commodore Hotel, Beach Rd, Kewstoke, Weston-super-Mare, BS22 9UZ. Facing the sea, a FP leads out of the car park to the L, crossing Kewstoke Rd after 55 yards. Keep following the FP to Worlebury Hill, until you reach a bridleway path to the R. Follow this path 1 mile to the hill fort through the wood.

51.357424, -2.985153

Blake's Pools, Severn Estuary

In winter, thousands of dunlins flock to this Severn Estuary coast between Weston-super-Mare and Clevedon. Watch graceful grebes and egrets feed at low tide from hides. Barn owls at dusk. Tides can hamper sea wall access. Contact the Avon Wildlife Trust for disabled access information. www.avonwildlifetrust.org.uk/reserves/blakes-pools

51.392864, -2.902975

Wain's Hill, Severn Estuary

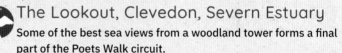

High ground occupied most recently by Iron Age hill fort overlooking a natural harbour facing SW into the Bristol Channel. Wales on the horizon. FP circles the fort foundations like an island mount above vast rabbit warrens.

➤ **Find** St Andrew's Church, Old Church Rd, Clevedon, BS21 7UE. Walk past the church towards the shore and the Poets Walk. Turn R looking out to sea and walk 370 yards to the hill point.

51.431652, -2.877710

Gullhouse Point, Clevedon, Severn Estuary

Coastal view of Blackstone rocks and path along the shore above a quiet stone shingle beach.

➤ **Find** St Andrew's Church (see above), and walk 1 mile SW on Clevedon Coastal Path via Land Yeo waterway.

51.426185, -2.882155

The Lookout, Clevedon, Severn Estuary

Some of the best sea views from a woodland tower forms a final part of the Poets Walk circuit.

➤ **Find** St Andrew's Church (see Wain's Hill), and walk 400 yards NE on Poets Walk towards Clevedon Marine Lake.

51.435311, -2.870802

Sand Bay, Kewstoke

LA MARINA, PORTISHEAD MARINA

Italian cooking by the table or takeaway a few yards from the Portishead Marina with views of the water. Weekly fish nights.

Lockside, Portishead, Bristol, BS20 7AH
www.lamarina
restaurant.co.uk

CAPTAINS CABIN, PORTISHEAD MARINA

Favourite stopover for cyclists who want fast food and a cuppa by the lock.

37–39 Lockside, Portishead, Bristol, BS20 7QH
01275 841 941

Clevedon Marine Lake

Clevedon Marine Lake

Safe swimming, crabbing and great views over Salthouse Bay.
➤ Find Clevedon Salthouse Park, off Salthouse Rd, Clevedon, BS21 7TU. From the large public car park, walk on down to the marine lake, with The Salthouse Bar and Restaurant on your L.

51.435529, -2.867939

Seafarers Memorial Stone, Portishead, Woodhill Bay

Ship watch at high tide from Portishead Point. Fossils can be seen in the stone and along the foreshore at Battery Point. There's an open-air lido right next to the point.
➤ Find the Portishead Open Air Pool, Esplanade Rd, Portishead, Bristol, BS20 7HD. Walk up the steps from the public car park on to the tree-lined ride. Turn L while looking out to sea and walk 220 yards. To avoid the stairs, walk around the front of the pool and turn R.

51.494170, -2.771548C

Woodspring, Kewstoke

DUKE OF CORNWALL, PILL, RIVER AVON

Lovely riverside pub that's popular among walkers and cyclists for a beer or cuppa.

Pump Square, Pill, Bristol, BS20 0BG
Facebook: The Duke of Cornwall - Pill

THE LAMPLIGHTERS, BRISTOL, RIVER AVON

Views over the mouth of the River Avon and the village of Pill. Food is freshly made and locally sourced. A popular haunt of seafarers from around the world who visited during long periods of anchorage in Hung Rd.

Station Rd, Bristol, BS11 9XA
www.thelamplighters
.co.uk

THE ANCHOR INN, OLDBURY-ON-SEVERN, RIVER SEVERN

On the original banks of the river, the Anchor has a history dating back to the Iron Age. At the end of the huge garden, boules is played, with 30 teams regularly taking part. Food and accommodation.

Church Ln, Oldbury-on-Severn, Bristol, BS35 1QA
www.anchor-inn-oldbury.co.uk

East Wood Fort, Portishead, Severn Estuary

Ancient woodland on a vast limestone platform between Portishead and Portishead Pier.

➤ **Find** the car park beside The Windmill Inn, Nore Rd, Portishead, Bristol, BS20 6JZ, and walk S a few yards to the FP. Turn E facing the water and walk 1 mile to the fort.

51.493510, -2.762654

Leigh Woods, River Avon

Wooded shores of the Avon Gorge. Walk with the shore on your L shoulder into Bristol Harbour.

➤ **Find** Leigh Woods Coffee Co, Forestry Commission Car Park, Leigh Woods, Bristol, BS8 3QB, a few yards from the public car park. The main path circles L after the cafe and then heads N following the line of the River Avon. After ⅔ mile, take a R turn and then another R turn down to the water, 1 mile from the car park. From the riverbank, either walk L for another 2.6 miles along the river to Ham Green and Pill village or turn R and walk 1.8 miles to see one of Isambard Kingdom Brunel's masterpieces, the Clifton Suspension Bridge.

51.465115, -2.636350

Aust Cliff, River Avon

The foundation stone to the Severn Bridge, on the English mainland. The cliffs here are red and white: the top a sand bed full of reptile bones, fish remains and teeth. Considered to be one of England's most productive sites from the Triassic period, a time 200 million years ago that ended with a mass extinction. Severn Bridge Viewpoint is a few mins' walk just under the bridge to the N.

➤ **Find** the riverside along New Passage Rd, Bristol, BS35 4BG, off the A403 at Aust, right next to junction 1 of the M48. Facing the river, get down on to the foreshore at low tide and walk R towards the bridge. Keep walking past the former Aust Ferry Landing until you reach the cliffs, where Aust Wharf Rd ends.

51.60334, -2.62888

Littleton Brick Pits, River Severn

Migrating birds feed along this chain of estuary reed beds, 1 mile E of the Severn Rd Bridge. Good for reed warblers, reed buntings and whitethroats.

➤ **Find** the White Hart pub, Littleton-upon-Severn, Bristol, BS35 1NR. Keeping the pub on the R shoulder, keep on for 330 yards to the T-junction and turn L for Whale Wharf. The lane ends (BS35 1NP) after ¾ mile at the riverside. Facing the river, turn R.

➤ Kissing gates so no wheelchair access. Take a dip. Shelter in a little hut when the weather turns bad (51.611272, -2.610611). Permit access only, details from AWT. Parking for permit holders only in Littleton-upon-Severn.

51.617860, -2.593933

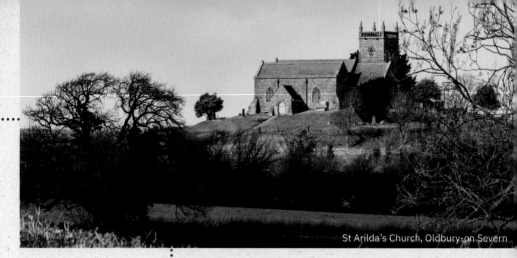

St Arilda's Church, Oldbury-on Severn

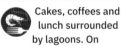
St Arilda's Church, Oldbury-on-Severn, River Severn

Sacred mound with beautiful sunset views from the church.
Information boards give the history of the church and the area.
The church is named after a female saint who was murdered
nearby, probably in the 5th century. Two churches are
dedicated to Arilda; the other is at Oldbury-on-the-Hill.

➤ **Find** the church in Church Ln, Oldbury-on-Severn, Bristol,
BS35 1QG. There's a small parking area. The nearest pub is a
½-mile walk from here at Oldbury-on-Severn. Facing the church,
there is a FP to the L of it. Follow it straight and then slightly L
after ½ mile, to reach the coast 1 mile away.

51.624636, -2.567232

Oldbury-On-Severn Submerged Forest, River Severn

Tree stumps discovered by the tidal rez next to Oldbury-on-
Severn power station embedded in peat. Best seen at low tide
with binoculars, as access across Oldbury Sands is extremely
difficult.

➤ **Find** the Anchor Inn (see opposite). Facing the pub, turn L along
Church Ln a few yards and then turn L on to the Severn Way for
1½ miles.

51.646953, -2.581819

Tites Point, River Severn, Gloucester & Sharpness Canal

Fish, mollusc, seed and plant fossils exposed at low tide.
Walk L (facing the water) ¼ mile around the coast for Purton
Ships Graveyard, Berkeley, GL13 9HX.

➤ **Find** the Church of St John the Evangelist, 1 Hesterville Villas,
Purton, Berkeley, GL13 9HS beside the canal. There's a public car
park opposite, next to the bridge. Cross the canal bridge and walk
along the path to the Severn point and sands, ⅓ mile away.

51.738745, -2.452992

THE OLD PASSAGE INN, ARLINGHAM, RIVER SEVERN

 Seafood restaurant beside an ancient ford across the River Severn. Lobster, oysters and other seafood specials. En suite rooms with river views, close to the Forest of Dean.

Arlingham, Gloucester, GL2 7JR

www.theoldpassage.com

THE ANCHOR INN, EPNEY, RIVER SEVERN

 Wonderful beer garden that fronts on to the river at a bend in the road.

Epney, Gloucester, GL2 7LN
www.anchorinnepney
.co.uk

Splatt Bridge, Gloucester & Sharpness Canal

Beautiful bridge across the canal, beside St Mary's Church, Fretherne, Arlingham, GL2 7JF. Views and FP down to the Severn Estuary, which is just ⅓ mile away. The church is known as a Mini Cathedral of Gloucestershire.

➤ **Find** Splatt Bridge over the Severn Way, Frampton on Severn, Gloucester, GL2 7EJ. Parking is available.

51.758678, -2.375268

Hock Cliff, River Severn

Tree-lined cliff tops of Long and Smith's woods. Fossils in the limestone and shale.

➤ See the directions at Splatt Bridge (above). Cross the bridge from the car park and turn immediately R on to the Severn Way. Follow the FP 2 miles to the point.

51.77845, -2.39236

The Awen Stone, River Severn

Stone carving linked to St Mary's Church, Arlingham, by a ½-mile-long bridleway, in a horseshoe curve of the River Severn.

➤ **Find** St Mary's Church (see Splatt Bridge, above), just ¼ mile from the village. After the church, take the first L and follow the FP to the stone and, eventually, the river.

51.786927, -2.414607

Splatt Bridge at Frampton on Severn on the Gloucester & Sharpness Canal

THE WHARF HOUSE, HIGHNAM, RIVER SEVERN

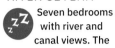 Seven bedrooms with river and canal views. The Wharf House is an old lock keeper's cottage on the banks of the River Severn. The house is run by the Herefordshire & Gloucestershire Canal Trust, a charity that is working to rebuild the 34 miles of historic canal between Gloucester and Hereford.

Horseshoe Dr, Highnam, Gloucester, GL2 8DB
www.thewharfhouse.co.uk

THE WHITE HORSE, GLOUCESTER, RIVER SEVERN

 Outdoor tables riverside, with the path running along the edge of the beer garden.

Sandhurst Ln, Gloucester, GL2 9NG
www.thewhitehorse chineserestaurant.co.uk

THE RED LION, NORTON, RIVER SEVERN

 Iconic pub by the riverside. Best seasonal fruits and vegetables from the Gloucestershire countryside. Afternoon teas during the summer served in a snug area overlooking the river.

Wainlode Ln, Norton, Gloucester, GL2 9LW
www.redlionwainlode .co.uk

Garden Cliff, Westbury-on-Severn, River Severn

Rapidly eroding cliff that's good for fossil hunting. Take the diversion FP at Severn Mill to the church ⅓ mile away. Westbury Severn Gardens is next door, free to NT members.

➤ **Find** The Lyon Inn, Bell Ln, Westbury-on-Severn, GL14 1PA, off the A48. Continue down Bell Ln past the Church of St Mary, St Peter and St Paul, and then take the FP to the R at the end of the lane. The FP loops 765 yards from the church to Severn Mill. Turn L at the river and walk 220 yards to the cliff.

51.81699, -2.41453

Longney Sands, River Severn

Lagoon-like bulge in the river. Huge flocks of birds roost and feed on these sandbanks at low tide.

➤ **Find** The Anchor Inn (see page 207). Facing the river, turn R on to the Severn Way and walk 1¼ miles to the sands.

51.810847, -2.358926

Alney Island, River Severn

This flood plain has escaped development because of its high water table. It's dripping in wildlife and wilderness.

➤ **Find** the Gloucester Castle Mead Car Park, Castle Meads Way, Gloucester, GL2 5HQ, on the southbound A430/Llanthony Rd. Facing the river, turn R on to the Severn Way and follow for 1 mile to explore the island's SW shore.

51.863231, -2.260473

Canal swing bridge pier of the Severn railway bridge

Wainlode Cliff

SEVERNSIDE CARAVAN SITE & BOAT PARK, APPERLEY, RIVER SEVERN

 Caravan and boat park with views over the river and Malvern Hills. Waterside pub next door has a one-bedroom apartment. Coalhouse Inn gets its name from barges travelling to the old coal wharf at Coombe Hill via a now-defunct canal.

Gabb Ln, Apperley Nr Tewkesbury, GL19 4DN
www.static-caravan.co.uk

THE YEW TREE INN, CHACELEY, RIVER SEVERN

On the W bank of the river, between Tewkesbury and Gloucester. The Mill House is a detached self-contained one-bedroom apartment in the Yew Tree grounds. Short- or long-stay moorings available.

Gloucester, GL19 4EQ
www.yewtreeinn.co.uk

Over Bridge, Over, River Severn

Well-engineered stone bridge, crafted by Thomas Telford, and made redundant by the A40 carriageway. Perfect as a quiet seat upon which to escape, above the narrowing river where you can watch the Severn Bore.

➤ **Find** The Wharf House (see opposite). From Horseshoe Dr, walk under the A40 by the river and then up on to the old bridge. It's possible to cross the bridge and walk N along the West Channel to explore the N part of Alney Island. The FP loops back along the W Channel too, but it's a 3-mile walk back to the old bridge via the path along the N side of the railway line. (Also see the directions for Alney Island opposite. The bridge is on the R, at the end of the mile walk.)

51.874440, -2.267771602

Wainlode Cliff, Norton, River Severn

Wooded cliff face that towers over the Severn. Keep an eye out for cliff falls as good fossils can be found.

➤ **Find** The Red Lion. Parking is for customers only. The cliff is a few yards away.

51.93002, -2.22592

Odda's Chapel, Deerhurst, River Severn

Three for the price of one... Odda's Chapel next to St Mary's Church. And only a 200-yard walk from the river and Severn Way.

➤ **Find** Odda's Chapel, off the B4213, Deerhurst, Gloucester, GL19 4BX, right next to a little car park. The FP to the river is opposite the chapel.

51.966918, -2.192055

Formby

CHESHIRE & LIVERPOOL

WILD THINGS TO DO BEFORE YOU DIE:

SWIM with man-sized statues.

SMELL 50 different flowers at Warburton's wild wood.

TOUCH the Godstone by a tree-lined beach.

WATCH hen harriers at Burton Mere.

FOLLOW Stone Age footprints before they vanish on the tide.

SEE bee-eaters and shrikes – England's rarest birds.

RIDE a horse on Thurstaton Beach.

WALLOW in the Hilbre Island shallows at low tide.

COUNT the hand-made bricks in England's oldest (brick) lighthouse.

EXPLORE all England's canals in one afternoon at the National Waterways Museum.

LISTEN to screeching swifts over Burton Mere.

FIND the red squirrels at Formby.

LOOK for goldcrests over dune heath.

THE SHIP INN, CHESTER, RIVER DEE

Pub inside the Chester city walls. Views overlooking the river.

18 Handbridge, Chester, CH4 7JE
www.theshipchester.co.uk

THE HARP INN, LITTLE NESTON, RIVER DEE

Secluded track overlooking the marshes. Beer garden and benches looking over the river.

19 Quayside, Little Neston, Neston, CH64 0TB
www.harpinnneston.
foodanddrinksites.co.uk

THE LITTLE TEAHOUSE, NESTON, RIVER DEE

Tea by the sea. Lovely views over the estuary.

South Cottage, The Pde, Parkgate, Neston, CH64 6SA
www.thelittleteahouse
parkgate.com

Thurstaston Beach

Grosvenor Park, Chester, River Dee

Park on the banks of the River Dee, a short walk from Chester city centre. Feed the squirrels while exploring the church ruins. The park overlooks a former Roman fort and castle across the water, and has a cafe and open-air theatre.
➤ **Find** the Grosvenor Car Park, Newgate St, Chester, CH1 1EA, a 2-min walk from the Chester Roman Amphitheatre. Walk through the theatre grounds, into the church and then into the park.

53.189602, -2.880691

RSPB Burton Mere Wetlands, Dee Estuary

Raptors, hides and walks at the entrance to the Dee Estuary. Drinks and snacks with wardens on site who are knowledgeable on wildlife and local history. Best for avocets, marsh harriers and swifts.
➤ **Find** RSPB Burton Mere Wetlands, Burton Rd, Puddington, Neston, CH64 5SF. There's parking.

53.254163, -3.029925

Thurstaston Beach, Wirral, Irish Sea

Peaceful sands and tree-lined cliffs, with views over N Wales. Good for horses. Visitor centre and boat launch.
➤ **Find** Flissys Coffee Shop, Bank Side Station Rd, Thurstaston, Wirral, CH61 0HN. Keeping the shop on your R shoulder, continue 200 yards to the public car park on the R and on the Wirral Way. Walk down to the beach and turn R while looking out to sea. Thurstaton Beach is ½ mile on. The foreshore and beach gets more interesting and isolated the further you walk.

53.336967, -3.141661

Red Rocks Marsh, Hoylake, Irish Sea

See the rarest birds in England: bee-eaters, shrikes and wintering snow buntings. Views out towards Hilbre Island. Small brackish pools that sometimes form around the sand dunes are home to natterjack toads. Their loud calls can be heard in the breeding season.

SHELDRAKES, LOWER HESWALL, RIVER DEE

High-tide lunches and afternoon teas on the terrace of the former Dee sailing club. Spectacular views across the Dee Estuary and the Welsh mountains.

Banks Rd, Lower Heswall, Wirral, CH60 9JS
www.sheldrakes restaurant.co.uk

NUMBER FIFTEEN, HOYLAKE, IRISH SEA

Old merchant's house by the golf course and beach. Rooms with a view over the dunes and Little Eye island. Try the smoked salmon and scrambled egg for breakfast.

15 Stanley Rd, Hoylake, Wirral, CH47 1HN
www.numberfifteen.co.uk

➤ **Find** Hoylake Station in Carr Ln, Hoylake, Wirral. At the level crossing, with the station on your R shoulder, continue straight on the Wirral Trail over the roundabout. After 330 yards, turn L into Stanley Rd (by the red-brick St Hildeburgh's Parish Church). Follow the dead-straight road ¾ mile to the bottom where it meets the beach. Once on the beach, turn L (walking S) ¼ mile.

53.383246, -3.195233

Dove Point, Hoylake, Irish Sea

At low tide, discover shrimps and crabs and look for the submerged forest where prehistoric artefacts are often found.
➤ **Find** Leasowe Lighthouse Car Park, Lingham Ln, Birkenhead, Greasby, Wirral, CH46 4TA. Walk 1½ miles W on the ECP to the point.

53.406501, -3.157998

West Kirby Beach, Wirral Peninsula

Look out for seals. Wild; biblical in scale and senses. The entire area from here N to Red Rocks is a former Mesolithic site. Stone Age weapons and tools have been discovered in the clay below the sand. In between looking, wallow in the shallows of low tide.
➤ **Find** the car park at Croft Dr, Birkenhead, Wirral, CH48 2JL, and walk 2 miles NW to marine lake.

53.372135, -3.188836

Hilbre Island, Irish Sea

Wallow in the shallows at low tide. Chance to see sea lions and seals here, across the Dee estuary sandbanks or near the old lighthouse end of the island. Kayak out from the mainland, though tidal creeks are powerful so care is needed. Be wary of quicksand and mud, as the seabed is constantly changing.
➤ Follow the same directions as Red Rocks Marsh (see opposite) up to the beach. Looking across the bay, see the island on the horizon 1.2 miles away.

53.378696, -3.216336

Red Rocks, Formby

SNACK BAR, LEASOWE, IRISH SEA

 Handy little roadside tea hut next to parking by the sea.

Leasowe, Wirral, CH46 4TH

LEASOWE CASTLE, MORETON, IRISH SEA

 Built in 1593 as 'New Hall', the door was about 6ft above ground to protect it from high tides. The walls were 3.2ft thick. Luxury rooms and a restaurant for residents and non-residents. Less than 220 yards from the coast path.

Leasowe Rd, Moreton, CH46 3RF
www.leasowecastle.com

THE DERBY POOL, WALLASEY BEACH, IRISH SEA

 Terraced views over the grassy banks that fall down to the beach. Great-value food.

Bayview Dr, Wallasey, CH45 3QS
www.harvester.co.uk

CAFFE CREAM OF NEW BRIGHTON, WALLASEY, RIVER MERSEY

 Family-run coffee shop. Selection of vegan and fruit drinks, brunches and lunches.

1 Marine Point, Wallasey, CH45 2PB
www.caffecream.co.uk

Leasowe Lighthouse, Irish Sea

The UK's oldest brick lighthouse, built from 660,000 hand-made bricks in 1763. Migratory birds stop over in spring and autumn, including redstarts, ring ouzels and wheatears. There are some lovely stories that surround the lighthouse. It opens occasionally, usually on the 1st or 3rd Sunday of each month. Two FPs and a bridleway lead in and around the lighthouse from S and W, the latter across a stream called The Birket.
➤ **Find** Leasowe Lighthouse on Lingham Ln, Moreton, Greasby, Wirral, CH46 4TA. There's a car park opposite.

53.413084, -3.126039

The Gunsite, Wallasey, Irish Sea

Mass of dunes and sand trails. Site was formerly used as a WWII anti-aircraft gun location to protect Liverpool from attack. Good views from the gunsite and sandhills. Historically important as a common, a status it retains.
➤ **Find** the Green Ln Car Park at Green Ln, Wallasey, CH45 8LW. Multiple paths lead out from the car park and Green Ln towards the beach, dunes and over the gunsite.

53.424219, -3.089879

Fort Perch Rock, River Mersey

Napoleonic fort built at the mouth of Liverpool Bay to defend the port. Good views across the Mersey and docks. At low tide, walk out to the much newer New Brighton Lighthouse, built almost 200 years ago. No access, but good photos.
➤ **Find** New Brighton Beach, off Marine Prom, Wallasey, CH45 2JU. There's a public car park beside the huge marine lake. The fort is 230ft from the lake on the foreshore.

53.442479, -3.041056

Wallase[y]

Wirral

Marine Lake, Wallasey

Communal pool area at which to watch and wait as the world passes by. Right next to sandy New Brighton beach.

➤ **Find** Perch Rock Car Park, Marine Promenade, New Brighton, Wallasey, CH45 2JS, next to the lake.

53.441894, -3.041222

Port Sunlight, River Mersey

Green, riverside area recovered from industrial wasteland. Views over Liverpool are best at sunset, with both cathedrals visible. Paths are wheelchair friendly.

➤ **Find** Dock Rd North, Birkenhead, Wirral, CH62 4TQ. Walk into the park.

53.356828, -2.979346

Eastham Country Park, Eastham Channel

Vast woodland along ½-mile stretch of Eastham Channel, known as The Warrens. There are many trails to explore. Find the bridleway that trails away from the river and back towards town, and New Chester Rd. Stunning views of the river from Eastham Ferry Point. Also walk the shore N to Job's Ferry. Pubs, cafe and toilets.

➤ **Find** The Tap Pub, 1a Ferry Rd, Birkenhead, Wirral, CH62 0AU. Keep on into the park with the pub on your L shoulder. Lots of parking bays with river views.

53.327470, -2.957749

THE REFRESHMENT ROOMS, BIRKENHEAD, RIVER MERSEY

 Somewhere to stop for a drink on the river.

2 Bedford Rd E, Birkenhead, CH42 1LS
www.refreshmentrooms.info

THE FERRY TAVERN, PENKETH, RIVER MERSEY

 Historic riverside pub. Fish and chips or pies.

Station Rd, Penketh, Warrington, WA5 2UJ
www.theferrytavern.com

THE MERSEY HOTEL, WIDNES, RIVER MERSEY

 Rooms next to the Silver Jubilee Bridge. Large beer garden by the waterside.

146–148 Mersey Rd, Widnes, WA8 0DT
www.merseyhotel.com

CARGO, LIVERPOOL, RIVER MERSEY

 A fish restaurant and bar at the heart of Liverpool, ⅔ mile from the famous Cavern bar where the Beatles once played. Right by the river.

Alexandra Tower, 19 Princes Pde, Liverpool, L3 1BD
www.cargofishrestaurant.co.uk

National Waterways Museum, Ellesmere Port

History and showcase of England's great canals. Listen to recordings of people who have lived on the water and boats of old. If the museum is impressive, the location is spectacular: Ellesmere Port and Manchester Ship Canal that leads into the rivers Weaver and Mersey. Museum and cafe.

➤ **Find** the port and museum at South Pier Rd, Ellesmere Port, CH65 4FW. There's a massive car park opposite.

53.287893, -2.891971

Warburton's Wood, River Weaver

Ancient woodland beside the river. More than 50 species of wild flowers bloom here, including wood anemone, yellow archangel, giant bellflower, common violet, primrose, bluebell and pale wood violet. The wood is fed by springs and wells, the most important being Brine Spring at the wood's centre. Herbs and grasses run down to the river around the N of the wood. Explore Well Wood and its waters next door via a FP that turns inland at the turn in the river.

➤ **Find** Ball Ln, Kingsley, Frodsham, WA6 8HL, off the B5153. If arriving from Kingsley, the lane will fork after ¼ mile. Take the L fork. Continue on another ⅔ mile, through Well Wood and then to the river. Washburton is a few yards along the water path. Back in the village, The Red Bull Inn, The Brow, Kingsley, Frodsham, WA6 8AN, cooks up decent food.

53.282313, -2.667597

Moore Nature Reserve, River Mersey

Lakes, ponds and a river lined by numerous paths and bird hides. Takes a few hrs to walk.

➤ **Find** the small car park for Moore Nature Reserve, Lapwing Ln, Warrington, Cheshire, WA4 6XE, right between the Manchester Ship Canal and the River Mersey.

53.370680, -2.646538

Formby Point

**PREMIER INN
LIVERPOOL
CITY CENTRE,
LIVERPOOL,
ALBERT DOCK**

Budget rooms surrounded by docks and river traffic.

East Britannia Building,
Albert Dock, L3 4AD
www.premierinn.com

Festival Park, Liverpool, River Mersey

Oriental gardens and woodland for cycling or walking. Best in summer when the flowers are in bloom. It's a 1-hr walk into the city from here.

➤ **Find** Riverside Drive Car Park, Riverside Dr, Liverpool, L3 4EF. Walk across the road to the waterside. Turn L and walk ¼ mile into the gardens.

53.372500, -2.959586

Brighton le Sands, Crosby Channel

Walk among the 100 Antony Gormley beach statues at low tide ... then watch the sculptures vanish as the water comes in. A magical swim.

➤ **Find** the Crosby Beach car park, Mariners Rd, Liverpool, L23 6SX, looking R across the dunes. The statues are right in front of you.

53.482582, -3.055066

Formby footprints, Formby, Irish Sea

Ephemeral, prehistoric footprints from humans who walked these shores thousands of years ago. They are found sometimes in the silt along a 3-mile stretch of coast from Lifeboat Rd to Gypsy Wood (or Formby Point and the Ribble Estuary). Look roughly 55–110 yards offshore from the dune edge. The prints are a snapshot of people and animals that walked across the mud before their imprints were baked by the sun, and before these in turn were covered in hardened silt. These silt layers are occasionally eroded by the 21st-century tides. The footprints survive for one day only, before the waters return 12 hours later and wipe them out ... forever. Heartbreakingly wonderful, it's enough to bring a grown adult to tears. Footprints have also been found at Ainsdale Beach, near Shore Rd.

➤ **Find** the large car park beside the dunes on Lifeboat Rd Car Park, Formby, Liverpool, L37 2DD.

53.548210, -3.106243

Ainsdale Sands

Formby

1 The Corpse Stone, The Cross Stone, Formby, Irish Sea

An 18in marker stone known as The Godstone is found in St Luke's churchyard. The carved stone features a cross on a stepped platform with a circle on top. The stone's purpose is unknown but it is thought to be at least 1,000 years old. The church sits on the edge of conifer plantations along the dune-lined beach.

➤ **Find** St Luke's Church, 3 St Luke's Church Rd, Formby, Liverpool, L37 2DF.

53.551801, -3.087167

Formby, Irish Sea

Stunning. Pine trees, beach and swimming.

➤ **Find** Formby Beach Car Park, Victoria Rd, Formby, Liverpool, L37 1LJ.

53.576166, -3.096401

Freshfield Dune Heath, Irish Sea

Goldcrests and red squirrels flit around the birch and pine woodland. This is the largest lowland heath in the NW. What makes it so special is its location over tidal dunes. Although once common around the shores, woodland, coast and heath are a rare mix in 21st-century England. Look out for water voles around the Wham Dyke.

➤ **Find** Freshfield Station, Victoria Rd, Formby, Southport, L37 7DD. Montagu Rd runs parallel with the station on its E side. Follow the road ⅓ mile until its ends at the woodland path. Walk on another ¼ mile and turn L over the railway line. This final path leads another 1 mile, all the way over the dunes to the beach. Kissing gates mean no wheelchair access.

53.576550, -3.075551

Morecambe

LANCASHIRE

SWIM and wild camp the Ribble Estuary.

TOUCH a labyrinth carved into rock.

EXPLORE a magical well in a rocky square.

LOOK for rutting roe deer in Freeman's Wood.

KAYAK into the mouth of the River Ribble.

FIND tombs carved into Heysham sandstone.

CLIMB a pine cliff over Jenny Brown's Point, or Lancashire's only sea cliffs.

SMELL the coconut-scented gorse over Barnaby's Sands.

LISTEN to the 'bubbling' call of curlews.

VISIT Sambo's grave.

WALK around Lancaster Castle.

LOOK out for wild orchids at Warton Crag.

THE DOLPHIN INN, PRESTON, RIBBLE ESTUARY/RIVER DOUGLAS

Traditional pies, steaks and casseroles and all-day breakfast on the mouth of the estuary, next to the River Douglas.

Marsh Ln, Preston, PR4 5JY
www.greencrabpubs.co.uk

RIVERSIDE BREAKFAST BAR & COFFEE SHOP, PENWORTHAM, RIVER RIBBLE

Tiny cafe beside the river bridge.

1–3 Leyland Rd, Penwortham, Preston, PR1 9QH
01772 752 762

NEW CONTINENTAL, PRESTON, RIVER RIBBLE

Riverside pub that hosts arts events and performances.

South Meadow Ln, Preston, PR1 8JP
Facebook:
@new.continental

THE BOATHOUSE AT PRESTON MARINA CAFE, PRESTON MARINA

Cafe at Preston Marina. Ice creams, home cooking and baking.

Ashton-on-Ribble, Preston, PR2 2FS
www.prestonmarina.co.uk

Ribble Estuary

Follow the path on to vast sands or kayak for wild camps.

➤ **Find** the car park at the junction of Marine Dr and Marshside Rd, Southport, PR9 9PJ. Facing the sea at low tide, walk 0.8 mile out to the sandbank.

53.678689, -3.001995

Banks Marsh, Ribble Estuary

Explore the mouth of the River Ribble at low tide. Follow the FP from Fiddler's Ferry out to the Marsh via Old Hollow Farm. The Banks Sand are beyond the marshes.

➤ **Find** the bus stop at the junction of Hundred End Ln and Marsh Rd, Southport, PR9 8DZ. With your back to the Hundred End Ln T-junction, turn L into Marsh Rd and then immediately R on to FP after 250 yards. Follow the FP 1 mile to Banks Marsh. At the water, turn L and follow the FP along the sea wall 2¾ miles to Fiddler's Ferry.

53.706684, -2.904328

Longton Sands, River Douglas

Mouth of the River Douglas as it enters the River Ribble.

➤ **Find** All Saints Old Church, at the end of Becconsall Ln, Hesketh Bank, Preston, PR4 6RR, next to Douglas Marine Boatyard. Follow the FP between the R of the church and the L of the boatyard, 2.3 miles along to where the River Douglas meets the River Ribble.

53.733206, -2.861651

Penwortham, River Ribble

Church and ancient camp mound (motte) at a bend in the river. River FPs runs 9 miles (as the crow flies) to the estuary; 16 miles via the River Asland enforced detour. It's a 1-mile walk to Preston centre.

➤ **Find** The Parish Church of St Mary's Church, Church Av, Penwortham, Preston, PR1 0AH. Through the churchyard, next to the car park, find the river FP. Facing the water, turn L and follow the path.

53.755928, -2.722664

Ribble Estuary

CLIFTON ARMS HOTEL, LYTHAM ST ANNES, RIBBLE ESTUARY

 Four-star, upmarket family hotel right on the seafront. 48 en suite bedroom with room service. Afternoon teas and breakfasts. Grass promenade and estuary to the front.

4 West Beach, Lytham St Annes, FY8 5QJ
www.cliftonarms lytham.com

FAIRHAVEN LAKE CAFE, LYTHAM ST ANNES, FAIRHAVEN LAKE

 Right beside the water, with benches over the water.

Inner Prom, Lytham St Annes, FY8 1BD
www.fairhavenlakecafe .co.uk

BEACH CAFE FYLDE, LYTHAM ST ANNES, RIBBLE ESTUARY

 Great-value lunch deals include curries and pies. Chilled, infused coffee, seasonal smoothies and cocktails.

South Prom, Lytham St Annes, FY8 1NW
www.beachcafefylde.co.uk

Lancashire and the England Coast Path

Lytham Windmill Museum, Ribble Estuary

Windmill built on the marshes before the area was drained and tourists arrived. Many interesting and sad stories to discover, including the one about the schoolboy who playfully grabbed a sail (much longer than today), was swept into the air and died from the fall.

➤ **Find** St John the Divine Church, 24A East Beach, Lytham St Annes, FY8 5EX. The museum is opposite.

53.735649, -2.955570

Nut Wood, River Brock

Conifer and broadleaf woodland on inland tidal water known as River Brock and Blay Rook. 3 miles E of St Michael's on Wyre via St Michael's Church (53.862865, -2.819577).

➤ **Find** Light Ash Farm Shop and Cafe beside the River Brock bridge, St Michael's Rd, Bilsborrow, Preston, PR3 0RT. Walk N, with your back to the river, ⅓ mile then turn sharp L down towards the trees and river bridge.

53.862162, -2.787282

Barnaby's Sands & Burrows Marsh Nature Reserve, River Wyre

Wigeon, pink-footed geese and peregrines on saltmarsh and mudflat. Many coastal wildflowers in spring, including purple sea lavender and lilac sea aster. Smell the coconut-scented gorse.

➤ **Find** the bend in the road at the junction of Brown's Ln and Corcas Ln, Poulton-le-Fylde, FY6 0JG. Follow the FP N 2.1 miles all the way to Knott End-on-Sea along the River Wyre. Alternatively find Knott End Car Park, Wayside, Knott End-on-Sea, Poulton-le-Fylde, FY6 0EA, and walk back S the other way.

53.906963, -2.990883

Lane Ends, Morecambe Bay

Wooded area by the shore with views over Morecambe Bay. Park on the sea wall and walk in either direction. It's 3½ miles W to Knott End-on-Sea for a cuppa.

➤ **Find** park and lagoons next to the car park in Backsands Ln, Preston, PR3 6AU, off the A588.

53.937887, -2.894898

Meldham Wood, Lancaster, River Lune

Pine and broadleaf wood on sandy foreshore. FP between Glasson to S, and Lancaster, 4 miles N.

➤ **Find** Cafe D' Lune in Corricks Ln, Lancaster, LA2 0AN, beside the River Lune and creek bridge. There is a public car park a few yards N of the cafe. Facing the river, turn R on to the path and walk nearly 1 mile to the wooded shore.

54.009026, -2.831020

Morecombe

KNOTT END CAFE, KNOTT END-ON-SEA, RIVER WYRE

Family-run business since 1946, on the waterfront. Home-cooked food made from local produce.

3 Ramsay Ct, Knott End-on-Sea, Poulton-le-Fylde, FY6 0EA
www.knottendcafe.co.uk

THE BOURNE ARMS PUBLIC HOUSE, KNOTT END-ON-SEA, RIVER WYRE

Sea view restaurant over Morcambe Bay and the Lake District. Easy access to walk along the River Wyre.

Bourne May Rd, Knott End-on-Sea, Poulton-le-Fylde, FY6 0AB
www.bournearms.co.uk

BANK HOUSE COTTAGE, THURNHAM, RIVER LUNE/ MORECAMBE BAY

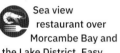

Hot tubs and sea views. Self-catering rooms and caravan rental 110 yards from the coast, looking over Morecambe Bay.

Slack Ln, Thurnham, Lancaster, LA2 0AY
www.bankhousecottage.co.uk

River Lune Estuary

Lancaster Castle, River Lune

12th-century castle overlooking a strategic ford. The Saxon fort was demolished to make way for this Norman castle, built around 1088. Still used today as a Crown Court and open to guided tours.

➤ **Find** Quay Meadows, 27 St George's Quay, Lancaster, LA1 1RD, beside the river. Facing the water, turn R and walk along the quayside all the way to the new Millennium Bridge. From here, double back on to the FP around the Roman Bath House, Lancaster Priory Church and finally, Lancaster Castle, 2 Castle Park, Lancaster, LA1 1YQ.

54.04981, -2.80562 1

Freeman's Pools, Freeman's Wood

One of the UK's rarest trees stands here: a mature native black poplar. More saplings have now been planted, and are protected from roe deer and otters that sometimes visit. The pools and ponds are home to wedge warblers, reed buntings, oystercatchers and ringed plovers.

➤ **Find** the Lancaster–Glasson cycle path 330 yards before the end of New Quay Rd, Luneside, LA1 5QS. The path turns towards the river away from the road.

54.046582, -2.832310

St Helen's Church, Morecambe, Lune Estuary

Ancient church dating back to 11th century. Beside the Lune Estuary and Chapel Pool. Find the sandstone cross base and shaft in graveyard.

➤ **Find** St Helen's Church, Church Grove, Overton, Morecambe, LA3 3HZ.

54.0112181, -2.8552697

Chapel Pool, Overton, Lune Estuary

Tiny creek that feeds into the vast Lune Estuary. The path from St Helen's Church leads down to the water's edge and the pool. The churchyard contains the war grave of a WWI airman.

➤ **Find** St Helen's Church (see page 225).

54.0112181, -2.8552697

Sambo's Grave, Sunderland Point, Lune Estuary

Historic grave on an isolated, sandy peninsula of the Lune Estuary's N shore. The story goes that Sambo arrived in 1700s from the West Indies as a servant. He died shortly after arriving and was buried in this grave a few yards from the shore.

➤ **Find** the harbour car park, First Tce, Morecambe, LA3 3HR. Facing the water, turn R and follow the river path S. At the end of the houses, turn R into The Lane, up towards Mission Church. Keep walking to the other side to meet the water and then turn L. The grave is 110 yards along the shore.

53.9963107, -2.8827755

 Heysham Nature Reserve, Heysham Docks

An oasis for butterflies, dragonflies and birds near Heysham docks.

➤ **Find** the car park to the reserve off the wooded Money Close Ln, Heysham, Morecambe, LA3 2XA.

54.033459, -2.906861

 Heysham Half Moon Bay

Beach cove between Heysham Point to the N and the Serly naze

➤ **Find** Half Moon Bay Cafe (see left). From the public car park opposite, walk across the road to the beach and bay opposite.

54.039210, -2.907866

 The Barrows, Heysham Half Moon Bay

The only sea cliffs in Lancashire. Woodland, open grassland over sand beach and rock pools.

➤ See Half Moon Bay (above). Find the sea cliffs at the Nern end of the beach and bay.

54.044674, -2.904950

Heysham Labyrinth, Heysham Half Moon Bay

A pre-Roman stone carving of a labyrinth. One of only two in mainland Britain. The other is at Tintagel, Cornwall. Barrows line the ridge of the Heysham Head leading up towards the ruins of St Patrick's Chapel on the N headland from the town. Continues N 1½ miles along the coast to Morecambe Bay. Don't panic, there are teashops.

STONE JETTY CAFE, MORECAMBE BAY

Toasties, coffee and cakes on a jetty out into the bay.

Morecambe, LA4 4NJ
www.inmorecambebay
.co.uk

BAYVIEW CAFE, MORECAMBE BAY

Cafe by the bay next to Happy Mount Park and a huge public car park.

Morecambe, LA4 6AJ

➤ Close to St Patrick's Chapel and St Peter's Church, Heysham. The rock carving is on the foreshore. Follow directions for The Barrows (see opposite) and keep walking N another ⅓ mile.

54.046939, -2.907155

Rock-cut tombs, St Peter's Churchyard, Heysham Half Moon Bay

Two sets of tombs cuts into the sandstone at St Peter's Churchyard, thought to be more than 1,000 years old. Series of straight and body-shaped graves with holes at the top, which may have once held wooden crosses. Bodies were excavated in the 1970s. Also an ancient cross in the churchyard.

➤ See directions for Heysham Labyrinth (above).

54.047070, -2.901659

Hunting Hill, Keer Estuary

Ancient settlement mound over the Keer Estuary where it feeds into Morecambe Bay. Several ancient tracks circle the hill. Good views over Warton Crag.

➤ **Find** the rickety river bridge in Shore Rd, Carnforth, LA5 9HR. Facing the River Keer, turn L on the shore road and walk 1 mile, then turn L on to the FP (at 54.126701, -2.785876). Hunting Hill is ⅓ mile up the FP to the NE.

54.129161, -2.781476

Lancaster

Lancashire Coastal Way

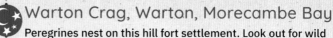 Warton Crag, Warton, Morecambe Bay

Peregrines nest on this hill fort settlement. Look out for wild orchids. Several bridges cross the railway line on to the marshes less than 1 mile away.

➤ **Find** the car park at Warton Crag Local Nature Reserve, Crag Rd, Warton, Carnforth, LA5 9RY. The peak is ⅓ mile N from here.

54.147600, -2.779220

Badger Hole, Warton, Morecambe Bay

Small cave about 65ft up the W face of Warton Crag (see above). Inhabited by humans for thousands of years. Various finds date back before the last ice age, 10,000 years ago.

➤ **Find** access via New Rd from Warton to Silverdale. After passing the caravan park and old lime kiln there is a lay-by on the R. The cave is found by a short but steep scramble up the bank above the lay-by.

54.148846, -2.794860

Dog Holes, Warton, Morecambe Bay

Series of caves, chambers and passages in the limestone rock. Bolton Museum holds various finds, including tools and bones recovered from the caves. The caves are on private land with a gated entrance, so ask for permission.

➤ See Badger Hole (above).

54.150479, -2.792599

Jenny Brown's Point, Morecambe Bay

Views over the estuary and lakes as the sun sets. Walk from Gibraltar Farm.

➤ **Find** where the road forks between Slackwood Ln and New Rd, 330 yards S of Silverdale Station, take New Rd S and follow for 0.6 miles, then turn R on to the lane to a small car park over the railway line. Follow the FP E towards the coast 1 mile.

54.157480, -2.830331

Jack Scout, Morecambe Bay

Mixture of pine and broadleaf forest that falls down to the rocky foreshore and beach just N of Jenny Brown's Point.

➤ **Find** The Silverdale Hotel, Shore Rd, Silverdale, LA5 0TP. Follow the road E towards the water's edge where vehicles park by the beach. Facing the sea at low tide, turn L and walk around the headland to the point 1 mile away.

54.157480, -2.830331

Woodwell

Ancient well that falls from the rock face into a basin, and then into a huge square pool. Trees grow about the place, giving it a magical feel.

➤ **Find** the well 200m N of Jack Scout (see above).

54.158956, -2.828439

Fishermen's cottages at Silverdale

Ravenglass

CUMBRIA

WILD THINGS TO DO
BEFORE YOU DIE:

DANCE round a stone circle on
Birkrigg Common.
WASH tired feet in the natural spa
at Gutterby.
TRACK otters on the River Esk.
EXPLORE the caves at Humphrey
Head Point.
WALK through a kaleidoscope of
butterflies.
ENJOY a flutter on the River Eden
(hundreds of moths here in summer).
LISTEN to the mating call of
natterjack toads.
WATCH England's only nesting black
guillemots.
SWIM the wood shore at White Creek.
LISTEN to Brent geese honking
on Foulney Island.
WATCH Cumbria's grey seals at
South Walney.
WALK where coast (almost) meets
Coniston.
FIND Morecambe Bay's most sacred
island or the puffins at St Bees.
WILD camp the River Duddon.

ARNSIDE INDEPENDENT HOSTEL, CARNFORTH, MORECAMBE BAY

Watch sunsets over the bay from the garden with a warming fire pit.

Oakfield Lodge, Carnforth, Red Hills Rd, Arnside, Carnforth, LA5 0AT
www.arnsideindependent hostel.co.uk

PLANTATION COTTAGE B&B, MILNTHORPE, KENT ESTUARY

Heavy plank doors and oak-beamed bedrooms. Perfect stopover for anyone taking on the famous Cross-Bay Walk; the starting point for the walk is a few mins away.

Milnthorpe, LA7 7JU
www.plantationcottage arnside.co.uk

THE VILLA LEVENS, LEVENS, RIVER KENT

Dog-friendly hotel with 22 bedrooms set in 14 acres between the coast and the lakes.

A590, Levens, LA8 8EA
www.thevillalevens.co.uk

EMMA'S CAFE, GRANGE-OVER-SANDS, MORECAMBE BAY

Shortbread on the shore. Right on the waterside.

Grange-over-Sands, LA11 7DS

White Creek, Morecambe Bay

4 sq miles of pine forest over Morecambe Bay. Walk or swim the shore from Arnside in the N to Silverdale in the S. Get on to Arnside Knot if you want to get above the tree canopy.

➤ **Find** the fork at 59 Red Hills Rd, Arnside, Carnforth, LA5 0AY, and take the R fork in to Knott Ln. Follow the lane 0.4 miles to the car park in the trees. On entering the car park on foot, turn up the hill to Arnside Knott a few yards away for views. Afterwards, drop back down into the car park and follow the FP 1.1 miles down though the park, trying to find the shore at Blackstone Point, circling the caravan park, with views over the estuary. From here, turn R and walk down to White Creek.

54.183799, -2.864105

Humphrey Head, Morecambe Bay

Breathtaking woodland ramp where peregrine nest and bluebells flower. The rock reaches more than a mile out into Morecambe Bay like a natural pier. Fed by freshwater springs, spas and streams. Explore arches and caves at the head point.

➤ **Find** the end of Holy Well Ln, Grange-over-Sands, LA11 7LY, where there is a small car park. Beware the incoming high tides. Fill your boots.

54.158106, -2.932695

Roudsea Tarn, Ulverston Channel

Explore via a series of wooded tracks and river paths. This is Morecambe Bay's NW limit. It's just 5 miles from Windermere, along the River Leven.

➤ **Find** The Ship Inn & Greenodd Brewery, Main St, Greenodd, Ulverston, LA12 7QZ. Facing the pub, turn L down Main St a few yards, then leave the road L by the stone wall and the FP sign. Follow the path L and then R over the A590. Over the road, turn L again at the River Leven and then go across the river bridge. Follow the path 1 mile around the river and into Roudsea Wood.

54.237315, -3.030896

Humphrey

SEA WOOD B&B, ULVERSTON, LEVENS ESTUARY

On the shores of Levens Estuary, with views of Lancashire and Cumbrian Fells. Shore and canal fishing. Secure storage for bicycles.

Seawood, Ulverston, LA12 9EN
www.seawoodbandb.com

THE BAY HORSE HOTEL & RESTAURANT, ULVERSTON, RIVER LEVEN

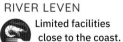

A 17th-century coaching inn where travellers would rest before making the journey by horse coach across the sands to Lancaster. Famous for being the birthplace of Stan Laurel, with many art festivals.

Canal Foot, Ulverston, LA12 9EL
www.thebayhorsehotel
.co.uk

PRIORY VIEW CAMPING & CARAVAN SITE, ULVERSTON, RIVER LEVEN

Limited facilities close to the coast.

Sandhall, Ulverston, LA12 9EQ
Facebook:
@CampPrioryView

Rushland Pool, River Leven

Where woodland estuary meets lakeland fells. The Rutland Valley is within spitting distance of the fells; the shortest distance between Coniston and the coast. Well worth deviating inland for time to take in some of the best views in England.

➤ **Find** The White Hart, Wear Bridge, Bouth, Ulverston, LA12 8JB. Facing the pub, turn L into the main street below and follow it around the R bend into The Causeway. Follow the road ½ mile and just before the river bridge turn R on to the FP along the river. The pool is another 330 yards on. Cross the river bridge to walk along the facing bank all the way past the A590 to the start of the tidal estuary 1 mile away.

54.254456, -3.027870

Beach Wood, Leven Estuary

Best at sunrise. Broadleaf woodland over Morecambe Bay's sandy W shore.

➤ **Find** the end of Cooper Ln, Ulverston, LA12 9RA, past the factory unit. Park next to the shore. Facing the water, turn L and walk N ⅔ mile along the FP or beach to the shoreside wood.

54.171873, -3.059390

Chapel Island, Leven Estuary

A 7-acre wooded island, less than 1 mile from the shore. Over time, it has been a refuge for people caught out by the tide while walking the bay. The island lies roughly on the line of an ancient crossing between Cartmel and Conishead.

➤ Island is closest to the shore from Beach Wood (see above). Seek advice as tides and sands are constantly shifting. At low tide, find The Bay Horse Hotel & Restaurant, Ulverston, LA12 9EL, next to the public car park. There is a greenway from here that leads out on to the Cartmel Sands but it should not be attempted without someone with knowledge or a guide.

54.173706, -3.041066

Sunbrick Stone Circle, Birkrigg Common, Morecambe Bay

Double stone circle on an ancient common surrounded by FPs. Twelve stones inside 20 more. Great views.

➤ **Find** the junction where Coast Rd/A5087 meets Main St, Bardsea, Ulverston, LA12 9QU. There's a waterside car park here that looks out across the sea. Walk into Main St, with the sea to your back. Take the first L and follow the road 250 yards to the fork, then turn L following the road another ⅔ mile as it loops S of Hag Wood and then leads on a straight path up to Birkrigg Common.

54.156555, -3.085196

Chapel Island

St Cuthberts, Ulverston, Morecambe Bay

Peaceful graveyard sloping down to the beach. The 12th-century church has a small leper's hole in the E wall of the chancel. Small car park outside the church with toilet facilities.
➤ **Find** the church on Coast Rd, Aldingham, Ulverston, LA12 9RT, overlooking the sea.

54.1299714, -3.0980504

Foulney Island, Morecambe Bay

Island of pebbles formed by glaciers that 'rolled 'em round' during the last ice age. Terns nest on the island's shingle banks, but it's not a good time to visit. Best at low tide and sunrise. Arrive in autumn when thousands of Brent geese, curlew, dunlin and knot fly in over flowering sea aster. Connected to the mainland by a man-made causeway.
➤ **Find** the Rampside Lighthouse, in Roa Island Rd, Barrow-in-Furness. With your back to the sea, turn L along the Roa Island coast road and follow it to Roa Island, around the sharp bend ⅔ mile to the car park. The causeway is to the L. At low tide only, but take care due to tides and shifting sands.

54.066398, -3.153592

Piel Castle, Barrow-in-Furness, Piel Harbour

Ruins of a 14th-century castle that guarded the harbour. Monks monitored traffic passing through Piel Harbour to Ireland and the Isle of Man before Henry VIII took ownership.
➤ **Find** the Piel Island ferry land station in Pier St, Barrow-in-Furness, LA13 0QQ. Free and open access. There are public toilets a short walk back and a cafe at Bosun's Locker (see left).

54.0626, -3.1733

THE QUEENS ARMS,
BIGGAR VILAGE,
PIEL CHANNEL

Food, drink and
accommodation.

Biggar Village,
Barrow-in-Furness,
LA14 3YG
Facebook:
@TheQueensArmsBiggar

South Walney, Barrow-in-Furness Harbour

The Walney jaw of Barrow-in-Furness Harbour. Actually more gentle claw than jaw. The shingle hook curls around the sands and harbour like a long arm bent at the elbow to protect the only grey seal colony in Cumbria. More than 250 species of bird have been recorded here.

➤ **Find** the lifeguard huts at 1–27 Niobe St, Barrow-in-Furness, LA14 3QP. There is a public car park here. Facing the sea, turn R and walk along the FP to NE Point, overlooking Piel Castle just ½ mile away. Try to visit at all sections of the tide. Walk across on to the other side of the shore for very different views. The beach walk to Walney Lighthouse is beautiful.

54.045252, -3.195601

Roanhead Beach, River Duddon

Sandy beach and dunes, with views up to the Lakeland mountains. Listen to the rare mating call of natterjack toads. Thousands of waterfowl and waders in winter. Good for wild camps. Hawthwaite Ln, Barrow-in-Furness, LA14 4QT.

➤ **Find** the end of Hawthwaite Ln where it meets the dunes at Barrow-in-Furness, LA14 4QT. There is a beachside car park here, literally in the dunes. Walk a few yards for epic views.

54.1714727, -3.2287749

Waberthwaite Cross,
St John's Church, Waberthwaite

This church is a worthy of the diversion. A 1,000-year-old 'cross' is daubed in Viking and early Anglian period art. OK, the top is missing, but the 6ft shaft is impressive, not least for the detail of the bird and animal markings.

➤ **Find** Newbiggin Cottages, Stockbridge, Waberthwaite, Millom, LA19 5YQ. Look for the FP across Whitrow Beck on the N side of the road, and once across the ford, walk ⅔ mile to the church. Explore the ford to the W side of church at low tide but take care.

54.343483, -3.385474

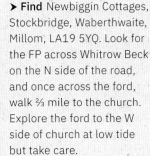

Ulverston

PRINCE OF WALES, FOXFIELD, RIVER DUDDON

Brewery and B&B close to the river.

Inglewood Tce, Foxfield, Cumbria, LA20 6BX
https://princeofwales foxfield.co.uk

THE DOWER HOUSE, DUDDON BRIDGE, RIVER DUDDON

Country house for self-catering or B&B. On an old packhorse inn overlooking the estuary.

High Duddon Cottage, Duddon Bridge, Broughton-in-Furness, LA20 6ET
www.dowerhouse.biz

THE OLD PUMP HOUSE, MILLOM, DUDDON ESTUARY

Cottage that sleeps six on the banks of the Black Beck. At the Nern end of an ancient ford crossing over Duddon Sands.

The Old Pump House, A5093, The Green, Millom, LA18 5JA
www.theoldpumphouse millom.co.uk

HARBOUR LIGHTS CAMPSITE, MILLOM, DUDDON ESTUARY

Camping 50 yards from the beach on the edge of the Lake District.

Moor Moss Ln, Haverigg, Millom, LA18 4NG
www.harbourlights campsite.co.uk

Giants Grave, Millom, Duddon Estuary

Two giant standing stones with sea views.

➤ **Find** the FP next to the railway track where it crosses the A5093, Millom, LA18 5LN. With the rail hut on your R shoulder, cross the railway line and turn L into the tiny lay-by where the path leads 210 yards to the stones. A 1-mile diversion via Kirksanton.

54.218343, -3.326297

River Duddon Estuary

Gutterby Spa, Silecroft Beach

Spa next to freshwater spring on the beach. The well has been used for thousands of years. There were stone circles here, ¼ mile back from the foreshore. They've been destroyed but one can still be seen on Google Earth. Walk N along the beach to the FP at Bog Hole. Follow the path inland a short distance to the small woodland area known as The Mosses.

➤ **Find** the Silecroft Beach Cafe (Silecroft, Millom, LA18 4NY). There is a large car park here. Looking out to sea, turn R and walk 2⅓ miles to Gutterby Banks and the Spa.

54.247155, -3.379435

Haverigg

HINNING HOUSE, RIVER ESK

 Bridging the link between tidal and fresh fells. Set in 12 acres of pasture and woodland with red squirrels, deer and barn owls to look out for.

Hinning House, Birkby Rd, Ravenglass, CA18 1RT
www.hinning-house.co.uk

HARTLEYS BEACH SHOP & TEA ROOMS, ST BEES BEACH

 Wonderful sea views from outside tables. Good place to stop for a food and drink after a cliff top walk.

Beach Rd, Saint Bees, CA27 0ES
Facebook: @hartleysbeachshop

Eskmeals Dunes, River Esk

Otters around the mouth of the River Esk. The dunes and shingle spit are home to more than 300 plant species, including pyramidal orchids. One of the few places in Cumbria to see or hear natterjack toads.

➤ **Find** the bend in Stockbridge Rd where the railway line crosses the S shore of the River Esk Estuary. Where the cars park in the bend, and looking across the water (keeping the railway on your R), walk around the sea path. The path ends after about 110 yards. Keep walking if you dare. This is a danger area, but some do risk it.

54.342258, -3.413584

Muncaster Castle, River Esk

Bluebell woods and history tours. If tours are not your thing, keep walking 7 miles into Miterdale Forest, Caddy Well ... and then another 2 miles to the 660 yards over Wast Water. You'll be ready for a double-poster bed at the B&B on your return.

➤ **Find** Muncaster Church, Ravenglass, CA18 1RJ. Walk through the car park to the Castle 220 yards away. Alternatively, walk 1½ miles through the wooded hills from the River Esk at Ravenglass.

54.354944, -3.384026

Glannoventa, Roman Fort, Ravenglass

Ancient settlement now lost to the sands of time. This natural harbour is formed by the coming together of the three rivers – Irt, Mite and Esk – but it's hazardous to explore even at low tide, by foot or kayak. There is a danger area marked on OS just to the S. The ECP is a bridleway here that trails N and S between Ravenglass and Newbiggin via Esk Ford below. A safer option than venturing on to foreshore.

➤ **Find** Ravenglass Station, Ravenglass, Cumbria, CA18 1SW, and walk S 1½ miles on the ECP to Eskmeals ford. Eskmeals Dunes are W, across the ford at low tide.

54.342222, -3.416659

Grey Croft Stone Circle, Seascale, Irish Sea

Stone circle framed against the power station. Access comes and goes, depending on the landowners and intervention or funding by the relevant government agencies.

➤ **Find** the railway crossing at South Pde, Seascale, CA20 1PZ, and follow the road to the beach, where there's a large public car park. Facing the sea, turn R on to the FP trail between the railway line and the beach. Follow for 1 mile to where a FP turns away from the beach and across the railway line and across Seascape Golf Course. The circle is ⅓ mile further on.

➤ **Access** on S side of FP down to the beach over the railway line between Calder to the N and Seascale to the S.

54.407661, -3.490714

Workington towards Maryport

Whitehaven West Pier Lighthouse, Whitehaven Harbour

A 19th-century lighthouse built into the Old Quay. Wonderful views and walk around the harbour to North Pier on the other side.

➤ **Find** the end of West Strand Rd, Whitehaven, CA28 7LY, where it meets the car park looking over the harbour. Facing the harbour, turn L and walk ¼ mile along the pier to the lighthouse.

54.552739, -3.598490

Lowca Beck, Parton Bay, Whitehaven

This stream once served a Roman fort. Lowca Beck runs into Parton Bay beach, next to St Bridget's Church. Rare plant fossils and coral can be found around the foreshore and cliffs.

➤ **Find** St Bridget's Church Moresby, High Lowca, Whitehaven, CA28 6PJ, off the A595. Facing the church, walk R and walk 330 yards before turning L into Foundry Rd. After another 220 yards, turn R off the road into the open area and keep walking under the railway line and on to the beach next to the beck.

54.57003, -3.58400

Crosscanonby, Allonby Bay

Rabbits love this sheltered wood set back 100 yards from the path. Bluebells and yellow flag iris in spring. A place to take a rest from heat or storm.

➤ **Find** the small car park at Crosscanonby Nature Reserve, Maryport, CA15 6SL, just off the B5300.

54.743073, -3.453894

Senhouse Roman Museum, Maryport, River Ellen

An award-winning museum.

➤ **Find** the museum in Sea Brows, Maryport, CA15 6JD. There's a car park right on the seafront opposite.

54.7213049, -3.4956846

Bowness-on-Solway Village, River Eden

More than 380 species of moth and 20 species of butterfly flutter around this river mouth in summer. Nice place to swim. Marks the end of Hadrian's Wall on the W coast. It's the place to skip across to the E shore, to start walking back to London...
➤ **Find** RSPB Campfield Marsh, off the coast road, Wigton, CA7 5AG. Facing the sea, continue on the coast road ½ mile R. Park on the verge at the nature reserve entrance. Please do not obstruct the farm track through the reserve.

54.943614, -3.241024

King Edward's Monument, Burgh by Sands, Solway Firth

Monument to King Edward I, who died here with his army while waiting to cross the Solway estuary into Dumfries and Galloway.
➤ **Find** the main crossroads in Burgh by Sands, Carlisle, CA5 6AP. Follow the sign towards 'Monument' into The Pack Ln. Follow for ¾ mile, then take the FP/lane L. Just past the lay-by area, take the FP to the R and follow for ½ mile to the monument.

54.938413, -3.053947

St Mary's Church, Rockcliffe, River Eden

Old cross in St Mary's churchyard on the SE that may date back to the 10th century. Lovely views over the River Eden. Rockcliffe Beck is to the N.
➤ **Find** St Mary the Virgin, Rockcliffe off the main road at Rockcliffe, Carlisle, CA6 4AF. There's not much parking.

54.945098, -3.002363

THE KINGS ARMS INN, BOWNESS-ON-SOLWAY, RIVER EDEN

Good food ¼ mile from the waterside.

Bowness-on-Solway, Wigton, CA7 5AF
www.kingsarmsbowness.co.uk

SHORE GATE HOUSE B&B, BOWNESS-ON-SOLWAY, RIVER EDEN

At the end of Hadrian's Wall Walk.

Bowness-on-Solway, Wigton, CA7 5BP
www.shoregatehouse.co.uk

MIDTOWN FARM B&B, EASTON, RIVER EDEN

B&B 500 yards from Hadrian's Wall path and cycleway.

Easton, Kirkbride, Wigton, CA7 5DL
www.midtown-farm.co.uk

HIGHFIELD FARM, BURGH BY SANDS, SOLWAY FIRTH

B&B right on the Hadrian's Wall Walk and the Coast-to-Coast cycle route.

High Field, Boustead Hill, Burgh by Sands, Carlisle, CA5 6AA
www.highfield-holidays.co.uk

Allonby

NORTHUMBERLAND TO HARTLEPOOL

WILD THINGS TO DO BEFORE YOU DIE:

SWIM the cool North Sea waters on the quiet side of Holy Island.

LOOK for red squirrels at Druridge Bay.

FOLLOW the tidal creek over Long Nanny bridge.

EXPLORE Durham's largest caves.

CATCH a ride on a boat to the Farne Islands.

SEARCH for the 'sunken forest' of prehistoric stumps at Druridge Bay.

WALK 2 miles of headland at Dunstanburgh Castle.

EXPLORE Bamburgh Castle.

North Gare Sands over Redcar

River Tweed

Berwick Castle, Berwick-upon-Tweed, River Tweed

Castle ruin on N riverbank. Walk S under the railway line and Berwick Bridges to ancient Fisher's Fort on sand. Views and walks around the harbour are wonderful.
➤ **Find** Berwick Railway St, off Castlegate Rd, Berwick-upon-Tweed, TD15 1NF, and the large car park. Castle is right next door on the other side of the line.

55.7738, -2.0116

High Pool, Berwick-upon-Tweed, River Tweed

Woodland along ½ mile of riverbank E of town. Explore the sandbanks wherever possible.
➤ **Find** the river path in front of the castle ruin. Facing the water, turn R and walk ¾ mile to wooded section of river.

55.772358, -2.031082

Scremerston, Berwick-upon-Tweed, River Tweed

Plant and coral fossils in sandstone. Best where the rocky cliffs give way to pools and golden beaches before Chiswick Sands.
➤ **Find** Cocklawburn Beach and public car parks on the coast road, Berwick-upon-Tweed, TD15 2SY. Facing the sea, walk L back along the road about ½ mile to the bend on the road and then turn R down to the beach. Alternatively, walk along the beach and rocks all the way at low tide.

55.73883, -1.96464

BUDLE FARM CAMPSITE, BUDLE BAY, NORTH SEA

Right beside the sandy bay. Limited facilities.

B1342, Bamburgh, NE69 7AL
01668 214 357

BLACK SWAN INN, SEAHOUSES HARBOUR, NORTH SEA

Overlooking the harbour with sea views. Serves freshly cooked, locally sourced food.

2 Union St, Seahouses, NE68 7RT
www.blackswaninnsea houses.co.uk

The Coves, Holy Island, River Tweed

Swim on the far side of Lindisfarne around the quieter cove and bays.

➤ **Find** Holy Island Car Park, Chare Ends, Holy Island, Berwick-upon-Tweed, TD15 2SE. Walk back on to the main road and turn R. Walk 220 yards around the bend L, then turn R on to the FP. Follow for another mile straight and then bearing R to the bays.

55.684529, -1.786463

Bamburgh Castle, Bamburgh, North Sea

The Vikings destroyed everything on this naze in 993. The Normans rebuilt the castle 70 years later. Open to the public, entrance charges apply. Much like Holy Island, you really need at least two days to take it all in.

➤ **Find** the bend in the road where the B1340 meets Links Rd at the large public car park, Bamburgh, NE69 7BJ. Cross the road to the castle and dunes.

55.608, -1.709

Bowl Hole, Bamburgh, North Sea

Wooded exit and entry to the Bamburgh fortification, linking dunes and coast to mainland. A rare example of what the pre-Neolithic English coast looked like before the introduction of farming.

➤ **Find** 10 Links Rd, Bamburgh, NE69 7AX, and the shoreside car park. Walk over the dunes to the beach. Turn L at the sea and follow the shoreline 0.4 mile before turning inland back over the dunes into the trees.

55.606988, -1.706493

Bamburgh Castle

Annstead Dunes, Beadnell Bay, North Sea

Exmoor ponies graze across 33ft-high dunes. Colony of common lizards on site. The beach is trapped inside a 1-mile-long rocky spit that runs 330 yards offshore. See the Farne Islands on a clear day. Boat trips available (MV Golden Gate–Farne Island Boat Trips, North Sunderland Harbour, Seahouses, NE68 7RN).
➤ **Find** Annstead Farm Camping, Beadnell, Chathill, NE67 5BT. Facing away from the farm, opposite its L edge, take the gate and FP on to the dunes. Between Beadnell and Seahouses on the B1340.

55.567658, -1.644778

Little Rock, Benthall Round Cairn or Benthall Cists, St Ebba's Chapel (alternative name: Ebb's Sneuk; Ebb's Nook), North Sea

A natural pier that blends into the commercial harbour. Prehistoric burials have been uncovered by erosion around the foreshore.
➤ **Find** Beadnell Bay Boat Launch in the car park, Beadnell, Chathill, NE67 5BN. Facing the sea, turn L around the beach and walk 260 yards to the small harbour. Pass the harbour and walk along the sea wall another ¼ mile to the rocky point. The chapel and cairns once stood in the surrounding area.

55.551478, -1.621719

Long Nanny Bridge, Beadnell Bay, North Sea

Beautiful bridge over tidal creeks, one of which, called Long Nanny, twists N.
➤ **Find** the same car park as St Ebba's Chapel (see above), turn R instead of L along the beach and walk 1 mile to the creek. There is an alternative FP through the Beadnell Bay Caravan Park Holiday Cottages.

55.5374146, -1.641574

Dunstanburgh Castle, Embleton, North Sea

Among the largest forts in England. The ruins and their rock defences span almost 2 miles of headland that have been occupied for thousands of years. The entire site can be walked between Craster Harbour and Embleton Bay along the coastal path, or ½ mile inland along the Sustrans cycle path and bridleway. Good for nesting birds.
➤ **Find** the Dunstan Stands beach road, Craster, Alnwick, NE66 3DT. From the end of lane, turn R before the beach and golf course, and follow the path 1 mile to the castle.

55.4911, -1.5932

LINKHOUSE FARM, LOW NEWTON-BY-THE-SEA BEACH, NORTH SEA

 12 cottages, ranging from traditional farm cottages to stone-built and timber lodges. Walk through dunes to the beach of Low Newton-by-the-Sea.

Newton-by-the-Sea, Alnwick, NE66 3DF
www.linkhousefarm.co.uk

THE SHIP INN, ST MARY'S HAVEN, ALNWICK, NORTH SEA

 Locally caught fish, vegetarian food and old-fashioned puddings.

Alnwick, NE66 3EW
www.shipinnnewton.co.uk

JOLLY FISHERMAN INN, CRASTER BEACH, NORTH SEA

Fresh fish catches on the menu, including crab soup.

Haven Hill, Craster, Alnwick, NE66 3TR
www.thejollyfisherman craster.co.uk

THE FISHING BOAT INN, BOULMER, NORTH SEA

Old smugglers' haunt. Now a seaside pub/ restaurant virtually on the beach with panoramic sea views. Also a B&B.

Boulmer Village, Boulmer, Alnwick, NE66 3BP
www.thefishingboatinn
.com

Craster Harbour Wall, Craster, North Sea

Lovely place to sit and watch the tidal traffic. Walk S 1 mile for large sandstone and limestone boulders containing fossils.
> **Find** Howick Hall Gardens entrance at Alnwick, NE66 3LB. Keeping the entrance on your L shoulder, continue R down the lane E until the bend in the road after ⅔ mile. At the lay-by, walk on down to the beach another 275 yards and turn L at the water. Hunt for fossils along a ⅔-mile stretch.

55.45164, -1.58780

Sugar Sands/Howick/Whitefin Spring/ Crow Wood, Craster, North Sea

The oldest Stone Age settlement in England dating to 7,800BC was found here in 2002. More than 18,000 pieces of flint were recovered, as well as charred animal bone, hazelnut shells and red ochre. The site was also occupied into the Bronze Age, reinforcing its status as one of the most important sites in England.
> **Find** the lay-by at Craster Wall, but instead of walking down to the beach, keep walking S ⅔ mile along the greenway FP to the wonderful springs, woods and beach.

55.442599, -1.592949

Up river on the Tyne

THE OLD BOATHOUSE OR THE FISH SHACK, AMBLE HARBOUR, NORTH SEA

Two wonderful waterside eateries run by the same group offering fresh catches and seafood suitably sourced locally. Try a seafood platter.

www.boathousefood group.co.uk

THE DRIFT CAFÉ, CRESSWELL BEACH, NORTH SEA

Popular with cyclists and walkers. Coffees and lunches.

Cresswell, Morpeth, NE61 5LA
www.thedriftcafe.co.uk

BLYTH BOATHOUSE, RIVER BLYTH

Seafood restaurant and port heritage centre. Seafood fresh from the very boats that sail past the venue.

Quay Rd, Blyth, NE24 3PA
www.blythboathouse.co.uk

THE KING'S ARMS, WHITLEY BAY, NORTH SEA

Overlooking the famous Seaton Sluice Harbour. Front grassed area with views all the way to the Cheviots.

Whitley Bay, NE26 4RD
www.thekingsarms
-ne.co.uk

Cambois, S of Alnmouth

Alnmouth Wall Rock, Alnmouth Common, North Sea

The cup-marked stone was found on top of the Alnmouth Wall. There's still debate about whether it is Stone Age art or created by nature. Walk the harbour, the looping River Aln estuary and Alnmouth dunes.

➤ **Find** the coastal road down to Alnmouth Beach, Alnwick, NE66 3NJ. There's a large car park at the end. Walk back up the beach road and look for the FP up and over the wooded hill to the common 330 yards away. The wall is in the top N edge.

55.392415, -1.609756

Warkworth Castle, River Coquet

A medieval castle in the loop of the River Coquet. Walks to the beach and inland.

➤ **Find** Warkworth Castle, Castle Tce, Warkworth, Morpeth, NE65 0UJ, off the A1068.

55.3447, -1.6105

Low Huxley, Druridge Bay, North Sea

Stone-lined burials with cremated human have been uncovered here by mass erosion. Ancient tree stumps can be seen at low tide. Red squirrels in a pine forest (55.313962, -1.552514).

➤ **Find** Hauxley Ln, High Hauxley, Morpeth, NE65 0JW, off the A1068. Coming from the main road, continue along Hauxley Ln ¾ mile until you reach the beachside car park. Facing the sea, walk R 1 mile along the beach or the coast path.

55.309475, -1.554140

Hauxley Haven, Morpeth, North Sea

Look for red squirrels in the pines, over fresh lagoons and dunes. Explore rock pools at low tide.

➤ **Find** the car park at Low Hauxley Beach, Morpeth, NE65 0JS. Facing the sea, turn R and walk S ⅔ mile to the centre.

55.313962, -1.552514

THE VIEW, TYNEMOUTH LONGSANDS, NORTH SEA

At the beach with views towards Cullercoats and Tynemouth. Range of dishes from fish to home-made pizzas. Terrace outside the restaurant fitted with canopies and heaters. Outside beach huts fitted with heat lamps.

Longsands Beach Volleyball League, Grand Pde, North Shields, NE30 4JA
www.theviewtyne mouth.com

Cresswell Foreshore & Pond, North Sea

Five species of crab live in these rock pools. The 'pond' is a brackish lagoon created by a collapsed mine works, and is connected to the sea by Blakemoor Burn.

➤ 1 mile N of Cresswell Village. Find two roadside car parks that lead down to the beach at Morpeth, NE61 5EH. The pond is across the other side of the road, away from the beach.

55.242988, -1.556457

St Mary's Lighthouse, Whitley Bay, North Sea

Tidal causeway over to the island and lighthouse. Watch seals and suck in the sea air. Good for rock pooling.

➤ **Find** loos and parking off The Links, Whitley Bay, NE26 4RS. Walk to St Mary's Island Causeway and the lighthouse.

55.0717259, -1.44968

Tynemouth Castle, Tynemouth, River Tyne

Three kings are buried in this moated castle, within the ruins of the Benedictine priory.

➤ **Find** Tynemouth Sailing Club, on Pier Rd, Tynemouth, North Shields, NE30 4DB. A public car park is next door. Walk 330 yards around the beach and past the sailing club to the priory and castle ruins.

55.0175, -1.418889

Tynemouth

THE MERCHANTS TAVERN, RIVER TYNE

Good place to sit outside for a cuppa overlooking the marina.

1 St Peter's Wharf, Newcastle-upon-Tyne, NE6 1TZ
01912 759 000

TYNE VIEW COTTAGE, RYTON WILLOWS, RIVER TYNE

Cottage overlooking the river.

River Lane, Ryton Willows, NE40 3QF
Facebook: Tyne View Cottage

SHIPWRIGHTS HOTEL & RIVERSIDE PUB, RIVER WEAR

Restaurant and hotel on the banks of the River Wear. The river was once famous for navy ships that press-ganged men into the service.

Ferryboat Ln, Sunderland, SR5 3HW.
www.theshipwrights.co.uk

TONIA'S CAFE, SEAHAM, NORTH SEA

Lunches, ice cream and hot drinks over a vast beach and open space.

Seaham Hall Car Park, North Rd, Seaham, SR7 7AG
Facebook: @Tonias.Seaham

Tynemouth Pier Lighthouse, River Tyne

Huge stone pier extends 900 yards out to sea to protect the harbour. The walkway leads out to the lighthouse.

➤ See directions as for Tynemouth Castle (see page 249).

55.0145911, -1.4027328

Newcastle Castle Keep, River Tyne

William the Conqueror's eldest son built a castle here in 1080 to stop the Scots invading. It was rebuilt in stone by King Henry II around 1175.

➤ **Find** the castle in Castle Garth, Newcastle-upon-Tyne, NE1 1RQ, 110 yards from the tidal River Tyne, 275 yards from the Tyne Bridge and 220 yards from Manors Train Station.

54.9688, -1.6105

Nose's Point, Seaham, North Sea

Caves and prehistoric beach at Nose's Point. Visit at low tide to make the best of exploring the caves. Lovely waterfall (54.821373, -1.322679) a few hundred yards S of the caves.

➤ **Find** the NT car park at Nose's Point Car Park, E Cliff Rd, Seaham, SR7 7PS. The point is 150 yards away on the coast.

54.823251, -1.3230050

Fox Holes Dene, Peterlee, Horden Burn

Best in early or late spring when the valley is carpeted in snowdrops, wild garlic and bluebells. Look for roe deer in the avenue of ash, elm and yew. Listen for the small waterfall where the valley meets the sea. Good shelter in all seasons.

➤ **Find** Easington Colliery Coastal Car Park, Camp St, Easington, Peterlee, SR8 3RB. Walk S to the bottom of the car park and find the trail across the railway line to the shore. Fox Holes Dene is 400 yards further on.

54.784609, -1.310594

Teesmouth, Redcar

PORTALS PLACE, HARTLEPOOL MARINA, NORTH SEA

Mediterranean-inspired restaurant and cafe next to the marina. Steaks, fresh seafood, pasta and vegetarian dishes. Fresh, locally sourced produce.

Neptune House, Slake Tce, Hartlepool, TS24 0YB
www.portalsplace.co.uk

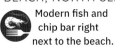

SURFSIDE FISH BAR & RESTAURANT, SEATON CAREW BEACH, NORTH SEA

Modern fish and chip bar right next to the beach.

3 Seaton Reach, Coronation Dr, Hartlepool, TS25 1XN
www.surfsidefish.co.uk

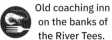

BLUE BELL, STOCKTON-ON-TEES, RIVER TEES

Old coaching inn on the banks of the River Tees.

663 Yarm Rd, Stockton-on-Tees, TS16 0JF
www.bluebellatyarm.co.uk

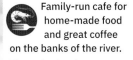

PIER 22, STOCKTON-ON-TEES, RIVER TEES

Family-run cafe for home-made food and great coffee on the banks of the river.

Thornaby, Stockton-on-Tees, TS17 6BN
www.pier22online.co.uk

Blackhall Rocks & Cross Gill, Hartlepool, North Sea

Low-tide caves in the reef-limestone cliffs are the largest in Durham. Kelp forest over the rocky reef is home to cuttlefish, lobsters and sea slugs.

➤ **Find** Blackhall Rocks Picnic Area, off Station Rd, Blackhall Colliery, Hartlepool, TS27 4AR. There is a public car park. Steep steps leading down to the beach. The coastal FP runs along the cliff tops.

➤ South E of Blackhall Rocks. Turn L off the A1086 under a railway bridge to Blackhall Rocks car park.

54.741059, -1.268388

Saltburn, North Sea

Wooded river valley to walk inland to Hazel Grove and Skelton Brook. The Jurassic cliffs at Saltburn Scar yield ammonites and other fossils.

➤ **Find** the Saltburn Valley Gardens, of Saltburn Bank, Saltburn-by-the-Sea, TS12 1NY. There is a large public car park. With your back to the beach, walk S keeping the Skelton Brook on your R shoulder. For the Scar, face the sea and walk R along the coast path for ½ mile or walk down to the beach and do the same to look for fossils.

4.583803, -0.968355

Skelton Beck

Flamborough Head

YORKSHIRE

WILD THINGS TO DO BEFORE YOU DIE:

WATCH minke whale and porpoises around Spurn Head.

WALK the wooded cliffs of Brunswick Bay.

WATCH kittiwakes from the beach at Hunt Cliff.

EXPLORE caves at Thornwick Bay.

QUIETLY sit at Bowesfield Marsh and look for otters.

HIRE a mackerel fishing boat on Staithes Harbour's cobbled streets.

SEE the Milky Way in dazzling clarity over Filey Brigg.

SWIM the 'inner lake' channel protected offshore by the High Scar rocks.

STAND under a waterfall at Beast Cliff.

WATCH puffins and auks over Flamborough Cliffs.

WALK a submerged forest at low tide.

LISTEN to curlews calling from the Humber at dawn.

FIND the church clock with a 13th hour.

THE STRAY CAFE, REDCAR BEACH, NORTH SEA

Nicely set back on the grassy promenade overlooking the sea. Lots of parking.

Coast Rd, Redcar, TS10 3AX

Facebook: @strayette

Bowesfield Marsh & Portrack Marsh, Stockton-on-Tees, North Sea

Otters returned to the Tees marshes in 2004 after a 30-year absence. Sand martins and common terns come back each summer.

➤ **Find** the end of Kingfisher Way, Stockton-on-Tees, TS18 3NB. The river Tees is 220 yards away. Once waterside, turn R to explore the lagoons and marshes around the river loop that brings you almost all the way back.

➤ From the A66, follow signs for Tees Barrage, head straight over the roundabout and R into Whitewater Way. Follow the road to the Talpore. Portrack Marsh is a short walk from Stockton-on-Tees and Middlesbrough.

54.542664, -1.317756 & 54.347, -1.165054

Redcar Beach

Hunt Cliff, Saltburn-by-the-Sea, North Sea

Kittiwakes land here in Feb on the highest cliffs along the E English coast. Watch the nesting kittiwakes, with their black wing tips, from either the beach below or the cliff top. The cliffs are also home to a colony of house martins. Grey seal, harbour porpoise and minke whale can also be seen here.

➤ **Find** access to the cliff top via the Cleveland Way, which leaves Saltburn Seafront next to the Ship Inn, Saltburn Rd, Saltburn-by-the-Sea, TS12 1HF. The cliff face, 1⅓ miles E around the coast path, can also be viewed from the beach. This site is well served by car parks at Saltburn and a well-constructed FP (with steps) runs to the cliff top. Interpretive panels at the Ship Inn describe the area's geological interest and at the top of Hunt Cliff a panel describes the bird life and flora of the area. Further along the coast path are a number of artworks linked to the Heritage Coast. This is the more isolated E side section of Saltburn but there's still beach below until you move further along 1 mile to the rocky cliff itself past Saltburn Scar.

54.584549, -0.962403

Hazelgrove, Saltburn-by-the-Sea

Forage for gooseberries and red currants in the wooded valley that follows the stream Pit Hills Skell into Saltburn beach. Hazel is now relatively scarce, but there is shelter in the overgrowth among pine, ash, sycamore and oak.

➤ **Find** Seafront Car Park, Saltburn-by-the-Sea, TS12 1HH. Walk 600 yards W on the ECP and then turn SW towards the FP and grove.

54.586076, -0.981794

Street House Farm Burial, Saltburn-by-the-Sea, North Sea

Bronze Age barrows have revealed human activity along this stretch of coastline dating back over 5,000 years.

➤ **Find** the Tiger Inn on the A174/Whitby Rd, Easington, Saltburn-by-the-Sea, TS13 4NE. A FP leads down the R side of the pub car park ¾ mile to a road. Turn L on to the road for another 300 yards. Opposite the farm and house on the L, turn R on to the FP (N). The burial was found to the L about 460 yards down this path. The coastal path is another 275 yards on. Turn L for Moss Seat, a well-known birdwatching area.

54.566274, -0.862430 & 54.566274, -0.86243

Staithes Harbour, North Sea

Cobbled streets and beaches that are good for ammonites and other fossils. Boats available for mackerel fishing.

➤ **Find** the car park in Staithes Ln, Staithes, Saltburn-by-the-Sea, TS13 5AD. Walk down ⅓ mile into the village and turn R for the harbour. Ammonites are found on the beach.

54.55992, -0.78462

TIDES, EAST ROW BECK, WHITBY BEACH, NORTH SEA

 Cafe in the perfect position overlooking the beach and river estuary.

E Row Bridge, Whitby, YO21 3SU
www.tidesbeachshop.co.uk

THE FISHERMAN'S WIFE, WHITBY BEACH, NORTH SEA

 Seafood restaurant with sea views over the bay from the Esk Estuary.

Khyber Pass, Whitby, YO21 3PZ
www.thefishermanswife.co.uk

THE DUKE OF YORK, RIVER ESK

 Historic pub with links to shipping and early Christian settlement. Right at the bottom of the 199 steps on to the waterside and pier.

124 Church St, Whitby, YO22 4DE
www.dukeofyork.co.uk

HORNBLOWER LODGE, NR SALTWICK BAY, NORTH SEA

 Cottage for two next to the Cleveland Way FP with views towards Highlights Lighthouse and the cliffs beyond.

Whitby, Hawsker, YO22 4JY
www.hornblowerlodge.co.uk

Densely Dale, Brunswick Bay, North Sea

Broadleaf woodland over a sandy cove. Sea views close to toilets and parking.

➤ Find the end of The Cleveland Way where it meets the sea at Runswick Bay, Saltburn-by-the-Sea, TS13 5HU. There are several car parks here. Continue around the bay R along the wooded beach.

54.53056, -0.74807

Hummersea Cliff, Loftus

Smell pyramidal orchids. The cliffs are home to nesting seabirds. Wooden steps down to the beach.

➤ Find Skinningrove Public Toilets, Beach Rd, Skinningrove, Saltburn-by-the-Sea, TS13 4BT. Walk a few yards N on to the beach FP and then continue 700 yards E to the cliffs.

54.571472, -0.885009

BAY HOTEL, ROBIN HOOD'S BAY, NORTH SEA

 An iconic walking landmark: the hotel marks the end of Alfred Wainwright's 192-mile Coast-to-Coast Walk from St Bees in Cumbria. The bottom bar of the Bay Hotel has been renamed Wainwright's Bar in his memory.

New Rd, Robin Hood's Bay, Whitby, YO22 4SJ
www.bayhotel.info

Kettleness High Cliff, Kettleness

The beach is good for ammonites. Listen to the waterfall and springs. Take great care around beach access and tides and cliffs are hazardous.

➤ **Find** the car park in Cleveland Way, Runswick Bay, Saltburn-by-the-Sea, TS13 5HU, and walk SE on the ECP. Keep going for 1½ miles to the High Cliff and Kettleness Miles.

54.53079, -0.72282

Saltwick Bay, North Sea

Sheltered sandy beach protected by rock on both sides. Best at low tide. Ammonites found along the foreshore or in nodules.

➤ **Find** the fork where Hawkster Ln and Green Ln meet, Whitby, YO22 4EY. There is a car park here. Turn L out of the car park and follow the road for 380 yards, past the ruined abbey, until it meets the Cleveland Way. Turn R on to the Way and walk another 1 mile through the caravan park to the top of the cliffs. There is a cafe in the park.

54.48456, -0.58897

Whitby

THE HAYBURN WYKE INN, SCARBOROUGH, NORTH SEA

An 18th-century coaching inn set in woodland.

Cloughton, Scarborough, YO13 0AU
www.hayburnwykeinn
.co.uk

THE PROMENADE CAFE, NORTH BAY, SCARBOROUGH, NORTH SEA

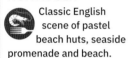

Classic English scene of pastel beach huts, seaside promenade and beach.

Scarborough, YO12 7TN
07866 414 101

The Coomb, Scarborough, North Sea

Seals, sloes and broadleaf trees along a cliff platform over the sea

➤ **Find** St Hilda's Church at the top of Raven Hall Rd, Ravenscar, Scarborough, YO13 0NA. Keep on down the lane to the parking bays at the bottom just before Station Rd. Facing the Raven Hall drive, take the FP to the L. Follow the FP for 330 yards and then keep bearing R towards the cliffs and into and along the top of The Coomb. There are other paths that lead further N towards the cliff edge.

54.404615, -0.489340

Hayburn Wyke, Scarborough, North Sea

Star watch and inhale the warm summer air around one of the most isolated stretches of cliffs along the Yorkshire coast.

➤ **Find** Ravenscar Tearooms, 1 Station Square, Ravenscar, Scarborough, YO13 0LU. Walk 150 yards NE on to the ECP and follow the trail 3 miles SE to the cliffs.

54.35949, -0.44689

Castle Cliff

THE GOLDEN BALL, SCARBOROUGH BEACH, NORTH SEA

Pub right on the harbour. Dog friendly and good value. Open fire in winter.

31 Sandside, Scarborough, YO11 1PG
01723 353 899

North Bay, Scarborough

Beast Cliff, Scarborough, North Sea

Springs, waterfalls and sea views.

➤ See directions for The Coomb (opposite). At Raven Hall, turn R and then L on to the FP for a 2-mile walk to the wooded cliffs.

54.380667, -0.459897

Scarborough Castle, Scarborough, North Sea

Fortified for thousands of years – more lately by the Romans, Saxons and Vikings – to control strategic crossings and approaches. Views across the North Sea, and walks around the castle grounds.

➤ **Find** Scarborough Harbour, 18 West Pier, Scarborough, YO11 1PD. There's a public car park right next door. Facing the sea, walk L around the harbour and up towards the castle ½ mile away.

54.287000, -0.388000

Cornelian Bay, Scarborough, North Sea

Swim the 'inner lake' channel protected offshore by the High Scar rocks.

➤ **Find** Sea Cliff Rd, off Holbeck Hill, Scarborough, YO11 3BJ. At the end of Sea Cliff Rd, next to the car park and facing the sea, turn R on to the Cleveland Way FP. The rocky, wooded bay is 1 mile away.

54.258044, -0.371809

Cayton Bay, Cayton, North Sea

Look for ammonites after high tides and storms. Take care on the path up and down from the beach – it's almost vertical.

➤ **Find** Cayton Bay Beach Car Park, Killerby Cliff, Cayton, Scarborough, YO11 3NR, and walk 400 yards NE to the bay.

54.243913, -0.359221

THE TEA BAR, SHUGA SHAK & THE GALLEY, FILEY BEACH, NORTH SEA

Try the fish and chips followed by a hot chocolate.

Coble Landing, Filey, YO14 9LF
Facebook: The Tea Bar, Shuga Shak & The Gally

GLEN GARDENS CAFE, FILEY BEACH, NORTH SEA

Classical cafe surrounded by trees and greens set back about 150 yards from the beach.

S Cres Rd, Filey, YO14 9JL
Facebook: Glen Gardens

BEACH CAFE, FILEY BEACH, NORTH SEA

Great breakfasts on the coast terrace. Steep road down to the beach.

Sands Rd, Hunmanby Gap, Filey, YO14 9QW
Facebook: Beach Cafe

THE NORTH STAR HOTEL, FLAMBOROUGH CLIFFS, NORTH SEA

Great-value rooms within 330 yards of the cliffs. It's worth checking out some fabulous all-inclusive winter specials.

N Marine Rd, Flamborough, Bridlington, YO15 1BL
www.thenorthstarhotel.co.uk

Filey

Spittals, Filey Brigg, North Sea

Wall of red rock jutting out into the North Sea. Sensational views back of Filey Bay.

> **Find** Filey Brigg Caravan Site, Church Cliff Dr, Filey, YO14 9ET. There is a large pay-and-display car park. Walk to the nearest cliff face and turn R towards the Brigg, ⅔ mile away.

54.214914, -0.264042

Thornwick Bay caves, North Sea

Series of four sets of caves along a ½-mile stretch of sand coves. Explore at low tide but great care needed due to rising tides.

> **Find** the Thornwick Bay Cafe, Flamborough, Bridlington, YO15 1BD. There's a car park next door that leads down to the beach and cliffs a few yards away.

54.131363, -0.113151

Danes Dyke & Naze, Flamborough, North Sea

Yorkshire's largest naze is the best place in England in which to find fossil sponges. The cliff plantation is also awash with wildlife, fresh water, beach and trees. It's only failing is that the cafe kiosk is often closed. There is, however, parking and toilets. Danes Dyke runs 2½ miles over Flamborough Headland, from this Sern point to Cat Nab on the Bempton Cliffs. Great place to explore woodland trails and seashore.

> Parking at the end of a lane off the B1255, at Danes Dyke, Flamborough, Bridlington, YO15 1AA

54.10431, -0.14204

THE SHIP INN, SEWERBY, NORTH SEA

 Village pub less than 220 yards from the cliff edge, overlooking the bay between Bridlington and Flamborough.

Cliff Rd, Sewerby, Bridlington, YO15 1EW
www.shipinnsewerby.co.uk

BELVEDERE CAFE, BRIDLINGTON BAY, NORTH SEA

 Perfect view with seating right over the bay. Donuts, burgers and hot drinks.

Princess Mary Prom, Bridlington, YO15 3LG
Facebook: @Belvedere CafeBridlington

CLIFF TOP CARAVAN PARK, HORNSEA, NORTH SEA

 Easy beach access and incredible views. Tents, motorhomes and caravans right on the cliff edge.

Cliff Rd, Hornsea, Atwick, Driffield, YO25 8DF
www.skirlington.com

FLORAL HALL CAFE, HORNSEA BEACH, NORTH SEA

 Licensed cafe run by volunteers next to the shore. Artwork by local artists on display.

Esplanade, Hornsea, HU18 1NQ
www.floralhall.org.uk

Flamborough

Flamborough Cliffs, North Sea

One of the most important seabird colonies in Europe. Tens of thousands of breeding auks, gannets, gulls and puffins, creating a memorable experience.

➤ **Find** Danes Dyke car park and toilets (see page 260). The lane is on the L ⅔ mile E of Flamborough. A short walk to the beach. There are also excellent walks through the wood near the car park and even picnic tables.

54.10431, -0.14204

Mappleton Beach, North Sea

A 25-mile beach running from Hornsea to Spurn Head, littered in seclusion and fossils. Great for wild camping.

➤ **Find** The Old Post Office Tea Rooms in 2 Cliff Ln, Mappleton, Hornsea, HU18 1XX. Follow Cliff Ln to the beach, where there is a public car park. Many fossils to be found, but as this is an old MoD site, be careful.

53.87571, -0.13378

Noah's Wood (Submarine Forest), Withernsea, North Sea

Submerged forests were once thought to be remnants of the biblical flood. This one near Withernsea still goes by the name of the lead biblical character in that particular tale. Sometimes seen at low tide.

➤ **Find** parking along North Prom, Withernsea, HU19 2DW, with easy access by steps on to the beach.

53.732989, 0.035905

Spurn Head

HUMBER TAVERN, RIVER HUMBER

Waterside Tce.
70 Main St, Paull,
Hull, HU12 8AL
www.humbertavern.co.uk

HOPE & ANCHOR, GOOLE, RIVER OUSE

Freehouse on the banks of the tidal River Ouse.

Main St, Goole, DN14 7YW
www.hopeandanchor
blacktoft.co.uk

RUSHOLME GRANGE HOLIDAY COTTAGE, DRAX, RIVER OUSE

Farm cottage on banks of the River Ouse. Working farm with horses and pigs.

Rusholme Ln, Drax,
YO8 8PW
www.rusholmegrange.co.uk

Spurn Head, River Humber

Harbour porpoise and minke whale swim here. Look out for startled flocks of waders over the skies when merlins and peregrines are hunting.

➤ **Find** Spurn Discovery Centre, Spurn Rd, Kilnsea, HU12 0UH. There is parking all along the strip. From here, walk out to the beaches and Spurn Head.

53.611436, 0.143460

Welwick Saltmarsh, Humber Estuary

Thousands of birds feed here, including hundreds of curve-billed curlews on the edge of the salt marsh. Look out for purple sea lavender and aster flowers in summer.

➤ **Find** the end of Humber Side Ln, where it meets the waterside at Hull, HU12 0QT. You have arrived.

53.651293, 0.022913

St Johns Church, Acaster Malbis, River Ouse

Acaster's beautiful waterside church is at the end of an 8-mile walk along the river path (via Bishopthorpe) out of York city centre.

➤ **Find** The Ship Inn. From the large car park, and facing the river, walk R along the FP 3½ miles to the waterside church.

53.8613622, -1.1284281

Beacon Lagoons, Easington

Winter roost for thousands of waders. Time your visit for high tide to see huge flocks of plover, knot, dunlin and sanderling that shelter in the grassy islands between the fresh and salt pools.

➤ **Find** the small car park on Easington Rd, Sandy Beaches, Hull, HU12 0UH. Walk 1 mile N to the pools and lagoons.

53.634521, 0.132051

JEMMY HIRST AT THE ROSE & CROWN, RAWCLIFFE, RIVER AIRE

Hand-pulled ales from independent Yorkshire breweries, on the river.

26 Riverside, Rawcliffe, Goole, DN14 8RN
www.jemmyhirst
.freeservers.com

THE PERCY ARMS, AIRMYN, RIVER AIRE

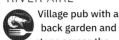
Village pub with a back garden and steps across the road up to the riverbank.

89 High St, Airmyn, Goole, DN14 8LD
www.thepercyarms
airmyn.co.uk

HALF MOON INN, REEDNESS, RIVER OUSE

Rooms, pub and restaurant on the S bank of the River Ouse.

Main St, Reedness, Goole, DN14 8ET
www.halfmoonreedness
.co.uk

BLACK HORSE HOTEL, DUTCH RIVER

A waterside pub and hotel wedged between the marina, canal and river. Great value.

Station Rd, Rawcliffe Bridge, Goole, DN14 8PU
www.review.anecu.com/
black-horse-hotel/

All Saints Church & Cawood Castle, River Ouse

An important church at an important tidal crossing. Known today as Cawood, the nearby ford was part of a prehistoric trade route that linked Scandinavia to Ireland. Cawood Castle came a little later, and is famous for the 'Great Feast of Cawood' in 1465. The local pub has more, but records show diners consumed some 104 oxen, 6 wild bulls, 1,500 chickens, swans and peacocks and … 25,000 gallons of wine. The castle grounds are free to walk in, off Thorpe Ln, a 15-min walk from the church.
➤ **Find** the B1222 bridge across the River Ouse next to The Ferry Inn. Facing the river next to the pub, turn R into Old Rd, and turn L along the river and the Water's Row FP. At the end of the FP, turn L into Church Rd. The church is 165 yards on the L. For the castle, retrace your steps and turn L at Old Rd after the FP and then R into Thrope Ln. The castle is a few yards up on the lane.

53.8333449, -1.1236983

St John's Chapel, Temple Hirst, River Aire

Tiny chapel next to the river and some open ground. May be possible to launch a kayak here with permission from the landowner to the L of the chapel.
➤ **Find** The Sloop Inn pub and campsite beside the River Aire, in Temple Hirst, Selby, YO8 8QN. Facing the pub, walk R 350m to the church.

53.7178613, -1.0847272

The Parish Church of St Mary Magdalene, Whitgift, River Ouse

Riverside church with a famous clock. Instead of 12, it shows 13 in Roman numerals (XIII). Somewhere to launch a kayak into the River Ouse on the flood tide.
➤ **Find** the church in Main St, Goole, DN14 8HQ. There is no parking for miles.

53.6944505, -0.7764791

Humber Bridge

Gibraltar Point

LINCOLNSHIRE

SWIM the sandy secluded waters of Huttoft Beach.

WILD camp around the dunes and woodland at Mablethorpe and Sutton.

FORAGE for samphire and sea purslane around Frampton Marshes on the edge of The Wash.

STAND on the Greenwich Meridian Line where longitude 0'0'0' passes through the UK.

WATCH seal pups from a viewing gallery over the Donna Nook sand dunes.

WAVE beside the Pilgrim Fathers Memorial – the place where the Founding Fathers of America are supposed to have set off on their voyage to colonise the New World.

WALK 2 miles along the Haven to Black Buoy Sands, to meet the tidal Wash and the edge of nowhere.

THE FERRY BOAT BAR AND KITCHEN, WEST BUTTERWICK, RIVER TRENT

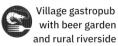 Village gastropub with beer garden and rural riverside views from the decking.

9 South St, West Butterwick, Scunthorpe, DN17 3JT
Facebook: @theferryboatbarandkitchen

THE WATERFRONT INN, DONCASTER, RIVER TRENT

Waterfront glamping pods right next to the pub, or rooms inside. Linked with the Chesterfield Canal, River Trent and River Idle. Bar meals and Sunday carveries. Teas and cakes in the canal-side tearoom.

Canal Ln, Doncaster, DN10 4ET
Facebook: @thewaterfrontWS

The Parish Church of St Oswald, Althorpe, River Trent

Church at the end of the inland river path. The 40-mile track from Newark towards the Trent Estuary ends at a FP to accommodate a railway bridge and the A18. It rejoins 1 mile later.

➤ **Find** Church Ln where it meets Main St, in Keadby, Althorpe, Scunthorpe, DN17 3HX

53.576531, -0.740607

Waterfront Harbour & Church, West Stockwith, River Trent

Like a Spaghetti Junction for waterways. Where the Chesterfield Canal, River Trent and River Idle all meet. Food and drink at The Waterfront Inn (see left). Pods for £40 a day, with dogs.

➤ **Find** The White Hart Inn (Main St, West Stockwith, Doncaster, DN10 4EY), St Mary the Blessed Virgin, and river car park.

53.442562, -0.818974

West Burton, Retford, River Trent

As far as it's possible to get from the coast without ever leaving it. Walk into the pine and broadleaf woodland on the FP that circles out from the river.

➤ **Find** Bole Church in East St, Retford, DN22 9EW. Facing the church, turn R down East St and walk ⅓ mile across the railway line and into the woodland. Through the wood crescent, follow the FP as it curves clockwise around 0.9 miles to the river. Turn L for the River Humber ... a modest 40 miles away.

53.370540, -0.791679

River Trent, Barrow upon Humber

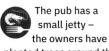

Beach Huts at Sutton on Sea

Spring Head, Sutton-on-Trent, River Trent

River walk down from the church.

➤ **Find** Beck & Trent, Church St, Sutton-on-Trent, Newark, NG23 6PD. Facing the church, turn L along Church St and walk 110 yards bearing R into Ingram Ln. The river FP is 55 yards on the R. Walk 765 yards to the river. Turn R and walk ⅔ mile to the river bend known as Spring Head.

53.180481, -0.795623

Cromwell Lock, Newark, River Trent

End of the tidal Trent. Cromwell Weir and locks are the first major restriction to river traffic arriving from the Humber Estuary. The tidal range here is negligible. It's unique in the sense that so few English rivers have been left open to the tide.

➤ **Find** St Giles Church, Great North Rd, Newark, NG23 6JE. Facing the church, turn R along the road and then first L into Church Ln. Follow the road 330 yards across the A1 bridge. Turn R over the bridge and keep walking along the FP another 985 yards to the River Trent. The lock and weir are to the L.

53.1417475, -0.7929042

Girton Lake, Newark, River Trent

Boating lake next to the river. A dead-straight green lane pierces the site N to S from Clifton Hill to Girton, tapering back to the river path at each end.

➤ **Find** the Trent Ln turning off the A1133, Newark, NG23 7JA, 4.6 miles S of Newton-on-Trent. Follow Trent Ln all the way along Girton Lake, to where it ends at the River Trent.

53.1943905, -0.7804435

St Peter's Church, Gainsborough, River Trent

Set just back from the FP close to a bend in the river. An earthquake in 2008 brought the steeple crashing down on to the altar. It's since been restored.

➤ **Find** The Ferry House pub (see left). Facing the river, walk L 260 yards to the church. There's a bench up on the sea wall for river views.

53.441513, -0.816692

The Cliff, Burton-upon-Stather, River Trent

Broadleaf wood that is threaded like a necklace along a uniquely straight 5-mile, N–S bridleway with churches at its two ends and centre: Alkborough in the N, Burton-upon-Stather in the middle and Fluxborough in the S. The Cliff is arguably the jewel in the necklace as its canopy hugs the riverbank.

➤ **Find** the dead-end lane at the 90-degree bend off Walcot Rd, Burton-upon-Stather, Scunthorpe, DN15 9HW. Picnic area and car park at the end. Entering the wood, take the R bridleway. The cliff woodland area is 650 yards to the N. The other bridleway from the car park leads down to the riverside through the campsite. The Ferry House Inn (see page 267) by the river is lovely.

53.663220, -0.688216

Julian's Bower Turf Maze, Alkborough, Rivers Trent, Ouse and Humber

One of the best views in England, where three rivers meet.
➤ **Find** St John The Baptist Church, Church View, Alkborough, Scunthorpe, DN15 9JF. Facing the church, turn R along Church Side and keep walking straight 200 yards until the brown sign marked 'Julian's Bower'. The maze is 88 yards from the road.

53.685254, -0.669015

Julian's Bower (maze) at Alkborough

South Ferriby Cliff, Barton-upon-Humber, River Humber

Find ammonites and other fossils along a wooded shore. Disused quarries are usually off-limits, but this one is accessible as it is eroded by the River Humber.

➤ **Find** the 90-degree bend in Far Ings Rd, Barton-upon-Humber, DN18 5RG, and take the dead-end lane down to the river. From the small car park and with your back to the water, walk back up the lane and follow Far Ings Rd R past the farm building and on to the coastal FP. Walk for ⅔ mile to the cliff and beach, 2 miles E of Humber Bridge.

53.686502, -0.493574

HUMBER BRIDGE COUNTRY HOTEL (FORMERLY REEDS HOTEL), BARTON-UPON-HUMBER, RIVER HUMBER

 Lakeside dining rooms next to the Humber Bridge on the S bank of the River Humber.

Far Ings Rd, Barton-upon-Humber, DN18 5RG
www.hbcountryhotel.com

HAVEN INN, BARROW-UPON-HUMBER, RIVER HUMBER

 Great-value rooms and food. Built in 1730 as a coaching inn for travellers using the nearby ferry. A dog-friendly hotel for long walks along the Humber.

Ferry Rd, Barrow-upon-Humber, DN19 7EX
www.thehaveninn.co.uk

Far Ings National Nature Reserve, Barton-upon-Humber, River Humber

Listen for the boom of bitterns from March. Watch swifts and swallows over the flooded clay pits in summer. The Humber bank clay waters are remnants of the old brick industry.

> **Find** Chowder Ness View Point Car Park, Far Ings Rd, Barton-upon-Humber, DN18 5RG. Walk E on the ECP and 1 mile to the Visitor Centre.

53.692770, -0.470375

Fairfield Pit, Barton-upon-Humber, River Humber

Favourite feeding site for curlews. No direct access to the four flooded clay pits, but the path runs right around the top along the Humber bank.

> **Find** the small car park next to the Old Boathouse, Waterside Rd, Barton-upon-Humber, DN18 5BD, and walk E 3 miles on the ECP over one FB.

53.703969, -0.365436

Killingholme Haven Pits, North Killingholme, River Humber

Flooded clay pits from which to watch spoonbills, avocets and egrets.

> **Find** the first flooded pit in Haven Rd, opposite Clough Ln, North Killingholme, DN40 3JP. Facing the water, continue L down Haven Rd towards around the pits and along the Humber Coast Path.

53.662614, -0.238389

Grimsby Dock Tower, Grimsby, River Humber

What was once the world's largest fishing port ... until it crashed on the rocks of time and competition. The Tower is usually closed to the public, but is still worth a visit and a photo. Walk along the working water that is River Freshney, on Alexandra Dock.

> **Find** New Clee Station, Thorold St, Grimsby, DN31 3SG, and walk ⅔ mile N to the tower.

53.58310, -0.07030

Tetney Marshes, Grimsby

Good for crabbing on inland waters or walking across vast sand flats. Beware sinking sand and mud. Walk 1½ miles S to Tetney Haven's tidal creek and FP between Tetney Lock and Stonebridge Farm via Louth Canal.

> **Find** the small car park on 1st Main Rd, Humberston, Grimsby DN36 4HE, and walk S to the marshes.

53.524469, 0.017495

THE SEAL SANCTUARY WILDLIFE CENTRE, MABLETHORPE BEACH, NORTH SEA

Family-run sanctuary that has been looking after seals since the 1970s.

Quebec Rd, North End, Mablethorpe, LN12 1QG
www.thesealsanctuary.com

SNACK SHACK, MABLETHORPE BEACH, NORTH SEA

Great-value cafe right by the beach and dunes, with tables outside.

North Prom, Mablethorpe, LN12 1EP
07833 914 043

MILLBROOK CAMPSITE, SUTTON ON SEA, NORTH SEA

Short walk to the beach, ⅔ mile away. Limited facilities, but clean.

Millbrook Huttoft Rd, Sutton on Sea, Mablethorpe, LN12 2RU
01507 442 084

ADMIRAL BENBOW, CHAPEL BEACH, THE WASH

This beachside pub, built with reclaimed wood from the breakwaters and groynes, was named after the inn from *Treasure Island*.

Promenade, Skegness, PE24 5BQ
www.admiralbenbowbeachbar.co.uk

Mablethorpe

🔟 Greenwich Meridian Line, Humberston, River Humber

Where longitude 0'0'0' passes through UK. Good place to visit if you are interested in map reading, geography and related things.

> **Find** the waterside car park at 4 Meridian Rd, Humberston, Cleethorpes, DN35 0AR. Facing the water, the line is several yards to the L ... depending on the accuracy of your GPS and your position by the water. Facing the water, turn R and walk 1¼ miles on the sands at low tide to see the wading birds at Tetney Marshes.

53.541645, -0.001820

Donna Nook National Nature Reserve, Louth, North Sea

Breeding colony of grey seals arrive in November and December, with more than 1,300 pups born annually. There's a viewing area at the foot of the sand dunes. Britain has about 40 per cent of the world's population of grey seals and its river is becoming an increasingly important habitat.

> **Find** the end of Marsh Ln, Donna Nook, Louth, LN11 7PD. MoD site. No entry when red flags are flying, although most of the dune area is accessible at all times.

53.475726, 0.141134

Rimac Nature Reserve, Louth, North Sea

Sea breezes and great views from the top of the dunes.

> **Find** the dead-end lane at Saltfleetby, Louth, LN11 7TS, off the A1031, 0.87 miles from Saltfleetby All Saints. Vast beaches to explore.

53.401741, 0.208088

Mablethorpe & Sutton on Sea, North Sea

Dunes and trees down to the sand and sea.

> **Find** Sea Ln (LN12 1NN) off the A1031, 2.6 miles N of Mablethorpe. Take the first R on Sea Ln into Crook Bank. After another ⅔ mile, at a sharp loop, turn L. The beach and dunes are another 765 yards on. There are several car parks.

53.282450, 0.31062

Huttoft Beach, Alford, North Sea

Sandy secluded beach.

➤ **Find** the dead-end lane to the beach, next to the golf course. The lane joins with Huttoft Bank Rd and Sea Ln, Alford, LN13 9RR. Parking by the beach.

53.282450, 0.310624

Anderby Creek, Skegness, The Wash

Sandy stretch of beach. Ammonites and shell fossils can be found in boulders.

➤ **Find** the car park by the beach in Sandy Ln, Skegness, PE24 5XW.

53.25960, 0.32503

Chapel Point

Chapel Point, Chapel St Leonards, The Wash

Little terns dive around in the shallows just ½ mile N of the point. Dunes, sandbanks and creeks to explore at low tide. Walk here from Skegness on the beach path.

➤ **Find** The Observatory on the beach, off St Leonards Dr, Chapel St Leonards, Skegness, PE24 5XA. There is a large public car park right next door.

53.233470, 0.339703

Gibraltar Point, Skegness, The Wash

Little terns dive around in the shallows. Unique combination of dunes, sandbanks and walks. Lots of creeks to explore at low tide. Walk here from Skegness along beach paths.

➤ **Find** Gibraltar Point Visitors Centre (see left). There's a large car park just before it. Keeping your back to the road, exit the car park on foot via the top R corner FP and walk over the marshes and dunes to the sands. Turn L while facing the sea and walk ½ mile along the path to reach some of the best views.

53.100442, 0.337090

Gibraltar Point

The Inner Trial Bank mound

 Pilgrim Fathers Memorial, Boston, The Wash

Next to a creek known as The Haven. Walks and wildlife abound. Where the Pilgrim Fathers are said to have set off on their voyage to the so-called 'New World', via mainland Europe.

➤ **Find** the Scalp Rd turning (signposted 'Pilgrim Fathers Memorial'). Just S of Fishtoft village, on Gaysfield Rd, Boston, PE21 0SF. Follow the road 1.2 miles all the way to the riverside car park. The memorial is 110 yards away.

52.941944, 0.023611

Clay Hole, Boston, The Wash

Possibly one of the most isolated places on the entire coast path – overlooking The Wash.

➤ See Pilgrim Fathers Memorial above, but turn L at Gulch Creek. Walk ⅔ mile to Haven marshes, where there is a FP on the R. It's possible to walk 2 miles along this path on the side of the Haven all the way to Black Buoy Sands! Much care needed as these marshes and creeks fill quickly with incoming tides.

52.931791, 0.077459

Frampton Marshes, Boston, The Wash

Hen harriers and merlins hunt over this part of The Wash. Defined by large creeks, one of which was the old course of the River Withal – and wild flowers, including sea lavender, sea aster and sea purslane. Lots of redshanks, oystercatchers and skylarks. South Lincolnshire Wildfowlers' Club patrol and manage the site.

➤ **Find** the 90-degree bend in Frampton Rd and turn into Wyberton Rd at Boston, PE20 1AY. Follow the dead-end road ⅔ mile where there is parking on the R before the road meets the marshes at Gulch Creek. From the water's edge, turn R and walk on 720 yards to a sharp bend in the sea wall. Much care needed as these marshes and creeks fill quickly with incoming tides.

52.916984, 0.012380

CHURCH KEYS WINE BAR & RESTAURANT, BOSTON, RIVER WITHAM

 Breakfasts, light lunches, afternoon teas and more. Said to be haunted. Murder mystery nights are a killer.

28–30 Church St, Boston, PE21 6NW
www.churchkeys.co.uk

THE SHIP INN, SURFLEET, RIVER GLEN, RIVER WELLAND

Traditional English dishes made from locally sourced produce and ingredients riverside. Rooms for B&B.

154 Reservoir Rd, Surfleet, Spalding, PE11 4DH
www.myshipinn.com

TRAVELODGE SPALDING, SPALDING, RIVER WELLAND

Budget accommodation 11 miles from The Wash along the river.

Springfields Outlet Centre, Camel Gate, Spalding, PE12 6EU
www.travelodge.co.uk

THE SHIP INN, FOSDYKE BRIDGE, RIVER WELLAND

 Pub beside the river bridge. Good walks from here.

Main Rd (A17), Fosdyke, Boston, PE12 6LH
Facebook: @theshipinnfosdykebridge

Wyberton Marsh, Boston

This can feel like the very edge of the world when the sun falls
behind a cloud and a winter wind whips over these marshes.
Wear good clothing, and walk 3 miles along the river out of
Boston to see hen harriers.

➤ **Find** the small car park at RSPB Frampton Marsh, Roads
Farmhouse, Frampton Roads, Boston, PE20 1AY. Walk 1 mile S
and then E to marsh and coast.

52.933754, 0.029464

Moulton Marsh, River Welland

Broadleaf woodland scrub and lake beside the River Welland.
Lagoons, creeks and salt marsh.

➤ **Find** where the A17 crosses the River Welland, keep the Ship
Inn pub (see page 272) on your L shoulder and continue another
⅓ mile before turning L into Middle Marsh Rd. Continue straight
for another 1¾ miles and at the bend in the road turn L down the
dead-end lane to the edge of the River Welland. There is a small
park here to explore next to a car park (Moulton, Spalding, PE12
6LL). Walk R if looking at the river for the two large lagoons with
islands. Keep walking 9 miles to Spalding. The walk to the R leads
22 miles around The Wash and along the River Nene to Wisbech.

52.881514, -0.014059

West Nene Lighthouse, Sutton Bridge, River Nene

Built in the early 19th century. It's tall, fat and white.

➤ **Find** the 90-degree bend in West Banks Rd, Sutton Bridge,
Spalding, PE12 9QJ. The lighthouse is in front of you.

52.8087404, 0.2110644

The Wash

NORFOLK

WILD THINGS TO DO BEFORE YOU DIE:

HIRE a boat to explore Scolt Head sands.

SWIM between the sun-kissed dunes of the River Burn.

WATCH osprey fish on Alderfen Broad.

INHALE the salt spit off Blakeney Point after a hike in winter hail.

EXPLORE Waveney Forest's river path.

CLIMB the 112 steps of Happisburgh Lighthouse.

FLOAT on your back at high tide at Holme beach.

TOUCH the carved wolf that sits outside Hunstanton Chapel.

LISTEN to the goosey calls of cranes over Hickling Broad.

VISIT Seahenges I and II in a single day.

BIVVIE on Barton Broad to catch a glimpse of otters.

Happisburgh

JENYNS ARMS, DENVER, RIVER OUSE

A 19th-century public house set on the riverbank.

6 Sluice Rd, Denver,
Downham Market,
PE38 0EQ
www.jenynsarms.com

HEAD FEN COUNTRY RETREAT, LITTLE DOWNHAM

Lodges overlooking the private fishing lake, with a view of Ely Cathedral.

Head Fen Drove, Little
Downham, Ely, CB6 2EP
www.headfencountry
retreat.co.uk

THREE PICKERELS, MEPAL, NEW BEDFORD RIVER

A family-run pub, overlooking the river. Rooms with river views, too.

19 Bridge Rd, Mepal,
Ely, CB6 2AR
www.thethreepickerels
.co.uk

PINECONES CAMPING, KING'S LYNN, RIVER GREAT OUSE

Tents and motorhomes less than 2 miles from the coast.

A149 Dersingham by-
pass, King's Lynn,
PE31 6WL
www.pineconescc.co.uk

New Bedford River, Denver

Lock and launch point 3 miles S of Downham Market. Walk the river and canal FP on either side.

➤ **Find** Great Ouse Marathon boating area, 6 Sluice Rd, Denver, Downham Market, PE38 0EQ. There's a car park here.

52.5636229, 0.3175984

New Bedford River, Ely

Launch and access to the tide.

➤ **Find** the bridge at Bridge Rd, Ely, CB6 2AT. Parking by the river.

52.410937, 0.1168141

Church Ruin, Watlington, River Great Ouse

One of three churches in the village, this riverside one was 'ruined' after falling into disrepair. The 'ruining' involved removing the roof and windows. No shelter, but an interesting shell to explore.

➤ **Find** the Magdalen Bridge at 207 Station Rd, Watlington, King's Lynn, PE33 0JG. From the car park on the E shore of the river, cross the first river and then just before the next, turn R on to the FP along the bank through the wooden gate. Follow the path 1.2 miles to the ruin. On return, stop for a drink at The Cock Inn, 39 Church Rd, PE34 3DG, on the other side of the river bridge.

52.6934055, 0.3719718

King's Lynn Museum, King's Lynn, River Great Ouse

Seahenge I is here, the Bronze Age timber circle controversially removed from Holme beach. The 4,000-year-old structure was discovered after heavy tides removed some of the silt and mud that had covered it up.

➤ **Find** the museum in Market St, King's Lynn, PE30 1NL.

52.753807, 0.399378

Wolferton Creek, Snettisham, The Wash

Tide and fresh waters meet over the sands of Shepherd's Port.

➤ **Find** the end of Beach Rd, Snettisham, King's Lynn, PE31 7PS. There is a car park here looking on to the sea. Turn R and walk just over ½ mile offshore along the sandbank to the creek at low tide.

52.869875, 0.443818

Statue of a wolf, St Edmunds, Hunstanton Chapel, The Wash

A carved wooden wolf sits near the ruins of the chapel. It marks the spot in legend where King Edmund first landed on these shores before he was killed by Viking invaders. The legend has it that after he was beheaded, a wolf was found nursing the

THE LIGHTHOUSE CAFE, OLD HUNSTANTON BEACH, THE WASH

Fish and chips or a cuppa with sea views, next to a large public car park and cliffs.

Lighthouse Cl, Hunstanton, PE36 6EL
Facebook: @timatthelighthouse

CANDLEFORD AT HOLME BEACH, HOLME-NEXT-THE-SEA, THE WASH

Bungalow backed by sand dunes and a pine forest, which leads to quiet beaches.

Broadwater Rd, Holme-next-the-Sea, Hunstanton, PE36 6LQ
www.holmebeach.co.uk

LITTLE SALTINGS, BRANCASTER STAITHE BEACH, THE WASH

Sleeps eight people in four bedrooms at the end of a track right on the coastal path. Decking overlooks 10 acres of salt marshes from which to watch geese, barn owls and migratory birds.

Broad Ln, King's Lynn, PE31 8AT
www.crabpotcottages.co.uk

---

severed head in nearby woodland. Stunning views from the famous red-and-white cliffs of Hunstanton. The rocks and chalk are full of fossils, including ammonites and sharks' teeth.
➤ **Find** the chapel at Cliff Pde, Hunstanton, PE36 6EJ. Get down on to the beach and cliffs nearby.

52.949125, 0.491539

Hunstanton Cliffs, Hunstanton, The Wash

Norfolk's best geological feature. These red-and-white cliffs are rich in spectacle, and sprinkled with ammonites, shells and sharks' teeth fossils.
➤ **Find** North Promenade Car Park, 2 Cliff Pde, Hunstanton, PE36 6DZ, and walk 100 yards N on the ECP.

52.942249, 0.486305

Holme Dunes, Hunstanton, The Wash

Natterjack toads, butterflies and dragonflies congregate here where The Wash meets the North Sea. In autumn, look for bright orange berries of the sea buckthorn. Good for migrating birds in winter.
➤ **Find** Holme-next-the-Sea Car Park, Beach Rd, Hunstanton, PE36 6LG, and walk 1 mile E on the ECP.

52.974048, 0.551176

Holme-next-the-Sea, The Wash

The original home of Seahenges I and II. Pine and broadleaf woodland over dunes filled by fresh water. It's also a wonderful place to take a swim. One of the two timber circles is still on Holme beach, the other is at King's Lynn Museum. Seahenge II comes and goes depending on the tides.
➤ **Find** the end of Beach Rd at the waterside, Holme-next-the-Sea, Hunstanton, PE36 6LG. There is a car park to the R before the shore. Walk 1.3 miles to the R either along the beach or the coast path. Seahenge II can be found about 275 yards offshore. Keep walking E (R) along the sands and slightly inland to explore the trees, Broad Water lake and the Holme Dunes.

52.977704, 0.548412

Brancaster

THE CRAB HUT, BRANCASTER STAITHE HARBOUR, THE WASH

Beside the harbour, freshly baked baguettes filled with seafood from the owners' boat, which fishes out of Brancaster Staithe. Simon Letzer also has a smokehouse where he smokes locally caught fish and prawns using traditional methods passed on from his father Paul Letzer.

Harbour Way, Brancaster Staithe, King's Lynn, PE31 8BW

www.letzersseafood.co.uk

Gipsy Lane, Brancaster, The Wash

Tree-lined lane between marsh (and dunes) and a sacred cross at St Mary's Church.

➤ **Find** the end of Broad Ln, Brancaster, King's Lynn, PE31 8AX. From the car park, walk away from the beach 365 yards and turn R around the marshes and creeks. Follow the path ⅔ mile to the scrub.

52.966252, 0.626189

Burnham Deepdale, The Wash

Mow Creek, behind the sand dunes of Brancaster Staithe. Surrounded by FPs and Brancaster village. Church at Deepdale.

➤ **Find** St Mary's Church, Main Rd, Burnham Deepdale, PE31 8DD. Facing the church, walk L for 110 yards and then turn R on to the FP towards the beach. Continue on another 220 yards to the waterside and turn L along the FP for a ⅔-mile stroll and creek views all the way to Brancaster Quay. Enjoy seafood at The Crab Hut (see left).

52.966701, 0.685954

Scolt Head, Holkham, North Sea

Seals and seabirds on a low-tide island. Kayak or paddleboard to get there, or hike to the pine woodland arch around the bay and wet sands. Best seen at low tide. Boats to hire at high tide. Even on the busiest summer days these sands are so vast it could accommodate a small nation and there would still be places to hide.

➤ **Find** Lady Anne's Dr, Holkham, Wells-next-the-Sea, NR23 1RG. Parking all the way down to the strip and entrance into the estate. Walk through the trees into a natural wonder. (FP from Turnham Deepdale's St Mary's Church to Scorl Head Island dunes via the marshes.)

52.966701, 0.685954

Holkam, towards Scolt Head Island

Holkham, towards Wells-next-the-Sea

THE BARN, BURNHAM OVERY STAITHE, RIVER BURN

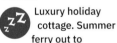
Luxury holiday cottage. Summer ferry out to Scolt Head Island bird sanctuary or a 30-min walk along the coastal FP across the marshes to the sandy deserted beach.

Norfolk Coast Path, King's Lynn, PE31 8JF

WELLS-NEXT-THE-SEA BEACH CAFE, NORTH SEA

Like a beach amphitheatre, with beach views.

Beach Rd, Wells-next-the-Sea, NR23 1DR
Facebook: @wellsbeachcafe

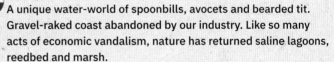

Holkham Gap, Holkham, North Sea

An arch of pine woodland around a vast bay of wet sand. Best seen at low tide. Even on the busiest day in summer, there are still places to hide.

➤ **Find** the large car park at Lady Anne's Dr, Holkham, NR23 1RG, and walk 400 yards N to beach and trees.

52.968691, 0.814486

Cley Marshes, Cley next the Sea

A unique water-world of spoonbills, avocets and bearded tit. Gravel-raked coast abandoned by our industry. Like so many acts of economic vandalism, nature has returned saline lagoons, reedbed and marsh.

➤ **Find** the car park at the Cley Marshes Visitor Centre, Coast Rd, Cley next the Sea, NR25 7SA, and walk N a few yards to the marsh and FP.

52.954035,1.056236

River Burn Estuary

A swim you'll never forget. Dunes, tidal estuary, surf and solitude.

➤ **Find** the coast path next to the public car park in Burnham Overy Staithe, East Harbour Way, King's Lynn, PE31 8JF. Facing the quay, turn R and follow the path 1.4 miles to where the dunes meet the sea. Turn L and walk another ⅔ mile to rejoin the mouth of the River Burn and wilder parts of the beach. Beware currents and tides.

52.9768, 0.75182

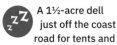

BLUE SKIES CAMPSITE, WELLS-NEXT-THE-SEA, NORTH SEA

💤 A 1½-acre dell just off the coast road for tents and touring caravans.

Stiffkey Rd, Wells-next-the-Sea, NR23 1QB
www.blueskiescampsite.co.uk

THE BLAKENEY HOTEL, BLAKENEY QUAY, NORTH SEA

💤 Quayside with views across the estuary and salt marshes to Blakeney Point. Try the bar terrace for afternoon teas, English breakfasts, light lunches and other menus for residents and non-residents.

The Quay, Blakeney, Holt, NR25 7NE
www.blakeney-hotel.co.uk

High Cape, Wells-next-the-Sea, North Sea

Broadleaf and pine woodland over dunes next to a boating lake and river estuary. Explore the lake and walk inland along Beach Rd and the East Fleet river path to Wells-next-the-Sea and breathtaking views over Wells' marshes.

➤ **Find** the beach at the end of Beach Rd, Wells-next-the-Sea, NR23 1DR. There is a huge car park. Walk to the end of Beach Rd and down the ramp on to the foreshore at low tide. From here, walk L to the pine woodland. If the tide is in, follow the FP L before the beach ramp.

52.974272, 0.842205

Blakeney Eye, River Glaven

Stand over the (buried) remains of Blakeney Chapel that stood on this islet for 200 years. Entirely surrounded by creeks and inlets known collectively as River Glaven. Walk on to Blakeney Point (52.979093, 0.979840). If Holy Island is the focus of human activity, this is nature's equivalent. Claw-shaped spit of sand shaped by tens of thousands of years of battering of immense energy and power into a natural harbour. Visit at low tide on a calm day.

➤ **Find** the end of Beach Rd and walk E along the sand past Cley Channel, The Hood, Longs Hills and Blakeney Point. It's 4 miles to the furthest point – 8 miles there and back. So take care and watch the tides. A 0.4-mile walk is enough to hop over the River Glaven that runs parallel with the shore on to the islet.

52.966021, 1.037482

Salthouse Marshes, from Weybourne

Sheringham

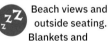

Salthouse Marshes

Explore salt tracks and greenways that link up with the coast path from Cley to Gramborough Hill. Most important greenway trails out of the front door at Salthouse crosses the A149 and leads down to Little Eye pools and dunes.

➤ **Find** the end of Beach Rd, Holt, NR25 7XW. The beach beckons.

52.955649,1.098044

West Runton, North Sea

Fossil hunt around the location of the famous 'West Runton Elephant' find. Mammal and fish remains are common, along with freshwater shells.

➤ **Find** the end of Water Ln, West Runton, Cromer, NR27 9QA. There is a car park here. Walk on to the shore and hunt for fossils to the R and L within 110 yards.

52.94173, 1.25137

RNLI Sheringham Lifeboat Station, Sheringham, North Sea

Learn about the savage seas of this coast by exploring a working lifeboat station and meeting its volunteers. The small shop is sometimes open. Look out for fossils in the chalk. Corals and shark remains have been found at this location.

➤ **Find** Cromer Lifeboat Station, Cromer Pier, The Espl, Cromer, NR27 9HE.

52.933014, 1.301140

Overstrand, North Sea

Chalk is exposed during winter at low tide and is full of fossils. Walk Foulness Beach to Cromer and then back along the cliff tops.

➤ **Find** the car park in 50 Pauls Ln, Overstrand, Cromer, NR27 0PF. Continue on foot down the ramp to the beach and walk ⅓ mile R. If the tide is in and high, walk along the promenade.

52.91666, 1.34769

SHIP INN, MUNDESLEY BEACH, NORTH SEA

 300-year-old pub beside the beach. Locally sourced food, beers and ales. Rooms with a view.

21 Beach Rd, Mundesley, Norfolk, NR11 8BQ
www.mundesley-ship
.co.uk

BEACH COTTAGE, MUNDESLEY, NORTH SEA

 Self-catering holiday cottage, situated by the sea on Mundesley sea front. Sleeps eight people – six in the main house and two in an en suite annex. Child and dog friendly.

13 Beach Rd, Mundesley, Norfolk, NR11 8BG
www.beachcottagenorfolk
.co.uk

SMALLSTICKS CAFE, CART GAP BEACH, NORTH SEA

Family-run cafe offering great home-cooked food from farmland next to the beach.

Cart Gap Rd, Happisburgh, Norfolk, NR12 0QL
www.smallstickscafe.co.uk

Mundesley All Saints Parish Church, Mundesley, North Sea

Beachside church with a rare organ in the corner of the churchyard! The church is also unusual in that it has no spire or tower. Good views.

> **Find** the church in 26 Cromer Rd, Mundesley, Norfolk, NR11 8FE, towering over the beach.

52.880635, 1.431288

Mundesley Beach, Mundesley, North Sea

Look for fossils along the beach. This was once a fossil-rich area because or erosion but, thankfully, sea defences have stopped the rot. Sponges and occasional mammal bones are still found around the N shore of the town.

> **Find** Mundesley Car Park, Sea View Rd, Mundesley, Norwich, NR11 8DQ, and walk 100 yards down to the beach.

52.882224, 1.431101

Mundesley

 # Happisburgh Lighthouse, North Sea

Climb the 112 steps when the lighthouse opens on bank holidays. Happisburgh is most famous for how quickly the coastline is eroding. The upside is the exposure of ancient life. Flint tools and butchered bones have been found on the beach dating back close to 1 millions years. Explore St Mary's Church, 4 Beach Rd, Happisburgh, Norfolk, NR12 0PP, for more (52.828471, 1.529970).

> **Find** what's left of the crumbling Beach Rd. There is still a car park over the beach. It's a wonderful place from which to look back at the lighthouse. Walk down the ramp on to the sands for long low-tide walks.

52.820501, 1.537132

Happisburgh Lighthouse

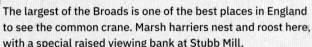 ## St John the Evangelist, Sea Palling, Waxham, North Sea

Church on a beach road at Waxham that dates back to the 12th century, although some parts predate this to the Saxon period around 850. Bike hire and cafe next door.

➤ **Find** Clink Rd Car Park, Sea Palling, Norwich, NR12 0UL, and walk 1⅓ miles S to the church.

52.778462, 1.617363

Barton Broad

Common terns nest on artificial platforms. Look out for otters, kingfishers and herons.

➤ **Find** Barton Broad Boardwalk, off Irstead Rd, Norfolk, NR12 8XR. Especially suitable for wheelchairs.

➤ Also, find the end of Staithe Rd, Norfolk, NR12 8AZ, where there's a small car park riverside.

52.733263, 1.492911

Hickling Broad

The largest of the Broads is one of the best places in England to see the common crane. Marsh harriers nest and roost here, with a special raised viewing bank at Stubb Mill.

➤ **Find** the end of Stubb Rd, Norfolk, NR12 0BW. From the car park, walk straight and then R along the path 800 yards towards the waterside.

52.742851, 1.595657

Hickling Broad boat houses

DECOY BROAD SCOUT CAMP, DECOY BROAD

A good reason to join the Scouts! 1 mile from the nearest public road. Group, District or County camps get to share this 20-acre Broad with almost no one but the odd angler. Direct access to the Norfolk Broads.

By river, Decoy Broad is located between Salhouse and Horning. Woodbastwick, Norfolk, NR13 6HN

TFI HORNING (FORMERLY FERRY INN HORNING), RIVER BURE

Free moorings and good food. Student discounts.

Ferry Rd, Norfolk, NR12 8PS
www.tfi-restaurants.co.uk

Alderfen Broad

Ospreys' stopover on migration. Alderfen contains some of the Broad's finest tussock fen and carr woodland.

➤ **Find** the N end of Long Rd, Norfolk, NR12 8XP. From the car park, walk back down Long Rd ⅓ mile to the T-junction. Turn R at the T-junction and then L around Water Ln until you find the FP on the R. Once on the FP, follow it straight, then turn L, then R, then L a final time into the woodland tails circling the Aldermen Broad. The FP can be muddy. There's a viewing area over the water.

52.723732, 1.482983

St Benedicts Church, Horning, River Bure

There's a bench by the river at the end of the church path.

➤ **Find** the large car park in Church Rd, Horning, Norfolk, NR12 8PZ, 55 yards from the church entrance. The path is down the side of the graveyard that leads to the river.

52.694146, 1.483173

WINTERTON DUNES BEACH CAFE, WINTERTON-ON-SEA

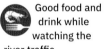 Serves hot and cold drinks, as well as food. Dog-friendly beach on which to eat and drink.

Beach Rd, Winterton-on-Sea, Great Yarmouth, NR29 4AJ
www.dunescafe.weebly.com

NORADA PUB & RESTAURANT, POTTER HEIGHAM, RIVER THURNE

Good food and drink while watching the river traffic.

Bridge Rd, Potter Heigham, Great Yarmouth, NR29 5JD
www.thenorada.co.uk

Winterton Dunes, Winterton-on-Sea, North Sea

Not a part of the Broads. This wooded dune and beach, known as The Common, escaped being classified and defined by post-peat industry evacuation. The Common is strangely riddled with FPs; seven run parallel out to the high-tide mark. Visit the Parish Church of the Holy Trinity and All Saints for more on the local area. The tower opens in the summer for views over the wood and dunes.

➤ **Find** the end of Beach Rd, looking out to sea, Winterton-on-Sea, Great Yarmouth, NR29 4AJ. There's a large car park here. Walk on to the beach, turn L and walk for ⅓ mile then turn L again on any of the trails into and over the dunes and scrub.

52.719228, 1.689434

Horse Fen, River Thurne

Boatyard and bridleway loop, opposite Toad Hall.

➤ **Find** the moorings and car park in Horsefen Rd, Ludham, Great Yarmouth, NR29 5QG. Looking across the water, turn L along Horsefen Rd and keep walking 700 yards until the road runs out and the FP takes over. The track leads along the wonderful Womack Water to meet the T-junction of the main River Thurne. Keep walking L and then L again, and L again on the bridleway to return.

52.699271, 1.549441

Caister-on-Sea

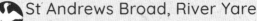

MUNCHIES, GREAT YARMOUTH, NORTH SEA

Cafe next to the beach with a boating lake and river to hire boats. Takeaway sandwiches, hot food and drinks or eat on the balcony with beautiful sea views. Beach hut hire, too.

2 North Dr, Great Yarmouth, NR30 4ET
www.munchiesgreat yarmouth.co.uk

St Andrews Broad, River Yare

Man-made Broad created by quarrying on the SE edge of Norwich. Views across the River Yare towards the city.

➤ **Find** parking in Whitlingham Ln, Trowse, Norwich, NR14 8TR. The Broad and waterside paths are just past the visitor centre. Circle the broad to walk along the River Yare path.

52.59460, 1.30408

Waveney Forest, River Waveney

Pine and broadleaf wood by the river.

➤ **Find** the car park in New Rd, Great Yarmouth, NR31 9HT. Either follow the paths to the river or walk to the bottom of New Rd and turn L on to the bridleway and follow the path all the way to the river's marshy edge.

52.552696, 1.624443

Humberstone Marshes

Isolated naze beside a path into the low-tide river.

➤ **Find** the church and parking at the end of Church Rd, Great Yarmouth, NR31 9QG. Facing the church, walk down the R side on to the river path and follow it around Breydon Water for 2.4 miles to the point at Humberstone.

52.603918, 1.690120

Sea Palling

Norfolk Broads

Chedgrave Common, River Yare

Remains of a communal stretch of river E of the town. Erosion has in the past closed the FP all the way to the 'lake' at Hardley Flood. Some still take the crumbling path on. The common area remains open.

➤ **Find** All Saints Church, Hardley Rd, Chedgrave, Norfolk, NR14 6NQ. Take the FP down the L side of the church to the river and turn L at the water. Follow to the end of the path.

52.540804, 1.511941

Surlingham Naze, River Yale

Wooded walk out of Surlingham Church (52.607417, 1.403468). Keep walking along the river valley path to Surlingham Broad.

➤ **Find** the Ferry House, 1 Ferry Rd, Surlingham, Norwich, NR14 7AR, beside the River Yale. From the grassy car park, walk S away from the pub along the riverbank 765 yards to the wooded bend in the river. Alternatively, find St Mary's Surlingham, in Church Ln, Norwich, NR14 7DF. Facing the church, walk L along Church Ln and keep walking all the way to the river woodland. At the river, turn R and walk for ⅓ mile to the wooded bend.

52.613965, 1.403839

Shingle Street

SUFFOLK

SWIM the secret lagoon at Benacre Broad.

TOUCH the devil's fingerprints at the 'Cathedral on the Marshes'.

HIDE among the brackish reeds of Dunwich Forest.

LISTEN to the booming bark of bitterns at Minsmere.

WILD camp around Sutton Ness and hunt for fish or fossils.

FORAGE for sea kale around Simpson's Saltings.

SWIM the Deben sandbanks.

FIND prehistoric flint tools beneath Pakefield Cliffs.

LOOK for sharks' teeth around Ramsholt Dock.

WATCH nesting avocets at Trimley Marshes.

EXPLORE a rare ship burial.

CATCH a ferry around England's largest spit.

RIDE Suffolk's oldest and smallest foot ferries.

EXPLORE the inland waters of Iken Cliff.

BELL INN, ST OLAVES, RIVER WAVENEY

This is where the ferryman waited for customers to ring when they wanted to cross the river. The bridge ended the service.

Beccles Rd, St Olaves, Great Yarmouth, NR31 9HE
www.bellinn-stolaves.co.uk

DUKES HEAD, SOMERLEYTON, RIVER WAVENEY

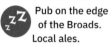 Pub on the edge of the Broads. Local ales.

Slugs Ln, Somerleyton, Lowestoft, NR32 5QR
www.dukesheadsomerleyton.co.uk

WHERRY HOTEL, OULTON BROAD

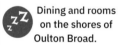 Dining and rooms on the shores of Oulton Broad.

Bridge Rd, Oulton Broad, Lowestoft, NR32 3LN
www.wherryhotel.com

THREE RIVERS CAMPING & CARAVANNING, BECCLES, RIVER WAVENEY

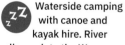 Waterside camping with canoe and kayak hire. River slipway into the Waveney River with a quay from which to launch vessels. BBQs, campfires and pets allowed.

Station Rd, Geldeston, Beccles, NR34 0HS
www.threeriverscamping.co.uk

Corton Cliffs, North Sea

Fossil beach peppered in reptile, ammonite and shell remains in the clay and rock around the sands and crumbling cliffs at low tide. The groynes and breakwaters are good for crabbing and shellfish.

➤ **Find** St Bartholomew Corton, Church Ln, Corton, Lowestoft, NR32 5HX; 2 miles N of Lowestoft, between the villages of Corton and Hopton-on-Sea. Facing the church entrance, turn R along Church Ln and keep walking ⅓ mile to the FP down to the beach on the L. Once facing the sea, walk ¾ mile to the L.

52.52986, 1.74110

Gunton Warren, Links Rd, North Sea

Sloping cliffs of shingle, sand, heathland and trees. A rare glimpse of how the ancient Suffolk shoreline looked before it was tamed and developed. Rare migrant birds (icterine and yellow-browed warblers) still come here to feed and roost over the sand dunes, marram grass and sea holly.

➤ **Find** the end of Links Rd beside the beach and dunes in Lowestoft, NR32 1UY.

52.499410, 1.753799

Oulton Broad, Suffolk Broads

More than 10 species of dragonfly flit around the inland, 'broad' tidal waters between the River Waveney and the North Sea. A gateway to the peat pools that make up the Norfolk Broads' Sern edge. Listen out for the plop of water voles.

➤ Carlton Marshes, Burnt Hill Ln, Carlton Colville. Less than a 1-mile walk from Oulton Broad Station, S river shore of Lowestoft. FP/bridleway loops NW along narrow watercourse drain and then back via River Waveney and Share Marsh.

➤ **Find** Suffolk Wildlife Trust building in Burnt Hill Ln, Carlton Colville, Lowestoft, NR33 8HU. With your back to the buildings and in the car park, walk over the marshes to the water 700 yards away.

52.473339, 1.686884

Six Mile Corner, River Waveney

Grazing marsh, fens and dykes. Marsh harriers and hobbies hunt over the reeds between the river wall and the water's edge where sedge and grasshopper warblers feed.

➤ Six Mile Corner is on the Waveney bend in the river via the old dam track, one of many. Walk Angles Way 5 miles E or W into Lowestoft or Beccles respectively.

➤ **Find** the car park close to the railway line in Wadehall Ln, Beccles, NR34 7QG. Cross the railway line and walk ½ mile to the riverbank.

52.462747, 1.634851

Pakefield Cliffs, North Sea

These cliffs have revealed evidence of England's earliest human inhabitants occupying East Anglia almost 1 million years ago. Flint tools dating back 700,000 years were found in 2005. Search for miles along the majestic, sandy beaches for ammonites, shells and reptiles in the boulder clay between Kessingland and Pakefield Cliffs.

➤ Find Beach Car Park, Marsh Ln, Kessingland, Waveney, Suffolk, NR33 7RU. Walk down to the sands and turn L. Walk 1.1 miles to just before Heathland Beach Caravan Park.

52.42971, 1.72915

Benacre Broad

Tidal lagoon surrounded by gorse, woodland, bogs, flowers and birdlife. Access is from the beach only. Fast tides and isolated.

➤ Find the Kessingland car park for Pakefield Cliffs (see above). Once on the beach, turn R instead of L and walk along a combination stone, sand and hard FP and beach 1¾ miles to the Broad.

52.387846, 1.719188

The Denes, Benacre Ness

Like a scene from Robinson Crusoe. Tramp an isolated lagoon trapped between Hundred River to the N, and Benacre Broad to the S. A special place for birdlife and fossils around the edges of shallow cliffs, dunes and gorse.

➤ Find Kessingland Beach Park, Church Rd, Kessingland, Lowestoft, NR33 7SF, and walk 1 mile S to The Denes.

52.398720, 1.727123

Benacre Broad

Covehithe Broad

Glorious saltwater lake that flushes at high tide, just S of Covehithe Cliffs. Fossils on the foreshore N. Take shelter in the ruined Church of St Andrew at Covehithe (52.3767327, 1.7057336). Newer 17th-century church built inside the shell of the other by villagers who gave up on the repair costs of the larger building. Visit soon before both are lost to the erosion of this coast.

➤ **Find** the Church of St Andrew Covehithe, towards the end of Mill Ln, Covehithe, NR34 7JJ. There is no parking here, so this part of the lane must be walked. Slightly back from the church on the L is the FP that leads 775 yards down to the beach and Broad. Alternatively, walk the longer way round, by continuing down Mill Ln to the beach and turning R.

52.368613, 1.705385

Covehithe Broad

Easton Broad

Wallow in the warm shallows while watching birdlife all around. Isolated on its own piece of foreshore. Southwold is 2 miles S, and Kessingland 5 miles N.

➤ Follow the directions for Covehithe Broad (see above). Keep walking along the beach another 1.2 miles.

52.354224, 1.695094 & 52.354284, 1.69500C

Easton Bavents, Southwold, North Sea

A rare opportunity to find fossilised mammals more than 1 million years old in red sediment, shells and sand in a formation known as Norwich Crag.

➤ **Find** Southwold Pier, 27 N Pde, Southwold, IP18 6LT. From the car park next door and facing the sea, walk L 0.9 miles.

52.343552, 1.689221

Southwold Harbour

Holy Trinity Church, Blythburgh, River Blyth

Incredible church, sometimes known as the 'Cathedral of the Marshes'. Built on sacred ground beside the River Blyth. During a huge storm in 1577, the vicar's morning service was struck by lightning, leaving the church's N door with scorch marks that can still be seen today. The marks were dubbed 'the fingerprints of the devil' after a man and boy died in the storm. The N exit leads down to the river path for a glorious 5-mile walk to Halesworth.

➤ **Find** Holy Trinity Church in Church Ln, Blythburgh, Halesworth, IP19 9LP.

52.3211977, 1.5948322

Walberswick Hill Covert, River Blyth

Wooded hill and heath above a tidal lagoon formed by a widening of the River Blyth. There are two unexcavated round barrows up on the hill but they're not obvious. Paths lead down through the pine and oaks on to the marshes and the water's edge. It's a wonderful 2-mile walk from here to Southwold Harbour's cafe's and pubs.

➤ **Find** the junction where The Street (B1387) meets Lodge Rd, in Walberswick, Southwold, IP18 6TQ. From Lodge Rd, continue along The Street for 1.3 miles to find a car park in the trees on the R. Take the FP L and follow it down to and across the water ⅓ mile away.

52.320016, 1.608186

BELL INN WALBERSWICK, WALBERSWICK BEACH, NORTH SEA

600-year-old pub with six bedrooms. Nice retreat in winter with open fires, quirky snugs and hidden alcoves. Outdoor dining in summer, overlooking Walberswick beach.

Ferry Rd, Walberswick, Southwold, IP18 6TN
www.bellinnwalberswick.co.uk

THE SHIP, DUNWICH BEACH, NORTH SEA

Old-fashioned bar with a nautical theme, beer garden and crackling fire. 16 bedrooms surrounded by heathland and beach. The seas have taken their toll. This medieval port was claimed by the waves during a terrible storm, but it's said you can still hear the peal of the church bells beneath the waves. Ruins of Dunwich monastery remain.

St James's St, Dunwich, Saxmundham, IP17 3DT
www.shipatdunwich.co.uk

Walberswick–Southwold Ferry, River Blyth

Ancient ferry crossing. Wonderful place to wander from the beach and up along the river path. Walk all the way round to the Southwold Harbour.

➤ **Find** car park end of Ferry Rd, B1387, Southwold. Return to Ferry Rd and walk NE 130 yards to the river. www.walberswickferry.com

52.3157159, 1.6679362

Dunwich Forest, Dunwich, North Sea

Wild horses graze over than 3 square miles of pine and broadleaf woodland. The trees and heath are separated from the beach by a ⅔-mile-wide strip of marsh, ditches and brackish pools. Look out for otters and water voles. A good place to shelter from all weathers.

➤ **Find** St James's Church, St James's St, Dunwich, Saxmundham, IP17 3DT. Facing the gate nearest the church door, turn L and continue on L at the road junction.

➤ **Find** Flora Tea Rooms, Beach Rd, Dunwich, IP17 3EN and the car park next door. Follow Westleton Rd for 150 yards before turning R on the FP towards the forest ⅓ mile away past the tearooms.

52.289950, 1.627029

Dunwich Heath, Saxmundham, North Sea

Woodland, heathland and gorse overlooking pebble beach and sea. Take care around the crumbling cliffs and when swimming.

➤ **Find** RSPB Minsmere Car Park, Sheepwash Ln, Westleton, Saxmundham, IP17 3BY. Walk 800 yards E and 1 mile N to the heath.

52.25273, 1.62707

Minsmere, North Sea

A jaw-dropping, wet-and-wild bird extravaganza. More than 300 species of birds, including bitterns, nightingales, avocets and nightjars. Best seen from the beach or hides. For a special treat, try an RSPB guide or a 4x4 Minsmere safari for groups of four. Details on the RSPB website. Cafe, parking and toilets.

➤ **Find** the RSPB Minsmere cafe and car park in Sheepwash Ln, Saxmundham, IP17 3BY. www.rspb.org.uk

52.247683, 1.618935

Goose Hill, Leiston, North Sea

Pine woodland 380 yards from the beach. Perfect hiding place for weary travellers.

➤ **Find** the dead-end lane Sizewell Gap where it meets the beach at Leiston, IP16 4UH. Facing the sea, turn L and walk 1 mile along the shore. There are several trails from here up to the woodland. Take any of them and walk 330 yards to find the woodland trails.

52.223897, 1.619493

SIZEWELL TEA, SIZEWELL BEACH, NORTH SEA

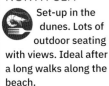

Set-up in the dunes. Lots of outdoor seating with views. Ideal after a long walks along the beach.

Sizewell Gap, Leiston, IP16 4UH
Facebook: @SizewellTea

ALDEBURGH CAFE, RIVER ALDE

Award-winning home-made pies, full English breakfast and afternoon teas. Walks down to the river.

Saxmundham Rd, Aldeburgh, IP15 5JD
www.aldeburghcafe.com

Thorpeness, North Sea

Miles of deserted beach, S and N of the old fishing village. Look out for fossilised blocks of coral and shell at low tide.

➤ **Find** Meare Shop and Tearooms looking across Thorpeness Meare, Thorpeness, Leiston, IP16 4NW. There is a large car park between the boating lake and the beach. Walk down to the beach between the houses, turn L and walk along the beach 8 miles to the quieter parts.

52.18878, 1.62294

Hazlewood Marshes, Saxmundham

Forage for samphire around one of Suffolk's oldest prehistoric settlements. Best explored by either kayak or packraft launched from Slaughden into Westrow Reach. Come in with the flood and out on the ebb for Cob Island and Barber's Point. Also access to the marshes via the car park.

➤ **Find** Hazlewood Marshes Car Park, off the A1094, Saxmundham, IP17 1PG, and ¼ mile W around the marshes on the ECP.

52.168297, 1.562503

Black Heath Wood, Saxmundham, River Alde

Pine and broadleaf wood that looks on to the stunning waters of Long Reach and Ham Creek at high tide. Actually, it's pretty special at low tide as well.

➤ **Find** Hazlewood Marshes Car Park (see above), and walk 1¼ miles W on the ECP.

52.165992, 1.543382

Suffolk pebble lagoons

Bawdsey Beach

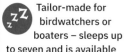

Iken Cliff, River Alde

Remote and quiet tidal water surrounding Iken Church. Salt marsh can be accessed by an eroded FP out into the watery depths. Swim with oystercatchers, grey plovers, pintails and dunlins.

➤ **Find** the three-way junction between Church Ln, Ferry Ln and Tunstall Rd, at Woodbridge, IP12 2ER. Follow the sign to Tunstall, and keep on the Tunstall Rd 1 mile before turning R at the brown park sign, into the car park down to Iken Cliff. Once in the car park, follow the FP to the R and then L down to the waterside.

52.151930, 1.505399

Iken

Chantry Point, River Ore

Naze with views over Havergate Island. From Orford Port, catch a ferry around the historic harbour and river. Walk from Orford Harbour along the River Ore. Return inland via the FP to Chantry Farm and up on to Orford Castle.

➤ **Find** the Jolly Sailor in Quay St, Orford, Woodbridge, IP12 2NU. A large car park is next door. From here, walk across the car park and on to the river. Turn L and keep on the river path 0.8 miles to the point.

52.080955, 1.537595

The Cliff, Orford, River Butley

Cutaway in the riverbank at the top of the FP that leads down to the E-shore ferry crossing.

➤ **Find** the castle ruin E of Orford and keep walking 1¼ miles E on FPs and road, through Gedgrave Hall to the riverbank 2 miles away.

52.084308, 1.497512

Butley Foot Ferry, River Butley

One of the oldest ferry services in England. Runs throughout the summer over the River Butley on weekends and bank holidays from 11am to 4pm. Apart from being quite wonderful, it prevents the need for a 7-mile walk or cycle around the river via Chillesford.

➤ Larger-sized parties mid-week subject to availability by emailing ferryman@butleyferry.org. or phoning 07913 672499. If these become redundant, Google 'Butley Foot Ferry' and follow the link. Woodbridge, IP12 3NJ, www.aldeandore.org.

➤ **Find** the point where Shingle St meets Shingle Beach at Hollesley, IP12 3BG. From the car park and facing the beach, turn L along the ECP or beach and walk 4 glorious miles along the River Alde to the ferry crossing. Alternatively, for a shorter hike, park at Orford and follow Gedgrave Rd and the FP past the castle ruins 2 miles W along the Sustrans bike route.

52.0803129, 1.4895136

Simpson's Saltings Nature Reserve, Ore Estuary

Breathtaking view of the unique and isolated Ore Estuary, with Orford Beach on the opposite bank. Rare plants, such as sea kale, sea pea, sea heath and sea kale, grow in the sand, shingle and salt marsh. If plants aren't your thing, watch the river traffic.

➤ Follow the directions from the Shingle St car park. Walk 1.6 miles. Alternatively, use the RSPB car park at HMP Hollesley Bay, behind Hollesley Bay Colony.

52.051851, 1.469643

MILL LANE B&B, BUTLEY, OLD MILL POND AND STREAM

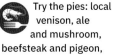

Great location between Woodbridge and Orford to overnight and explore hundreds of acres of woodland. No children or pets.

Mill Lane House, Mill Ln, Butley, Woodbridge, IP12 3PZ
www.milllanebandb.co.uk

THE FROIZE, WOODBRIDGE, RIVER BUTLEY

Try the pies: local venison, ale and mushroom, beefsteak and pigeon, free-range chicken with new-season asparagus.

The Street, Chillesford, Woodbridge, IP12 3PU
www.froize.co.uk

BOATHOUSE CAFE, BAWDSEY, RIVER DEBEN

 Hidden, wooden cafe at the mouth of the river. Enjoy home cooking and locally sourced food after or before boarding the Deben ferry. Alternatively, take a summer river trip; regular 1-hr river trips run to Ramsholt throughout the summer for up to 12 passengers at a time. Longer trips can also be arranged. Contact John on 07803 476 621, 01394 270 106.

The Quay Bawdsey Ferry, Bawdsey, Woodbridge, IP12 3AX
www.bawdseyferry.co.uk

THE RAMSHOLT ARMS, WOODBRIDGE, RIVER DEBEN

 The only S-facing pub on the river so make the most of the sun-soaked terrace. Beach and crab fishing jetty. Fresh, locally caught seafood in summer.

Dock Rd, Woodbridge, IP12 3AB
www.theramsholt arms.com

River Deben

Bawdsey Manor, River Deben

Woodland, beach and sandbanks. Good place to swim. The ferry to Felixstowe runs from the Bawdsey Quay across the River Deben at weekends during summertime.

> **Find** Boathouse Café (see left). There is parking all around.

51.989324, 1.394867

All Saints Church, Woodbridge, River Deben

River views from the round-tower church, beside the wooded shore. Walk along the FP ½ mile S from the church to Ramsholt Dock. Look for fossilised sharks' teeth, crabs and fish around the shore.

> **Find** Ramsholt Arms at the end of Dock Rd, Woodbridge, IP12 3AB, beside the river. Facing the water, walk R along the river FP and then veer R away from the river on the bridleway 765 yards up to the church.

52.023947, 1.361013

The Tips, Woodbridge, River Deben

Remote wooded point, at the centre of two coves. Perfect place for a secret swim or late-night star watching.

> **Find** Ramsholt Arms (see page 286) and walk to the river. Turn R at the water and continue along the bank for 3½ miles.

52.061170, 1.342058

Woodbridge

THE TEA HUT, WOODBRIDGE, RIVER DEBEN

 Cafe on the banks of the River Deben in Woodbridge. Next to a model boat pond.

River Wall, Woodbridge, IP12 4BB

www.theteahut.co.uk

QUAYSIDE ON THE RIVER DEBEN, WOODBRIDGE, RIVER DEBEN

Detached bungalow directly overlooking the river, with a conservatory.

Quayside, The Quay, Waldringfield, Woodbridge, IP12 4QZ

www.quaysidecottage.com

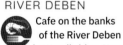 Sutton Hoo, Woodbridge, River Deben

One of England's most important archaeological sites. The 20 burial mounds shed new light on pre-Norman English history previously dismissed as myth and legend. The visitor centre explains the importance of the burials, in relation to the North Sea, and the heroic Old English poem *Beowulf*, which is set in Sern Sweden. There are original and replica artefacts of the ship-burial chamber on site. The burial field can be toured in the summer months, and at weekends and in school holidays year-round.

➤ **Find** Sutton Hoo off the B1083, Tranmer House, Woodbridge, IP12 3DJ, 1 mile from Woodbridge. From the visitor centre, follow the public FPs around the site and down to the wooded river at Ferry Cliff.

52.089322, 1.338411

Trimley Marshes, Trimley St Mary

The lagoon and islands attract migrating waders such as common sandpiper, curlew sandpiper and greenshank. Avocets and ringed plovers nest here in spring.

➤ **Find** the end of Cordy's Ln, Trimley St Mary, IP11 0UD, as it passes into the bridleway. There is a car park here. Keep following the bridleway and then turn R after ⅔ mile on to the Stour and Orwell FP. Follow the FP another 1½ miles past the containers and port to the marshes.

51.972092, 1.281768

Levington Lagoon, Levington

Brackish lagoon lit up by kingfisher and flowering sea lavender in spring. Sea purslane if you're peckish.

➤ **Find** the car park on Cordy's Ln, Trimley St Mary, Felixstowe, IP11 0UD. Walk SW on the BW to Stour and Orwell Walk, then turn NW towards Trimley Marshes. Walk 5 miles N to the lagoon and creek.

51.999002, 1.260755

Home Wood, Levington, River Orwell

Pine and broadleaf wood at Nacton Shore, Levington. Fossilised reptiles can be found around the cliffs and foreshore.

➤ **Find** St Peter's Church in Church Ln, Levington, Ipswich, IP10 0LQ, next to The Ship Inn (see left). Facing the church, continue L along the road and round the bend ¼ mile to the car park entrance on the R. Walk through the car park and continue on down the lane 100 yards to Levington Lagoon. Turn R on the Stour and Orwell Walk, and keep heading 800 yards down to the River Orwell. The wooded shore is another ½ mile.

52.001636, 1.241478

River Orw

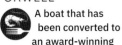

MARINERS RESTAURANT, IPSWICH, RIVER ORWELL

A boat that has been converted to an award-winning restaurant serving French food. Outdoor eating on the patio deck in fine weather.

Neptune Quay, Ipswich, IP4 1AX
www.marinersipswich
.co.uk

BUTT & OYSTER PIN MILL, IPSWICH, RIVER ORWELL

Made famous as a setting for one of Arthur Ransome's books and named after the oyster fisheries around the river.

Pinmill Rd, Ipswich, IP9 1JW
www.debeninns.co.uk

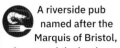

BRISTOL ARMS SHOTLEY GATE, IPSWICH, RIVER STOUR

A riverside pub named after the Marquis of Bristol, who owned the land and foreshore of Shotley Gate. Bristol Arms has overlooked the River Stour since the mid-1800s, serving the locals and sailors. Tea on the quay, milkshakes or ice creams.

Bristol Hill, Shotley Gate, Ipswich, IP9 1PU
www.bristolarms.com

Bridge Wood, Orwell Bridge, River Orwell

Peaceful, tree-lined beach under the shadow of Orwell Bridge.
➤ **Find** Orwell Country Park Car Park, off the A14, Ipswich, IP10 0JS. Follow the wooded paths ⅓ mile to the shore. Facing the water, turn L and walk another ¼ mile to the beach. You will pass an ancient oak close to the water's edge, believed to have been around since the days of Henry VIII, more than 500 years ago.

52.016017, 1.187360

Woolverstone Marina, Ipswich, River Orwell

The wooded remnants of what was once a vast park estate on the River Orwell, inherited and ruled by successive families dating back many generations. Explore the tree canopy and shore, 1 mile NW out of Chelmondiston, on the way into or out of Ipswich, 4 miles N.
➤ **Find** St Michael's Church at the end of the lane, opposite Glebe Ln, Babergh, IP9 1BD, off the B1456 Main Rd SE of Woolverstone. Follow the FP out of the back of the church ⅓ mile through the trees to the marina and to the river. Follow the FP past the marina into the woodland by the shore.

52.004743, 1.202035

Nacton Quay, Nacton

Look for fossiled reptile remains where sandy beaches give way to small, clay cliffs along the foreshore.
➤ **Find** Suffolk Levington Car Park, off Shore Ln, Nacton, Ipswich, IP10 0ES. Walk ½ mile W along the shore at low tide to find fossil sites and tree cover.

52.00619, 1.22373

Stutton Ness, Stutton, River Stour

Tree-lined sand-and-stone beach, miles off the beaten track. Wonderful place to wild camp and fish on the foreshore. Good for fossil hunting, too, with bones of mammoths and deer found here.
➤ **Find** the Kings Head Stutton, Manningtree Rd, Stutton, Ipswich, IP9 2SW. Next to the pub is a bus stop and opposite is a FP on the other side of Manningtree Rd. The FP leads 330 yards across a field to Hyams Ln. Turn R for 300 yards and then turn L into Crepping Hall Dr. Follow the FP 1 mile to Sutton Ness.

51.95554, 1.12285

ESSEX

WILD THINGS TO DO
BEFORE YOU DIE:

SWIM up a tarmac road that floods
each day on the tide.

EXPLORE a mammoth graveyard.

PICNIC at England's oldest and
prettiest chapel.

FIND the missing link between the
legendary King Arthur and Colchester
(Camalot) Castle.

FORAGE for wild oysters and
cockles.

DISCOVER an 11,000-year-old
oak woodland.

EXPLORE the smugglers' fate at
Fobbing.

FIND the sand hill with the best Essex
views.

SWIM the lagoon at Beeleigh Falls.

TRAMP England's most dangerous
road.

SEARCH for giant megalodon teeth
below Walton Cliffs.

WATCH bats hunt over gravel pits.

WILD camp Dengie's shell beaches;
kayak camp Walton Backwaters; or
hang a hammock in a riverside wood.

Tollesbury

Stone Point, Wrabness, River Stour

Look for fossilised bones of deer, horse and even whale from the
Red Crag. Shells and shark teeth are sometimes found inside the
cement stones and pyrite trapped in the London Clay.

➤ **Find** the small car park on Wheatsheaf Ln, Manningtree, CO11
2TF, and walk 400 yards N to the FP just past the first corner.
Continue down the FP another 400 yards N to the Wrabness and
Stone Point.

51.94675, 1.15870

Copperas Bay, River Stour

Majestic chestnut and hornbeam wood on the River Stour.
Owls hunt at dawn and dusk from the Bramble Creek hide,
where neighbouring Stour and Copperas woods fall down to
the water's edge. Spring is awash with bluebells, ferns and the
sound of nightingales. Ancient trees provide shelter in winter
or cool shade in summer.

➤ **Find** where Wall Ln and Wheatsheaf Ln meet, in Manningtree,
CO11 2TF. With Wall Ln on your L shoulder, continue straight along
Wheatsheaf Ln, 165 yards to the car park on the L. Continue along
the road another 0.4 miles past All Saints Church and turn L into
Stone Ln. Follow the lane ⅓ mile to the shore and then turn R. The
bay is 1⅓ miles along the beautiful path. There is a hide along the
river path offering stunning estuary views; it's not easy to get to,
which makes it all the more special.

51.940709, 1.196601

Walton Backwaters

THE CAFE ON THE
PIER, HARWICH,
STOUR ESTUARY

Home-made soups
and casseroles
with stunning views
over Harwich Harbour
and the Stour Estuary.

Ha'penny Pier, The Quay,
Harwich, CO12 3HH
www.cafeonthepier
harwich.co.uk

HARBOUR LIGHTS
RESTAURANT,
WALTON-ON-
THE-NAZE, RIVER
STOUR

Worth the visit
for the drive
and harbour
views alone.

Titchmarsh Marina, Coles
Ln, Walton-on-the-Naze,
CO14 8SL
www.harbourlights
carvery.co.uk

HIPKINS TEAROOMS,
WALTON-ON-THE-
NAZE, BLACKWATER
ESTUARY/
NORTH SEA

Fine service on an
outdoor raised
platform watching
the world go by along
miles of sandy beach.

32 Naze Park Rd,
Walton-on-the-Naze,
CO14 8JZ
07482 307 122

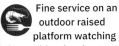 Marine Parade, Harwich, Dovercourt Bay

Fabulous shark teeth and plant fossils along the beach by
the sea wall of Dovercourt Bay. Walk or swim the beach as
it arcs southwards towards Colchester and Essex's unique
series of E-facing river valleys. If the W coast of Land's End
and beyond equals the deep and Wild Atlantic West and the
New World, it's the eastern sandy shallows that bridge to the
melting-pot magic of the past in Gaul, Scandinavia, Byzantine,
the fertile crescents of Babylon and ancient Egypt and India.
➤ **Find** Lower Marine Pde, Harwich, CO12 3RH, where it leaves
the B1414/Fronks Rd. Get on to the beach anywhere along the
parade where cars can park. Keep walking along the beach for
2 miles for some of Essex's most isolated dunes and tidal creeks.

51.93228, 1.27671

Skipper's Island, Walton Backwaters

Flooded causeway on to magical island of freshwater pools,
sea lavender, wild fowl and raptors. Home to the Fisher's
estuarine moth, found nowhere else in the world but Essex.
It feeds on a plant also found nowhere else in the world: sea
hog's fennel. Hamford Water lies beyond the island. Kirby
Creek to the E separates Skipper from Horsey Island.
➤ **Find** the end of Quay Ln, Beaumont, CO16 0BB, off the B1414
Thorpe Rd. Facing the water, turn R along the FP and walk 2½
miles to the causeway, along some of the best coast in Essex.
Low-tide access on to the island's foreshore by foot, ⅓ mile from
the mainland coast path. Hard and soft mud.
➤ Kayakers can launch from Titchmarsh Marina, Coles Ln, Walton-
on-the-Naze, CO14 8SL for a small fee 1¾ miles E. Access on to
the island's interior can be arranged by calling Essex Wildlife Trust
on 01621 862 960.

51.872247, 1.220585

Walton Cliffs, Walton-on-the-Naze, Blackwater Estuary/North Sea

Red cliffs down to a sandy beach that's good for swimming.
Search for the teeth of the greatest shark that has ever lived, the
megalodon. Giant, fossilised gnashers up to 4in long fall from
the cliffs after each tide. Combine fossil hunting with a walk out
to Stone Point.
➤ **Find** the Naze Tower (and sometime tearoom) at Old Hall Ln,
Walton-on-the-Naze, CO14 8LE, just past the large public car park.
Keep walking N and along the top of the cliffs until you find a path
down or the cliff runs out. If you get tired of fossils and the tide is
on the way out, consider walking the 2 miles to Naze Point (facing
out to sea and walking L). Be wary of tides coming in.

51.884019, 1.268637

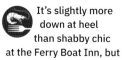

FERRY BOAT INN, POINT CLEAR, RIVER COLNE

It's slightly more down at heel than shabby chic at the Ferry Boat Inn, but the service is excellent and the views across to Brightlingsea are wonderful.

Tower Estate, Point Clear, CO16 8NG
01255 820 366

THE CREEK, GREAT BENTLEY, FLAG CREEK

Local produce. Formerly The Flag Inn, the pub was renamed The Creek when the owners saw the secret Flag Creek for the first time. There are many fabulous creek pictures all around the restaurant.

Flag Hill, Great Bentley, Colchester, CO7 8RE
www.thecreekgreat bentley.co.uk

COACH HOUSE COFFEE SHOP, BRIGHTLINGSEA, BRIGHTLINGSEA CREEK

A converted coach house next to Brightlingsea Harbour. It was once a Victorian watering hole on the edge of the hard, where boats still launched from the water's edge.

Waterside, Brightlingsea, Colchester, CO7 0AX
www.coachhouse brightlingsea.co.uk

John Weston, Walton-on-the-Naze, North Sea

The sandy entrance to Stone Point (2 miles further along The Naze Beach) where the water laps up and over the lagoon. If this feels isolated just wait until you get past Cormorant Creek and Stone Marsh on a hot summer's day. Deserted heaven.

➤ **Find** Naze Car Park, Sunny Point, Walton-on-the-Naze, CO14 8LD. Walk E on to the ECP and turn N, facing the sea. Walk 1 mile on the ECP to the Naze path.

51.873012,1.290386

Stone Point, Walton-on-the-Naze, North Sea

Arrive at low tide and let the incoming waters wash you into the mouth of Hamford Water. But only on a kayak. If on foot, it's best to arrive just after high tide. High risk.

➤ **Find** John Weston (see above). Where the ECP ends, keep on at low tide over marsh and sand.

51.884019, 1.268637

Jaywick Sands, Clacton-on-Sea, North Sea

The best beach in Essex is only a few mins' walk from Clacton, but several hundred yards offshore on a low tide.
Sand dunes, crabbing and summer breeze.

➤ **Find** the RNLI Clacton-on-Sea Lifeboat Station in Hastings Av, Clacton-on-Sea, CO15 1BW. There is a beachside car park opposite. Facing the water, turn R and walk L along the sands for 2 miles.

51.774921, 1.125784

Colne Point, St Osyth, River Colne

Porpoises come in with calves over the sandy Colne Bar in summer, when there's no wind and the tide is high. The low-tide foreshore is hauntingly good for exploring and getting lost in during winter. Beware sinking sands and plug holes if venturing out too far on foot. Make an effort to walk (or kayak) around the sea wall of Flag Creek (51.811451, 1.072595).

Alresford

ROSE AND CROWN, WIVENHOE, RIVER COLNE

Tables and chairs beside the river. Wonderful at sunset.

The Quay, Wivenhoe, Colchester, CO7 9BX
www.greeneking-pubs.co.uk

THE WHALEBONE, COLCHESTER, RIVER COLNE

Lovely in winter by the wood fire. More of a focus on local veg and British meat, but also bar snacks. Fishing pond with lawns down to the Roman River.

Chapel Rd, Colchester, CO5 7BG
www.thewhalebone inn.co.uk

Rowhedge

> **Find** the end of Beach Rd, Jaywick, St Osyth, Clacton-on-Sea, CO16 8TB. From the car park beside the sea wall, turn R if facing the sea and walk 2 miles past Lee-over-Sands village and across Brightlingsea Creek, to the Point and the Colne Bar.

51.770090, 1.041536

Alresford Grange, River Colne

Sandy ridge of oak and pine woodland to hammock down in next to the beach. The waterside flowers with pink tamarisk in June.
> **Find** the dead end of Ford Ln, Alresford, Colchester, CO7 8BB, beside Alresford Creek and ford. Facing the creek, turn R into the FP and walk ¾ mile to the beautiful wooded foreshore of the Colne.

51.846662, 0.981100

The Bench, Wivenhoe, River Colne

Resting place beside the river on a wooded path linking Colchester to Wivenhoe and Brightlingsea.
> **Find** Wivenhoe Woods, by the river and car park in Rosabelle Av, Wivenhoe, Colchester, CO7 9NZ. Walk to the river. Facing the marsh, turn R and walk ¾ mile to the bench. Keep walking another 3 miles to reach Colchester Castle.

51.870775, 0.941675

Colchester Castle Museum, River Colne

The largest Norman castle in Europe. Built above the richest Celtic port in Old Britain. The Witchfinder General, Matthew Hopkins, interrogated and imprisoned suspected witches here. No longer tidal, it's surrounded by park garden and river paths that lead down to the tidal River Colne and eventually the North Sea if you can muster the energy for the 3-hr walk.
> **Find** St Botolph's Priory, Church Walk, Colchester, CO2 7EE. There's a car park here next to Colchester Town Station. Walk N along St Botolph's St towards the castle and gardens ¼ mile away.

51.890589, 0.903047

MERSEA VINEYARD LTD, COLCHESTER, BLACKWATER ESTUARY

Locally produced wine and beer from a vintage tearoom set back from the coast path.

Rewsalls Ln, Colchester, CO5 8SX
www.vineyard.
merseabrewery.co.uk

COLCHESTER OYSTER FISHERY LTD, PYEFLEET CREEK

Oysters from the pure waters in Pyefleet creek.

Pyefleet Quay, East Rd, East Mersea, Colchester, CO5 8UN
www.colchesteroyster fishery.com

THE COMPANY SHED, WEST MERSEA, BLACKWATER ESTUARY

Join the queue for a seafood platter of local oysters.

129 Coast Rd, West Mersea, Colchester, CO5 8PA
www.thecompanyshed .co.uk

THE LOFT – TEA BY THE SEA, TOLLESBURY FLEET

Delightful tea-room on stilts.

Woodrolfe Rd, Tollesbury, Maldon, CM9 8SE
www.thelofttearoom.com

Fingringhoe Wick, Colchester, River Colne

Gravel pits down to hides over a wooded beach. Listen out for nightingales in May and June. Canoe camp on the foreshore at low tide in summer.

➤ Best explored by kayak. Launch from the tiny quay at the end of Ferry Rd, Colchester, CO5 7BX, next to the car park. Paddle L looking across to Wivenhoe for 1.8 miles just after high tide. Follow the tides out and return on the flood after 8 hrs.
➤ For daytime access, find the Essex Wildlife Trust car park at the end of Wick Ln, off South Green Rd, Fingringhoe, Colchester, CO5 7DN.

51.834746, 0.971109

Ray Island Nature Reserve, West Mersea

Remote, island backdrop to Sabine Baring-Gould's novel *Mehalah*. Fresh water, woodland and shelter, with direct access to the mainland via The Strood.

➤ There are only two ways here: 1) by canoe along the Ray Channel, setting off from the launch at the end of the Jetty, Coast Rd, West Mersea, Colchester, CO5 8RA; 2) by joining Essex Wildlife Trust (EWT) online (for a few pounds), which will grant you member access across the old drovers' path. Find the path with planks across the creeks, which joins The Strood at 51.801070, 0.915220. Much care is needed and advice can be taken with EWT before attempting.

51.794460, 0.903233

Cudomore Grove, East Mersea, River Blackwater

Prehistoric beach renowned for mammoths. A giant tusk was discovered here in 2018. Beachcombers can look out for monkey bones and prehistoric tracks across the river to Bradwell. Beware sinking sand when venturing too far offshore.

➤ **Find** the cliffs on the remote SW shore of the island at the end of Broman's Ln, Colchester, CO5 8UE. From the car park, follow the path ¼ mile to the East Mersea Flats, then turn R and walk along the shore towards the woodland.

51.791777, 0.996831

Shingle Head Point, Tollesbury Wick

Sandy and isolated headland at the end of grassy islands and shallow salt marshes. Perfect place for swims and wallowing. The open-air, saltwater swimming area of Woodup Pool, Woodrolfe Rd, CM9 8SE was dug out of the marshes more than 100 years ago and still survives. The Wick is far away enough from both Colchester and Maldon to make it isolated, but it's one of those perfectly spaced strolls for the slow, inquisitive

THE CHEQUERS INN, MALDON, RIVER BLACKWATER

 A 14th-century inn set back ⅓ mile from the river path.

The Square, 1 Church St, Goldhanger, Maldon, CM9 8AS
www.thechequersgold
hanger.co.uk

THE LOCK TEAROOM, RIVER BLACKWATER

 Looks across the waters of Heybridge Basin, where the Chelmer & Blackwater Canal meets the tidal Blackwater Estuary.

Basin Rd, Heybridge Basin, Maldon, CM9 4RS
www.tiptree.com

THE MALDON SMOKEHOUSE, MALDON, RIVER CHELMER

Smoked and fresh seafood beside the River Chelmer. Worthy of a special and remote location.

Maldon, CM9 4LB
www.maldonsmokehouse
.co.uk

THE BARGE TEAROOMS, HYTHE, RIVER CHELMER

 Experience tea-on-water on board a beautiful Thames barge.

Cooks Yard, Promenade Park, The Hythe, CM9 5HN
www.top-sail.co.uk

Fingringhoe

rambler who chooses to overnight, camp or B&B. For non-walkers, there's a free car park on the hill above the harbour, which floods at high tide.

➤ **Find** the public car park on the way down at Woodrolfe Rd, Tollesbury, Maldon, CM9 8RY. The marina is a ¼-mile walk from here. To find the Shingle Head, walk through the Tollesbury Cruising Club, past the restaurant and walk for 1½ miles along the coast path up and R of Woodrolfe Creek.

51.757333, 0.881138

Beeleigh Falls, Maldon, River Chelmer

Tidal lagoon separated from the freshwater river and canal by a weir. A unique opportunity to jump into salt water and then fresh water on either side of the bridge, all in less than 90 seconds.

➤ **Find** the car park in Promenade Park. At the waterside, turn L towards Old Maldon town 1 mile away. Cross the river at Market Hill Bridge and then turn L along the FP next to the Sunny Sailor, 1 Fullbridge, CM9 4LE. Keep walking another 1 mile, all the way along the river path, under the A414 bridge, and past the golf course to Beeleigh Falls.

51.743811, 0.663715

Statue Of Byrhtnoth, Maldon, River Chelmer

Statue of a 10th-century warlord set on an arching pier out into the River Chelmer. Byrhtnoth died at the hand of Viking invaders at The Battle of Maldon. The battle was later made famous by an Old English poem. The views from the end of the pier are stunning.

➤ **Find** the car park in Promenade Park, Park Dr, Maldon, CM9 5JQ, on the River Chelmer. Walk 765 yards to the riverside and turn R on to the pier towards the statue.

51.726305, 0.698709

THE STONE INN, ST LAWRENCE, RIVER BLACKWATER

Tranquil traditional pub on the shores of the river.

101 Main Rd, St Lawrence, Southminster, CM0 7NA
Facebook: @TheStoneInnStLawrence

Northey Island Causeway, Maldon, River Chelmer

Prehistoric crossing to a historic island. Walk the foreshore at low tide via the crossing, but beware tides.
➤ **Find** the car park in Promenade Park. Walk 220 yards to the riverside and turn R on to the FP. Walk another ¾ mile along the river to the large posts that mark the crossing point.

51.7187506, 0.7060709

Ramsey Marsh, Stansgate, River Blackwater

Isolated beach on the Blackwater's S bank. Sandier beaches at St Lawrence, once home to a thriving tourist industry that burned itself out on the lack of parking. Phosphate nodules containing lobsters and crabs can be found, with sharks' teeth and fish remains in the shingle.
➤ **Find** St Lawrence and All Saints in The Street, Steeple, Southminster, CM0 7RJ. To the R is a pub and a FP leads down the L side of the pub. Follow the path 2 miles over Ramsey Marsh to the river and Marconi Sailing Club. Once at the water, turn R and walk to the small beaches ⅓ mile away. Keep walking another 1 mile for The Stone Inn (see left). (If the FP is hard to find beside the pub, walk on another ⅓ mile and turn L down Stansgate Rd to the Marconi Sailing Club.)

51.71852, 0.79929

Blackwater Estuary, Osea Island

Sleep over in pods or bunk bed-style communal rooms. Prices include all food and are wonderful value. The birdsong at dawn is deafeningly sensational. Othona began as an experiment in Christian community back in 1946, but welcomes everyone.

East Hall Farm/East End Rd, Southminster, CM0 7PN
www.othonaessex.org.uk

Bradwell-on-Sea

Chapel of St Peter-On-The-Wall, Bradwell-on-Sea, Blackwater Estuary

The 7th-century chapel where pagan Britons were converted to Christianity. Swim after waking at dawn to the rising tide. You won't need an alarm clock. If the lapping tide sends you to sleep, the dawn-chorus birdsong blisters the ears as if they have been swamped in warm milk and honey. Lunch on salt air and the sea purslane that grows here.

➤ **Find** the end of East End Rd, Bradwell-on-Sea, Southminster, CM0 7PN, where there is a car park. Keep walking another 765 yards to the chapel.

51.735278, 0.94

SILVER ROAD CARAVAN PARK, BURNHAM-ON-CROUCH, RIVER CROUCH

Tents, caravans and motorhomes close to the River Crouch waterfront.

Burnham-on-Crouch, CM0 8LA
www.silverroadcaravan
park.co.uk

FERRY BOAT INN, NORTH FAMBRIDGE, RIVER CROUCH

Set back 220 yards from the riverbank. Friendly staff and classic pub food. Avoid during hot days in mid-summer as it gets very busy. The road up from the river floods at high tide, which makes for nice paddling and splashing about.

Ferry Rd, North Fambridge, Chelmsford, CM3 6LR
www.ferryboatinnessex
.com

FRASERS GUEST ACCOMMODATION, BATTLESBRIDGE, RIVER CROUCH

Guest house and camping close to the River Crouch. Uniquely set inside the largest antiques centre in England – more than 90 dealers housed in five period buildings. There are also two pubs.

Muggeridge Farm, Maltings Rd, Battlesbridge, Wickford, SS11 7RF
www.battlesbridge.com

Bradwell Shell Bank, Bradwell-on-Sea

Cockle and oyster shell bank for sea rocket, sea holly and rock samphire. This is one of the best places to see hen harriers, merlins, peregrine and short-eared owls. Best explored at low tide.

➤ **Find** St Peter's Chapel Car Park (see page 311). Walk ¾ mile E along the FP to the chapel and dunes.

51.734655,0.945705

Ray Sand & Shell Bank, North Sea

Seals, sand and shell beach. Needs to be explored at low tide. The Ray Sand (51.663047, 0.942089) reaches out here to Buxey Sand over the Ray Sand Channel. Come with an offshore wind, a friend, a boat in a backpack, paddles and an engine.

➤ **Find** the end of Grange Rd, Tillingham, Maldon, CM0 7UR, where it meets the FP (just before the sign for Grange Farm). Follow the lane ¼ mile as it swings N to the farm on the R. Just before the farm, find the FP R and walk ¾ mile to the shore. At the shore, turn R and follow the path 2½ miles to the shell beach.

51.647662, 0.935065

Bridgemarsh Creek, River Crouch

Fabulous birdlife around fens and river. Avocets, marsh harriers and barn owls.

➤ **Find** the end of Blue House Farm Chase, Chelmsford, CM3 6GU, off the Fambridge Rd, ⅓ mile S of Fambridge Station. From the Chase car park, continue on foot down the lane into the path and keep walking straight ⅓ mile to the river. Turn L and walk along the sea wall 1½ miles to the creek.

51.636985, 0.682113

Wallasea Island Wild Coast Project, Canewdon, River Crouch

The largest man-made bird reserve in Europe is one of the few places in England where you can see hen harriers. Boats trips available in summer to seal colonies on the mud flats.

➤ **Find** the end of Creeksea Ferry Rd, Canewdon, Rochford, SS4 2EY. There is a car park beside the river behind the huge sea wall.

51.619164, 0.776400

The Broomway, Southend-on-Sea, River Thames

A prehistoric path, officially dubbed the most dangerous road in England. It still has 'road' status and links Foulness Island to the mainland. No one has driven regularly here since stagecoaches went out of fashion ... and the MoD built road bridges across the creeks.

THE SMUGGLERS DEN, HULLBRIDGE, RIVER CROUCH

 A bar, grill and pub, where it's lovely to chill on the outside benches by the river enjoying a cuppa with gulls for company.

315 Ferry Rd, Hullbridge, Hockley, SS5 6NA
www.smuggsden.co.uk

PLOUGH & SAIL, PAGLESHAM, RIVER ROACH

 Traditional pub linked to the river by FPs.

Eastend, Paglesham, Rochford, SS4 2EQ
www.theploughandsail.co.uk

THE CROOKED BILLET, LEIGH-ON-SEA, LEIGH CREEK

 Sit outside on the cobbled streets by Leigh Creek.

51 High St, Leigh-on-Sea, SS9 2EP
www.nicholsonspubs.co.uk

SALVATION ARMY HADLEIGH TEAROOMS, BENFLEET, RIVER THAMES

 Super service from an army of volunteers, good-value food and glorious views.

Salvation Army Hadleigh Training Centre, Castle Ln, Benfleet, SS7 2AP
www.hadleighfarm.co.uk

Chapman Sands, off Two Tree Island

➤ **Find** the security-controlled barrier entrance to Qinetiq, the military weapons testing centre, in Stairs Rd, Southend-on-Sea, SS3 9XE. This is a public right of way that the MoD opens most Saturdays and Sundays. Drive to the end of Stairs Rd and park. The Broomway starts at the end of the stone walkway, just off the stone-and-sand beach.

51.548196, 0.840260

The Ray, Westcliff-on-Sea, River Thames

 Sandbanks and tidal creek are exposed once a day when the tide goes out. Get there by walking ½ mile along an old 'cockle path'. It's still used by bait diggers and foragers who pick oysters and cockles. Check tide times. Currents are strong and tides come in quickly.

➤ **Find** parking in Chalkwell Espl, Westcliff-on-Sea, SS0 8JH, near the bottom of Chalkwell Av. At low tide, the shingle FP can be seen next to the Crowstone pillar offshore, opposite Chalkwell Av. The Ray is ⅔ mile offshore. Grave danger if this is attempted without knowledge of tides and currents.

51.536231, 0.628579

Two Tree Island, Leigh-on-Sea

A vast forest of eel grass, salt marsh and flooded Atlantis-sand bank. Much as the west coast of Scotland is protected against tourism by midges, this estuary jewel is guarded by black sinking mud that only bait diggers or the foolhardy venture on to it. The views from the island car park are priceless, dawn until dusk. Best in winter for murmurations of migrant seabirds.

➤ **Find** the small car park just past the golf range and over creek bridge (Two Tree Island, Leigh-on-Sea, SS9 2GB). Cross the road and walk around the W side of the island towards the S car park and boat launching ramps. In summer, charges apply for kayaks launching from the slipway.

51.536231, 0.628579

THE LABWORTH BEACH CAFE, CANVEY ISLAND, RIVER THAMES

 On the water's edge with views over one of the busiest rivers in the world.

Canvey Island, SS8 7DL
http://thelabworthcafe
.co.uk

THE WORLD'S END, TILBURY, RIVER THAMES

 What it says on the tin. A truly unique place for a drink stop, with wonderful views upon the sea wall.

Fort Rd, Tilbury,
RM18 7NR
www.worldsendtilbury
.co.uk

 Hadleigh Castle, Hadleigh, River Thames

One of the best views in Essex from a 13th-century castle ruin that's always open.

➤ **Find** Hadleigh Bike Park Car Park, Chapel Ln, Hadleigh, Benfleet, SS7 2QH. Follow the FP S over Adders Hill for ½ mile on to the ECP. At the ECP, walk E 300 yards and then take the FP up to the castle.

51.5439, 0.6088

 Benfleet Downs, Hadleigh, River Thames

The highest peaks on the N Thames riverbank are still shrouded in ancient woodland: 4 square miles of down, thicket and grazing marsh. The River Thames trundled through just after the last ice age receded 10,000 years ago. Much like the daily tides, it's starting to creep its way back in again on rising tides of time.

➤ **Find** The Hub. Olympic Mountain Bike Cafe, at the end of Chapel Ln, Benfleet, SS7 2QH. Walk into the woodland from the car park.

51.549655, 0.594042

Fobbing Marsh, Stanford-le-Hope

A ghost river closed to stop counterfeit trade after centuries of smuggling. You can hear its ripple and tide in between the bulrushes and hare runs. The smugglers' tunnels still echo in history, running from the church to the town.

➤ **Find** St Michael's Church, in High Rd, Fobbing, Stanford-le-Hope, SS17 9JH. Facing the church, walk R down the hill 220 yards and find the FP on the R between the houses. Once away from the houses, the FP turns L along the course of the old River Fobbing. The houses along here used to back on to the quay. Locals still report finding marine paraphernalia in their back gardens.

51.533327, 0.472678

Crowstone

Mucking Creek

Mucking Creek, Stanford-le-Hope

Essex's most important archaeological site. Surrounding meadows brim with wild flowers, butterflies and views over neighbouring port. Creek is shallow and short but good fun to packraft on the flood tide.

➤ **Find** Thurrock Thameside Nature Park Car Park, Mucking Wharf Rd, Stanford-le-Hope, SS17 0RN. Walk 300 yards N to the creek.

51.498896,0.441996

Coalhouse Fort, East Tilbury, River Thames

Historic defence by the River Thames.

➤ **Find** the Church of St Catherine at the end of Princess Margaret Rd, East Tilbury, Tilbury, RM18 8RP, beside the River Thames. The fort is next door.

51.464508, 0.432384

Ghost Wood, Purfleet, River Thames

Fossilised oak stumps at low tide – remnants of the great forests that lined the Thames valley before the glaciers last cut them down about 11,000 years ago.

➤ **Find** the RSPB Rainham Marshes Nature Reserve at the end of the lane off New Tank Hill Rd, Purfleet, RM19 1ZX. The centre is wedged between the River Mar Dyke and the River Thames. Look out for the stumps along a 1-mile strip R of the visitor centre.

51.699657, 0.757269

North Bank, Putney Bridge

THAMES NORTH BANK

**WILD THINGS TO DO
BEFORE YOU DIE:**

PADDLE in shoes and socks around Chiswick Eyot.

WATCH cormorants fish from the concrete pillars between Tower and London bridges.

SMELL the roses in Middle Temple.

CANOE out from Barking Mouth.

VISIT the Museum of London Docklands.

WALK the tree avenue of Hurlingham Park at low tide.

SIT beside the riverside church at Syon Park.

STAND next to Boudicca on Westminster Bridge.

SKIP over the Thames at Teddington Lock.

CELEBRATE the view from London Bridge, as the sun sets over the greatest tidal city in the world.

 ## Barking Mouth, Barking, River Thames

A mini estuary where the River Roding enters the Thames.
Somewhere to watch seabirds and boat traffic. Used by kayakers
to launch. Perfect for London access on the incoming tide.

➤ **Find** Creek Mouth Open Space next to 72 River Rd, Barking,
IG11 0EG. Walk through the park and along the FP 220 yards
to the river, estuary and Barking Creek Barrier on to the River
Thames.

51.515661, 0.098749

 ## Thames Barrier

The redeveloped riverside area between the line and the River
Thames includes gardens, toilets and a cafe. Walk through the
park for a view of the Thames Barrier.

➤ **Find** Pontoon Dock station on the DLR line.

51.499427, 0.033209

Barking Mouth

Hackney Wick, Hackney Marshes, River Lea

One of the largest areas of common land in London; there's 136 hectares to explore. The tide once flowed as far as Hackney Wick.

➤ **Find** The Waterworks Visitor Centre, off Lammas Rd, Waltham Forest, E10 7NU. From the car park, walk to the riverside and across the river bridge. Keep walking along the path and across the to Friends Bridge, over the River Lea. Explore the Wick around the river walks on all sides.

➤ Lea Bridge station is a 5-min walk.

51.558773, -0.038135

The Bow Creek Ecology Park (formerly Limmo Peninsula Ecological Park), River Lea

A little island of woodland close to the E bank of Bow Creek. It's actually a bend in the river made up of streams, ponds and meadows. Best in summer when the wild flowers are out.

➤ **Find** Bow Creek Lighthouse, 64 Orchard Pl, Leamouth Peninsula, London, E14 0JW, at the mouth of River Lea and Bow Creek into the River Thames. Turning away from the Thames, follow Bow Creek path for 110 yards and cross to Canning Town DLR station. From here, turn L and walk 330 yards to the park.

51.511543, 0.003195

Island Gardens, Greenwich, River Thames

Views of Greenwich from a tree-lined green next to Greenwich Foot Tunnel.

➤ **Find** Mudchute station, Spindrift Av, Isle of Dogs, E14 9ZT. Exit on the East Ferry Rd and walk R ⅓ mile to Manchester Rd. Turn L another 240 yards before turning R again on to Douglas Path down to the River Thames, the tunnel and the gardens. There's a cafe in the park that's open most days.

51.486814, -0.007696

Museum Of London Docklands, Isle of Dogs, River Thames

Museum covering the history of the River Thames over 500 years. Built in warehouses on the Isle of Dogs, not far from Canary Wharf. Entry is free.

➤ **Find** West India Quay DLR station. Walk around the North Dock to the museum in West India Quay, Hertsmere Rd, Canary Wharf, E14 4AF. There are numerous car parks around Canary Wharf.

51.507581, -0.024036

THE GRAPES, LIMEHOUSE, RIVER THAMES

Riverside terrace for seafood and ales.

76 Narrow St, Poplar, London, E14 8BP
www.thegrapes.co.uk

From Greenwich Park with views to Canary Wharf

THE NARROW, LIMEHOUSE, RIVER THAMES

 Riverside FP alongside restaurant and toilet access.

44 Narrow St, London, E14 8DP
www.gordonramsay
restaurants.com/
the-narrow

PROSPECT OF WHITBY, WAPPING, RIVER THAMES

 Riverside in one of London's oldest pubs, next to the Shadwell Basin. Spectacular views over the River Thames, including from the beer garden and first-floor balcony and terrace.

57 Wapping Wall,
St Katharine's & Wapping,
E1W 3SH
www.greeneking
-pubs.co.uk

THE DICKENS INN, WAPPING, RIVER THAMES

 Pub with restaurant housed in a beautiful 18th-century warehouse in the heart of St Katharine Docks. Opened in 1976 by Cedric Charles Dickens, great-grandson to the famous author.

Marble Quay,
St Katharine's Way,
St Katharine's & Wapping,
www.dickensinn.co.uk

Wapping Foreshore, River Thames

Foreshore is accessible at low tide by various stairs along the N bank of the Thames. The foreshore is a mixture of sand, mud and rock. Hire a kayak at Shadwell Basin.

➤ **Find** Wapping Overground station, at Wapping High St, E1W 3PA. Facing the station, turn L along the High St and keep walking ¼ mile to the Prospect of Whitby (see left). Turn R on to the Thames path just past the pub and down to the small beach.

51.507389, -0.050315

Tower of London, River Thames

One of England most iconic buildings, epitomised by the phrase, 'sent to the Tower'. Its reputation for torture and death is partly based on the execution of seven people here; most deaths took place outside the Tower at the equally notorious Tower Hill, to the N of the castle, where more than 100 people were executed over a 400-year period. Sit under the shade or shelter of trees in the shadow of Tower Bridge. Direct water access ⅓ mile W along the shore via concrete steps.

➤ **Find** Tower Hill Underground station, London, EC3N 4DR. Walk down to the River Thames 295 yards away and around the vast Tower building set back from the shore.

51.506904, -0.075556

Middle Temple Gardens, River Thames

Trees, roses, river and temples. Savour the scene of Shakespeare's meeting between Richard Plantagenet and John Beaufort, which sparked the Wars of the Roses. The garden's real story is stranger than fiction. They were part

Tower of London

Boudiccan Rebellion Statue

THE OYSTER SHED, CITY OF LONDON, RIVER THAMES

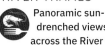
Panoramic sun-drenched views across the River Thames.

1 Angel Ln, London, EC4R 3AB
www.oystershed.co.uk

TATTERSHALL CASTLE, WESTMINSTER, RIVER THAMES

Old steam ferry converted to a pub. Fish and chips on the deck. Opposite the London Eye and between Westminster and Embankment Underground stations.

Victoria Embankment, Whitehall, SW1A 2HR
www.thetattershall castle.co.uk

of the headquarters of the Knights Templar until the band was dissolved in 1312. The gardens were taken over by the Knights Hospitallers until Henry VIII seized them in 1540. They passed to English barristers in 1608, and remain the HQ of the British legal profession.

➤ **Find** Temple Underground station, Victoria Embankment, London, WC2R 2PH. Facing the Thames, walk L along the river 260 yards to the National Submarine War Memorial. The park is opposite on the other side of the road.

51.511186, -0.110313

Boudiccan Rebellion, Westminster Bridge, River Thames

Statue on Westminster Bridge, with views of Westminster Palace, London Eye, Big Ben and the River Thames. Boudicca was a legendary queen of the Iceni tribe who led an uprising against the Roman armies in AD60. English artist Thomas Thornycroft spent 27 years working on the statue until just before he died in 1885. It was erected at Westminster in 1902.

➤ **Find** Westminster Underground station, London, SW1A 2JR. Walk 87 yards to Westminster Bridge across the Thames. The statue stands at the entrance to the bridge with the London Eye on the other side of the river in the foreground.

51.500803, -0.121852

PREMIER INN LONDON, PUTNEY BRIDGE, RIVER THAMES

 Budget accommodation 150 yards from Putney Bridge Underground station and 75 yards from the river path.

3 Putney Bridge Approach, Fulham, SW6 3JD
www.premierinn.com

THE BLUE BOAT, HAMMERSMITH, RIVER THAMES

 Open-plan kitchen for some real theatre of food.

Distillery Wharf, Parr's Way, Hammersmith, W6 9GD
www.theblueboat.co.uk

LONDON THAMES WALK, FULHAM, RIVER THAMES

 B&B in an Edwardian house just a 140-yard walk to the river path.

91 Langthorne St, Fulham, SW6 6JU

OLD SHIP, HAMMERSMITH, RIVER THAMES

 Cask-conditioned beers and a seasonal dining menu. Lovely views all year. Short walk from Ravenscourt Park, Stanford Brook and Hammersmith stations.

25 Upper Mall, Hammersmith, W6 9TD
www.oldship hammersmith.co.uk

Chelsea Embankment Gardens, Kensington, River Thames

Tree-lined avenues. Good views across Albert Bridge and the River Thames.

➤ **Find** South Kensington Underground station, in Pelham St, Kensington, SW7 2NB. Walk just under 1 mile to the river.

51.483470, -0.165756

Hurlingham Park, Fulham, River Thames

Boat launch or walk at low tide under the canopy of trees on the E side of the park.

➤ **Find** Putney Bridge Tube, Station Approach, SW6 3UH. Exit the E side of the station and walk 0.4 miles to Hurlingham Park, 17 Broomhouse Ln, Fulham, SW6 3DP. Pass through the public car park and make your way across the park to the exit in Broomhoouse Ln. Walk 200 yards to the bottom of the lane to the wooded area next to the river and the boat ramp.

51.464975, -0.197786

Chiswick Eyot, Chiswick, River Thames

One of the numerous small islands or eyots on the River Thames. Accessible from the N bank (Chiswick) during low tides. Not much to see apart from willow. Riverside parking and access to the river.

➤ **Find** riverside at the junction of Chiswick Ln South and Chiswick Mall. Only limited restrictions on weekend street parking. Nearest station is Stamford Brook Underground station, ½ mile N of the river.

51.487288, -0.247706

Chelsea

Hurlingham Park

BULLS HEAD, CHISWICK, RIVER THAMES

 Great-value food riverside with views from the river path over Kew Railway Bridge.

15 Strand-On-The-Green, Chiswick, W4 3PQ
www.chefandbrewer.com/ pubs/greater-london/ bulls-head/

THE WHITE SWAN, TWICKENHAM RIVERSIDE, RIVER THAMES

 Visit at high tide, when the garden may end up in the river, but never for long. Staff sometimes wade through the water with a few plates or glasses in hand.

Riverside, Twickenham, TW1 3DN
www.whiteswan twickenham.co.uk

Syon Park & All Saints Isleworth, Isleworth, River Thames

Wonderful church with parking access direct into the tidal Thames beside a stunning park with public access. Take in the view from both sides of the Thames. Sacred.

➤ **Find** All Saints Isleworth, Church St, Middlesex, TW7 6BE. Parking right beside the river. Facing the river, turn L back up Church St and turn R after 150 yards to explore Syon Park on the riverside.

51.471347, -0.319738

Marble Hill, Twickenham, River Thames

Walk through ⅓ mile of tree-lined path.

➤ **Find** Orleans Gardens beside public toilets and street parking on Riverside, Twickenham, TW1 3DJ. Walk down to the marina and, facing the water, turn L along the path and walk ⅓ mile to the wooded foreshore.

51.449232, -0.308374

Teddington Lock, River Thames

Tidal limit of the Thames. Complex of three locks in the London Borough of Richmond.

➤ **Find** where the river path meets Riverside Dr, Richmond, TW10 7RP. Just before the parked cars, follow the hard path 400 yards down to the Thames. The Teddington Lock Footbridge can be crossed to the other side of the river.

51.43009, -0.32211

TIMELINE OF EVENTS

The Never-ending Story

Once upon a time in the northern lands ... the Gods created the skies and a watery earth.

1 And the Gods went on to say: 'Let the waters under the sky be brought into one place and let the dry land appear'. And it came to be so.

2 And the Gods went on to say: 'Let us make people. And give them the land to explore and to look, and to see, and to enjoy'.

3 But the people went on to say: 'We can't get any bloody access to the land because someone has put up loads of fences'.

4 'We want access to mountain, moorland, heathland, downland and common land.'

5 So the Gods went on to say: 'Let there be paths'. And the Countryside Rights of Way Act (CRoW) came forth.

6 And most of the people were happy. But not the people by the coast without mountains or moor.

7 And so it began...

Kimmeridge, Dorset

Shingle Street, Suffolk

TIMELINE

2001
Essex Ramblers complain that CRoW is of little practical benefit to them because their county doesn't have much in the way of heath and no mountain or moor to access.

2002
Ramblers begin surveying coastlines. They find that access to the coast is limited due to missing links, eroded paths and routes that went so far inland that really you couldn't genuinely call them a coastal route.

2004
Essex Ramblers formally asked Ramblers HQ to campaign for access to the English coast. Ramblers HQ put together a campaign strategy.

2005
Labour Party includes a commitment to improve access to the coast in its manifesto.

2006
Labour government asked Natural England to explore the options for improving coastal access.

2007
Ramblers Association publishes its 'hit list' of some of the worst areas for coast access. These included:

- Sovereign Harbour in Eastbourne does not allow the public to cross the lock gates, an example of private companies buying up the coastline and restricting access.
- Cliffe Marshes on the Hoo Peninsular. Private beaches from Brighton to Folkestone.
- Isle of Sheppey – particularly the stretch between Minster and Warden, which were completely blocked to the public.

June 2007
David Miliband, Secretary of State for the Environment, arrives in Dover to set out the second phase of the Countryside and Rights of Way Act, proposing the coast path. He goes on to say: 'We are an island nation. The coast is our birthright and everyone should be able to enjoy it.'

June 2007
Gwyn Williams, RSPB head of reserves and protected areas, says: 'Our concerns have been taken on board and we are confident coastal access will be increased without harming important sites for wild birds.'

2009

The Marine and Coastal Access Act 2009 receives Royal Assent with cross-party support. The Act set out powers to create the path. The Act provides both a right to walk along the full 2,700 miles of England's coastline and a permanent right of access to a coastal margin around the coast, including beaches and access to sea cliffs.

early 2012

First stretch of England Coast Path is opened between Weymouth Bay and Portland Harbour to coincide with 2012 Olympic sailing events.

late 2012

Government extends path completion date from 2022 to 2032.

June 2013

Cuts to DEFRA budget and spending coincide with comments from Environment Minister, Richard Benyon, that the ECP is 'an expensive legacy'.

25 June 2013

Ramblers produce a report stating that expenditure on the path for 2012–15 was just £239,000; that the Wales Coast Path – which opened in May 2012 – was walked by 2.8 million people the previous year, bringing in an additional £16 million to the Welsh economy; and that the England Coast Path would be beneficial for struggling coastal towns.

July 2013

The Environment Minister, Richard Benyon, gives the green light for new sections of the Path in County Durham and Cumbria to open in 2014; Isle of Wight is removed from the Path route.

late 2013

Ramblers begin the Case for the Coast campaign, highlighting the economic, social and health benefits of an England Coast Path; 20,000 people sign the Path petition; the Campaign is joined by the National Trust, Outdoor Industries Association and the South West Coast Path Association to make the case for continued investment.

Isle of Wight is confirmed to be included in plans for the new Coast Path.

Daddyhole, South Devon

11 April 2014
Open: a 22-mile stretch from Allonby to Whitehaven, Cumbria.

2014
Deputy Prime Minister, Nick Clegg, announces that the government will accelerate the opening of the Coastal Path, bringing completion of the project forwards by more than 10 years, from 2032 to 2020.

Negotiating complex access agreements with landowners, the government is expected to have to release nearly £40 million to complete the Path.

4 December 2014
Deputy Prime Minister, Nick Clegg, announces that the government is committing £5.26 million in 2015–16 to speed up the opening of the seaside path.

December 2014
Open: 26 miles between Weybourne and Sea Palling.

2015
Comprehensive spending review after Cameron re-elected with a majority.

21 July 2016
Longest section of England Coast Path announced open in Middlesbrough – 68 miles from Filey Brigg through Scarborough and Whitby, Saltburn and Redcar.

19 July 2016
First section of Kent Coast Path opens from Camber just over the Sussex border to Ramsgate – a substantial section on the Sandwich peninsula that was completely inaccessible before. Three miles of new path have also been created at Sandwich, giving access around the peninsula for the first time. Walkers can enjoy new views along the River Stour across Pegwell Bay towards the cliffs at Ramsgate and overlooking the wonderful National Nature Reserve of Sandwich and Pegwell Bay.

July 2016
Later … the next section from Ramsgate to Whitstable is approved by the Secretary of State but the necessary signage and work to make the whole route usable is not yet in place.

24 October 2016
Open: 21-mile route between Hopton-on-Sea and Sea Palling, Norfolk – including 3 new miles of access between Horsey and Sea Palling.

Jonathan Stratford, General Manager at Haven's Hopton Holiday Village says: 'We are delighted to hear of the opening of the England Coast Path between Hopton-on-Sea and Sea Palling as it is a project that we have been actively supporting over the last couple of years. We encourage all our guests to explore the local area and this coastal path gives everyone the chance to discover more of this picturesque and unique coastline with ease.'

Combined with the opening in 2014, the paths cover 83 miles around the Norfolk coast as far as Hunstanton, creating the longest section of Coast Path in the east of England.

September 2017
Natural England announces that work has started on every stretch of coast in every county. Also, that more than 300 miles of the 3,000-mile coastline is now open.

26 July 2018
Tyneside and Northumberland's first England Coast Path section opens – 44 miles from South Bents to Amble. People can explore the coast around the River Tyne, linking the wild beaches and dunes of Druridge Bay to the resorts and ports to the south.

11 December 2019
Natural England completes the process of public consultation on the proposed path from Wallasea Island and Southend-on-Sea – almost 20 years after Southend-based Rambler Dave Hitchman began the original coastal survey that started it all off.

February 2020
Open: a 16-mile stretch around Walney Island.

Porthtowan Pool, North Cornwall

February 2022
The government announces the England Coast Path will be fully walkable, with bridges, signage and infrastructure, by the end of the current Parliament.

April 2022
Isle of Wight: Wootton Bridge to the Medina and Eastbourne to Camber stretches approved.

June 2022
Sutton Bridge to Skegness and Aldeburgh to Hopton-on-Sea approved.

July 2022
Another 5 miles of the England Coast Path are opened in Essex. Lord Benyon, Minister for Rural Affairs, says: 'We want to connect more people with nature. Essex has a dynamic and historic landscape and this path will support sustainable tourism.'

August 2022
New National Trail announced by Natural England. The £5 million Coast to Coast National Trail will link the England Coast Path between 192-miles of path from St Bees, Cumbria to Robin Hood's Bay, North Yorkshire.

late August, 2022
NEARLY THERE!
Out of almost 3,000 miles of path from the Scottish border to Land's End, less than 300 miles are still to be approved.

The Path Builders

If you worked on the England Coast Path and want to be included here email: **news@wildessex.com**

NATIONAL
Kate Conto
Richard Benyon
Nick Clegg
Kate Ashbrook
Tom Fewins
Neil Constable
Alison Hallass

RAMBLER
VOLUNTEERS

Somerset
Carl Earl
Les Stather
Rod Senior
Edward Levy
Eddy Hicks

Cornwall
Ken Sharp
Bob Fraser
Phil Howson
Anne Tryhorn

Devon
John Skinner
David Pawley
Joan Long

Dorset
Brian Panton

Hampshire
Alan Marlow
Richard C.
    Kenchington
Ian Backhouse
Ruth Croker
Peter Scott

Sussex
Inga Chapman
Julia Page
Con Geaney
Jerry Kind
Mike Riley
Geoff Cook
John Langford

Michael Bates
Barrie Brickle
Kay Chaffer
Keith Morgan
Murray Figgins
Peter Jarman
Gill Lamarque
Leslie Langford
Brenda Linfield
Peter Seed
Paul Bould

Isle of Wight
Mike Slater
Christine Armstrong
David Yates
Eileen Hollinshed
Sue Bradley
Jill Green
Helen Williams
Mark Elliott
Mike Marchant
Adrian Tavill
Doug Kelman

Graham Maddison
David Howarth
Janet Whiteman
John Whiteman
Keith Rose
Derek Baty
Alan Kennett
Kevin Byrom
Joy Allsop
Jim Catchpole
Janice Turner
John Turner

Kent
Ian Wild
Robert Peel

Suffolk
Alde Valley Ramblers,
Waveney Ramblers and
Ipswich Ramblers, and
in particular members
of Alde Valley working
party group

Dymchurch, Kent

Norfolk
Ken Hawkins
Catherine Hawkins
Roy Wheeler
Sue Wheeler
Ian Witham
Ian Mitchell
John Trevelyan
Allan Jones
Ray Longman

Lincolnshire
Barry Smith
Colin Smith

**Yorkshire
and Derwent**
Tom Halstead
Bill Dell
Dennis Barr
Les Atkinson
Peter Ayling
Martin Biggs
Robert Clutson
Tony Corrigan
Pauline Hakeney
George Malcolm

Colin Mullender
Brian Odell
Geoff Richardson
Eric Smith
Ray Wallis

Northumbria
Nuala Wright
Paul Wright
Richard Higginbottom
Vicky Ludbrook
Penny Ford
Diana Aynsley
Jacqueline Armstrong
Jenny Ellis
Julia Birchall
Neil Allender
Alan Mitcham

Berwick
Berwick Ramblers

**Lake District
Cumbria and North
Lancashire ramblers
and friends
Mid-Lancashire**
David Kelly
Brian Jones
Joy Greenwood
Hillary Bellis
Pam Gorham
Denise Copson
Roy Copson
 (deceased)
Lois Louden
 (deceased)

**Merseyside and
West Cheshire**
Merseyside and
West Cheshire
Ramblers and
friends

Essex
Ann McLaren
Dave Hitchman
Alan Goffee

Chris Marshall
Stanley Woolfson
Jeffrey Coe
Paul Fieldsend
Christopher Palmer
Mags Hobby
John Dowding
 (deceased)
Kevin Ascott
 (deceased)
Wally Webb
 (deceased)
Dianne Ingram
Gordon Bird
Richard Isles
Jackie Harrop
Roger Young
 (deceased)
Andrew Mackay
Dave Lemmy
Steve Gunn
Brian Bunn
Steve Hyde
John Payne
Keith Ling
Stephen Neale
 (author)

PROPOSED PATHS

16 places to which the England Coast Path could soon provide new access, subject to proposals being finalised.

KENT

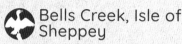 Bells Creek, Isle of Sheppey

Look for short-eared owls and marsh harriers around the edges of where brackish water merges with sea. A bird haven.
➤ Find (not yet open) Elmley Nature Reserve Car Park, beside Kingshill Cottages, Elmley, Minster on Sea, Sheerness, ME12 3RW, and walk ½ mile S to the coast. Turn E (L) at the water and walk 3 miles to the creek.

51.370745, 0.857083

 Grain Marsh, Isle of Grain

Explore one of the UK's most eco-rich marsh areas. More than 50 species of reptile, invertebrate and bird have been recorded here.
➤ Find (not yet open) Grain Beach Car Park, Grain Coastal Park, 55 High St, Isle of Grain, Rochester, ME3 0BS, and walk E a few yards to the coast. On the FP, turn N, and keep walking towards the new section of path that eventually turns inland towards Allhallows Marshes.

51.461071, 0.697943

SOUTH SOMERSET

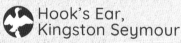 River Axe, Somerset

Walk the W bank of the River Axe.
➤ Find (not yet open) NT Brean Down Car Park, Brean Down Rd, Brean, Burnham-on-Sea TA8 2RS, and walk 3 miles E and then S on the FP and new access via the ECP.

51.309869, -2.989315

GLOUCESTERSHIRE & NORTH SOMERSET

Hook's Ear, Kingston Seymour

Smell the rare herb, sea wormwood, which still grows around this unique coastal area, but can be difficult to find. The plant was used in the past to cure fever and give appetite. Do some research on ID, but look for velvety white or greenish-silver stems, greenish leaves, and bright or pale yellow flowers.
➤ Find (not yet open) Clevedon Golf Centre, Lower Strode Rd, Clevedon, BS21 6UU, and walk 2 miles NW, then S along the coastal path to Hook's Ear.

51.412989, -2.889170

LANCASHIRE

 Cockerham Marsh, Cockerham

Star watch over the Lune Estuary from one of the most isolated places along the NW shore.
➤ Find (not yet open) the car park, waterside in Fluke Hall Ln, Preston, PR3 6HP and, facing the sea, turn NE (R) and walk 4 miles across Riling Marsh to Cockerham.

53.958705, -2.855418

CUMBRIA

 Summer View, Seascale, Irish Sea

Look around the N dunes in June and August for the tell-tale purple of seabind weed. The vine-like stems can be used as string.
➤ Find (not yet open) Seascale Car Park, S Pde, Seascale, CA20 1PZ and, facing the sea, walk S (L) ¾ mile on the new access FP to the dunes.

54.385541, -3.474639

Arrad Marsh, Ulverston

Walk the dismantled railway, along the edge of the coast where wintering birds roost.
➤ Find (not yet open) the public toilets on the waterside off the A590, Ulverston, LA12 7QX, and walk ½ mile S on the new access path.

54.218399, -3.053853

YORKSHIRE

 Fraisthorpe Sands, East Riding

Taste fresh bass, caught offshore in the shallows.
➤ Find (not yet open) Fraisthorpe Beach Top Parking, beside Auburn Farm, Fraisthorpe, Bridlington, YO15 3QU, and walk ⅔ mile S across sands.

54.040285, -0.216032

Sunk Island, River Humber

A rare patch of coastal woodland along Yorkshire's most isolated coastline.

➤ **Find (not yet open)** Stone Creek House Campsite, Stone Creek House, Cherry Cobb Sands Rd, Burstwick, Hull, HU12 9JX. Walk S and then N across and around Stone Creek, on to the ECP for 1½ miles.

53.640256, -0.112225

NORFOLK

Boathouse Creek, King's Lynn

Walk the line where two creeks come together. Boathouse Creek and Collard Creek have been important industrial hubs for more than 3,000 years, with prehistoric links to salt production.

➤ **Find (not yet open)** Snettisham Beach Car Park, Snettisham, King's Lynn, PE31 7PS, and find new access to the ECP on the waterside. Walk 2½ miles S along the sea wall to the creek.

52.844878, 0.456263

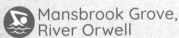
Vinegar Middle

Tidal access to Bulldog Sands from Old Lynn Channel, which runs through the Wash marsh and sea bank known as Vinegar Middle.

➤ **Find (not yet open)** Boathouse Creek (see above) and keep walking another 5½ miles S on the ECP.

52.796895, 0.370029

SUFFOLK
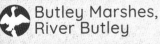
Mansbrook Grove, River Orwell

A secluded, semi-wooded, beach that time (almost) forgot.

➤ **Find (not yet open)** Bridge Wood Car Park off A14, Ipswich, IP10 0NZ, and follow the FP ½ mile S through Bridge Wood to the coast path. At the riverside, turn E (L) and walk another ½ mile to the grove.

52.014670, 1.200649

Butley Marshes, River Butley

Listen to waders and wildfowl that roost around the islands and lagoons offshore just to the N of the riverbank at Havergate.

➤ **Find (not yet open)** Shingle Street Car Park, Woodbridge, IP12 3BG, and walk E on the ECP 6 miles on to marshes.

52.091232, 1.494266

ESSEX

Abbot's Hall Saltings, Great and Little Wigborough

The most important new public rights of way (PRoW) access in Essex is the proposed new path from Salcott Creek to the banks of the E Strood, beside Mersea Island. A defining moment in the Essex ECP campaign, assisted by Essex Wildlife Trust and the Essex Ramblers, with much help from Natural England. A monumental achievement.

➤ **Find (not yet open)** St Nicholas' Church, Little Wigborough, CO5 7RD and walk ½ mile S to to the new section of path. Facing the water turn W (right) and walk another ½ mile to the N end of Saltings.

51.792737, 0.867114

Sutton Bridge Farm, River Roach

Listen to water lapping the river bank at high tide. Perfect location for an easy packraft launch into the S side. Previously only access from 1½ miles E at Ropers Farm sea wall.

➤ **Find (not yet open)** All Saints Church, Church Rd, Barling, SS3 0JS, and walk 500 yards E to the ECP. Facing the tide, turn N (L) on the FP and walk 3 miles along the sea wall to new access point. Exit by continuing to walk W 3 miles into Rochford.

51.577445, 0.745558

Mucking Creek, Thurrock

Smell the scent of dog rose upriver of Mucking Creek. Marsh and raptors all around.

➤ **Find (not yet open)** Enovert Community Trust Visitor Centre, Mucking Wharf Rd, Stanford-le-Hope, SS17 0RN, and walk 100 yards E to the ECP. Facing the tide, turn N (L) on the FP and walk ½ mile to new section of path.

51.501328, 0.435420

BY THE SAME AUTHOR

THE SOUTH WEST COAST PATH

1,000 Mini Adventures Along Britain's Longest Waymarked Path

Exploring the length of the South West Coast Path, this gorgeous and inspiring guidebook highlights 1,000 mini adventures to enjoy along its entire 630-mile route, from Minehead to Poole Harbour.

ISBN 978-1-8448-6617-5

WILD CAMPING

Exploring and Sleeping in the Wilds of the UK and Ireland

A revolutionary guide to the world of wild camping and foraging, showing how anyone can camp, sleep and wake in the UK's most secluded and beautiful places, with a Foreword by Ed Stafford.

ISBN 978-1-8448-6572-7

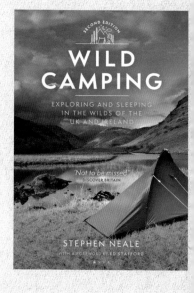

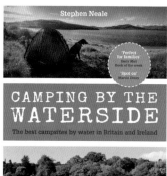

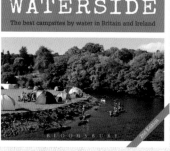

CAMPING BY THE WATERSIDE

The Best Campsites by Water in Britain and Ireland

This is the ultimate guide to camping near water – by the sea, lake, river or estuary – and covers planning your trip, gear to take, introductions to each activity (canoeing, sailing, angling etc) and the very best waterside locations in the UK and Ireland. With a Foreword by *One Man and a Campervan's* Martin Dorey.

ISBN 978-1-4729-4330-9